The City and the Region

The European City in Transition

Edited by Frank Eckardt
and Dieter Hassenpflug

Band 4

PETER LANG

Frankfurt am Main · Berlin · Bern · Bruxelles · New York · Oxford · Wien

Frank Eckardt (ed.)

The City and the Region

PETER LANG

Europäischer Verlag der Wissenschaften

Bibliographic Information published by Die Deutsche Bibliothek
Die Deutsche Bibliothek lists this publication in the Deutsche Nationalbibliografie; detailed bibliographic data is available in the internet at <http://dnb.ddb.de>.

Cover illustration:
The Regional Market in Marseille.
Photo: Frank Eckardt.

This publication is realised by the support of the European Commission and the Deutsche Forschungsgesellschaft.

ISSN 1619-375X
ISBN 3-631-52084-0
US-ISBN 0-8204-7789-3

© Peter Lang GmbH
Europäischer Verlag der Wissenschaften
Frankfurt am Main 2005
All rights reserved.

Printed in Germany 1 2   4 5 6 7

www.peterlang.de

The European Cities in Transition Series

Cities are a mirror of society and a motor of change. Especially the challenges produced by the growing interconnection of people and places find their spatial organisation in the world's metropolis. Globalization shapes new forms of economy, culture and social life and it comes all together in the historically grown European city. The increasing of mobility and communication brings forward the key questions of urban life again: How can the heritages of a European city been transmitted to a city in times of profound changes? What does it mean for political, cultural, social and architectural decision makers to act in an urban setting transformed by major societal trends?

The "European Cities in Transition Series" aims at publishing answers from all disciplines that are dedicated to find theoretical and practical solutions for the European City under the circumstances of the globalization and the unification of Europe. Edited by Dieter Hassenpflug and Frank Eckardt who both work at the Bauhaus-Universität Weimar, the tradition of the first Bauhaus is remembered: The Bauhaus architects like Mies van der Rohe and Walter Gropius have been searching for adequate solutions for the city of modernity. Today, this spirit has to be brought in, again. The post-national age requires new approaches for understanding, the European city. Bringing together the findings of research of scientists, city planers and architectures, the series will focus on different aspects of the current transition of urban life.

First volume: Consumption and the Post-Industrial City
Second volume: Urbanism and Globalization
Third volume: City Images and Urban Regeneration
Forth volume: The City and the Region

Forthcoming:

Paths of Urban Transformation

Contents

Contributors

Ageliki Anagnostou is a part time lecturer in Economic / Econometric and a Research Associate at the South East European Development Centre (SEED) at the University of Thessaly. In 2002, she completed her Ph.D at the University of Sheffield on Modelling Nonlinear Dynamic Behaviour of Time Series Data. She was a lecturer at the Brasenose College at the University of Oxford in 2000-2001 and a Research Fellow at the University of Warwick in 1999. Contact: aganag@uth.gr

Markus Beier, geographer, is a PhD student and researcher at the Leibniz-Institute of Ecological and Regional Development in Dresden, Germany. His research interests lie in the fields of spatial planning, regional governance and regional innovation systems.
Contact: M.Beier@ioer.de

Ingo Dallgahs is a PhD candidate in Social Geography at the Friedrich-Schiller-University of Jena. His research interests focus on social and urban theory under the condition of late modernity. He works in urban planning and publishes the monthly online-magazine "stadtanalyse.de".
Contact: ingo@dallgahs.de

Rémi Dormois is an urban planner working in the urban planning agency of Saint-Etienne (France) on housing and social and economic developments topics. He is also an associated member of the Centre d'Etudes et de Recherches sur l'Administration Publique de St-Etienne (CERAPSE), Rennes. He will defend his political science PhD on coalitions and action collective rules in the urban planning dynamics of Rennes and Nantes on winter 2004. Contact: remi.dormois@wanadoo.fr

Frank Eckardt is Junior Professor for the Sociology of globalization and is working as an urban sociologist at the European Urban Studies programme of the Bauhaus-Universität Weimar, where he is the local organizer of the "European Cities in Transition Conference" Series. He has finished his PhD at the University of Kassel in political science. Recent publication: "Soziologie der Stadt" (2004).
Contact: Frank.Eckardt@archit.uni-weimar.de

Simone Gabi, Dipl. Geographer and qualified NDS ETH regional planner, ETH Zurich. Member of scientific staff at the Institute for regional and landscape development, regional planning faculty, Netzwerk Stadt und

Landschaft. Main professional areas: sustainable regional and urban development, cooperative planning, open space planning.
Contact: simono.gabi@nsl.ethz.ch

Robert Grimm has been a PhD student at the Manchester Metropolitan University since 2001. His research started as a comparative study of three European cities but he finally focused on a small inner-city area in Marseilles where he conducted an ethnographic study among Algerian migrants over a period of three years. Robert's main interest is the relationship between globalisation and simple daily interactions as well as the relationship between place and transnational social space. The work is still in progress but, now in his fourth year, Robert hopes to submit his reseach findings in spring 2005.
Contact: grimmrobert@hotmail.com

Thomas Held, lic. phil. nat. (biology) and qualified NDS ETH regional planner, ETH Zurich. Member of scientific staff at the Institute for regional and landscape development regional planning faculty and chief assistant at the Netzwerk Stadt und Landschaft until March 2004. Proprietor of the held planning and sustainability office, Zurich. Main professional areas: sustainable regional development in research and practice, multifunctional landscape development in urban and rural areas.

Michael Janoschka has worked as Research assistant in Regional Planning and Investigation Chair at the Institute of European Urban Studies Bauhaus-University Weimar, Germany. Currently he holds a position at the University of Frankfurt.
Contact: m.janoschka@em.uni-frankfurt.de

Giorgos Kandylis is political scinetist and a PhD candidate in urban geography at the Department of Planning and Regional Development, University of Thessaly, Volos. The chapter in this volume is based on research carried out for his PhD thesis, 'Urban agglomeration and migration: social reproduction in Thessaloniki from a labour perspective'.
Contact: gkandyl@prd.uth.gr

Monika Krause studied Sociology at the Universities of Munich, Cambridge and the London School of Economics. She is currently a Ph.D. candidate at New York University. Her research interests include the critical theory of the state and citizenship.
Contact: monika.krause@nyu.edu

Jussi Kulonpalo is PhD candidate in urban studies at University of Helsinki, Department of Social Policy. He is currently working on his thesis focusing on urban governance in European cities and the role of cultural policies in urban regeneration, inter-city competition and urban cultural economy. Contact: jussi.kulonpalo@helsinki.fi

Antje Matern is a geographer and works at the regional planning department of the Technical University of Dresden, Germany. Her research interests include regional governance and spatial planning policies from European to regional level and with special focus on metropolitan regions. Contact: A.Matern@mailbox.tu-dresden.de

Sako Musterd is a Professor of Urban Geography at the University of Amsterdam, The Netherlands. His current research activities are in the field of urban regional transformations, spatial segregation, integration and social exclusion in large metropolitan areas in Europe. Special attention is given to large-scale analysis of 'neighbourhood effects and social mobility'. He coordinated the EU-funded URBEX programme and participated in several other large international research programmes. Recent publications include papers in Housing Studies, Urban Studies, the International Journal of Urban and Regional Research and the Journal of Ethnic and Migration Studies. Contact: s.musterd@uva.nl

Tom Nielsen is an architect/Ph.D, and is currently working as a post.doc.-researcher at the Aarhus School of Architecture. His research topic is contemporary urban development. His Ph.D. thesis (1997-2000) focused on the superfluous landscapes of the contemporary city. This project resulted in the book Formløs [Formless], (2001). In 2001-02 he worked on the project 'Ethics, Aesthetics and Urban Welfare, currently under publication. Tom Nielsen was co-editor on the book Urban Mutations (2004) and has been a partner in the architectural office TRANSFORM since 1996. For more information and links to publications and projects, see www.aarch.dk and www.transform-arkitekter.dk.
Contact: tom.nielsen@aarch.dk

Sotiris Pavleas (M.Sc) is a Ph.D. Candidate and a Research Associate of the South-East European Development Center (SEED) at the Department of Planning and Regional Development, University of Thessaly, Greece. He is at his second semester of his Ph.D. and his research interests include urban and regional economics. More specifically, he focuses on the evolution, the structure and the inter-relationships of the Greek urban centers. Contact: pavleas@uth.gr

George Petrakos (Ph.D.) is a Professor of Spatial Economics at the Department of Planning and Regional Development, University of Thessaly, Greece. His research interests include urban and regional economics, development, transition economics, Balkan studies and international economic relations. He has published several books and a large number of articles in international journals. Among others, he has edited or co-edited the volumes 'Integration, Growth and Cohesion in an Enlarged European Union' (Kluer 2004), 'The Development of the Greek Cities' (UTP 1999/2004), 'The Development of the Balkan Region' (Ashgate 2001), 'Integration and Transition in Europe: The Economic Geography of Interaction' (2000). Contact: petrakos@uth.gr.

Jefferey M. Sellers serves as Vice-Chair and Graduate Director in the Department of Political Science and has courtesy appointments in the Department of Geography and the School of Policy, Planning and Development at the University of Southern California. Prof. Sellers works on issues in urban studies, environmental and social policies and their politics from a global perspective. Recent book: "Governing from Below: Urban Regions and the Global Economy". Contact: sellers@usc.edu.

Alain Thierstein, Prof. Dr. oec., ETH Zurich, Institute for regional and landscape development, regional planning faculty. Former head of the regional economy faculty as well as director and member of the management of the institute of public services and tourism, St. Gallen University. Main professional areas: regional development and policy issues, innovation and technology policy, urban development, regional sustainability, and evaluation of policy measures.

The City and the Region
(Introduction)

The issue of regionalization has become a crucial point in the process of European Unification. As such, the region has become a major political institution in the process of European policy development. Key steps so far have been the implementation of the Council of the Regions, the DG Regions, the formulation of the principle of subsidarity, transnational regional cooperation policies, the definition of the NUTS system and others (Balchin/Sýkora/Bull 1999). Although it is obvious that the political use of the regionalization process by the European Union is also fostering and pushing it, it remains an open debate on how far this will happen and which meaning certain policies will have on the ground. Especially, the European Spatial Development Perspective (ESDP) has attracted a wider audience as it is here that many crucial ideas on how the European Union will be interlinked and spatially develop are mapped out. While the "region" has made a veritable career as a key word in the programmes of the EU; within the concerned discourse, the term remains attached to a variety of different definitions linked to spatial, historical, social, political and cultural discourses. The link—between the macro trends of globalization, the debate on political steering and the sociological perspective on the regionalization of life worlds seemingly fit together. In this short introduction, some links between the different understandings of the region are presented. To enable the analysis of problems and to contribute to their solution, it becomes necessary to clarify the terms we use to address the process of "regionalization." Therefore, in the following discourse, different approaches to theoretically embed the appearance of the "region" will be discussed. However, it remains unsatisfying to narrow the research down to the aspect of the particularities of places and therefore to the historically differing expression of what is here called "regionalization".

Regionalization and Globalization

This very basic assumption in urban studies is heavily under question today. Many recent developments and macro trends in society seemingly foster the idea that the "end of geography" has a transforming effect on the relationship between social organization and spatial forms. The appearance of new communication and information technologies has led to a new definition of distances and a reshaping of our immediate surrounding. Globalization, in all its facets, questions the societal pre-conditions to urbanism as a way of life. While it remains an open debate as to how we would live in the globalizing city in the future, the existence of cities as entities of societal organization has not been regarded as essentially challenged.

Regions are considered as being the other side of the coin of globalization. On a worldwide scale, regionalization is shaping two new phases of urbanization: first of all, regions are developing on a supra-national level as geographical regionalism where multi-nationalism is a dominating factor. Secondly, regionalization is replacing the nation state on sub-national level. Mega-cities are often seen to predominate the constitution of political systems and society (Costa 1998). Globalization has been contributing to this phenomenon in many ways. The key idea is that a globally evolving network society on the basis of new com-munication, transport and information technologies allows the reshaping of spatial entities (Castells 1996). While this speeds up the mobility of "flows" of migrants, goods, services and signs; the "time-space compression" (Harvey 1989) does not lead to an end of geography but, on the contrary, to a new process of concentration of economical activities and power (Sassen 1991). The trajectories of globalization on spatial developments, however, lead more to a mosaic of geographies and to a new colourful map of the world (Giddens 1990).

Regionalization from Economic Transformation

The discourses on regional development and particularly those claiming a wider significance of "regionalization" are mostly guided by economic theories. Since the early sixties, regional economic analyses have focussed on the patterns of settlement and investment decisions of firms with regard to geographical positioning processes (MnNee 1960). The focus was then broadened by including a wider concept of "investment resources" (Drèze 2001) which, as a consequence, led to works under-lining the importance of external growth factors in general. Regions, in this kind of analysis, have been regarded as merely passive victims of macro-economical activities (Bluestone/Harrison 1982). Simultaneously, it was considered by other authors that cooperative strategies and structure within the region should be taken into consideration as well (Chandler 1962). Slowly, the attention of scholars has been increasingly attracted by local economic cultures and informal network structures (Goodman/ Bamford 1991). And since the nineties, regions have gained a high priority in analysing innovation regimes and political governance (Cooke 1994).

In general, regionalization is often linked to certain transformations in the urban economies (Markusen/DiGiovanna 1999). The shift towards a regional organization of urban economies is regarded as having far reach-ing consequences for the establishment of new societal arrangements;

thus creating a "regional world" (Storper 1997a). While the growing interrelationship between core cities and surrounding areas is obvious in many cases, it has become difficult to identify the main direction of economic regionalization. Foremost, the loss of manufacturing industries and thereby a vast de-industrialization can be found in many regions which have once hosted classical heavy industries like steel and coal production, car manufacturing and ship building. It has become a common perspective to declare these regions as being in transition, which implies a certain time expectation and a presupposed end of de-industrialization. Furthermore, it appeals to evoke an image of a replacing new mass production. For a long period, the decline of regions, like the German Rhein-Ruhr area, has been addressed by rhetoric of "restructuring" (Massey/Meegan 1978). In reality, this perspective has not been expected to reflect the new type of regionalization. As a consequence, the debate on the new regions needs to take into consideration that certain regions are "restructured", "reindustrialised" and have regained economic growth, while other old industrial regions still remain in a desolate position and do not show signs of a new economic regime. Regionalization, therefore, is more about those areas which are seen as contributing to the growth of the transformed economy, in particular the new communication, transport and information technologies (DiGiovanna 1996).

Reorganization of the Regional Economy

The new dimension of economic restructuring of regions has different characteristics, not all of which are to be found in every case. Nevertheless, many scholars have pointed out that the emergence of inner regional networks or their intensified interference between firms is one of the most important features of the new regionalization (Harrison 1992). This leads to a more flexible management and cooperation which affects distribution lines and communication (Sabel 1989). The role of the new technologies has been regarded as crucial (Harrison 1994). Scale becomes another decisive issue. It is not that the disappearance of the old mass production sites and their total replacement by other industries signals the restructuring process as such. It is more likely that major enterprises are downsizing their productive capacities and a growing number of smaller firms organize a higher interlinked regional co-operation. This development is accompanied by a fragmentation of the supplier market (Piore/Sable 1984).

Another important reason for the reorganization of regional economy has been observed in the diversification of the production and consumption structure of the region, which follows an increasingly vertical disintegration (Christopherson 1993). As this leads to a clustering of production capacities and an outsourcing of productive activities and services, both competition and cooperation within a branch and between different sectors of industry are on the increase (Einem 1994). Economic competitiveness is the driving force behind regionalization processes; although the institutional contexts and cultural-legal political legacies are different (Herrschel/Newman 2002). It is evident that these economic changes in the regional structure are accompanied by a new valorization of the power relationships and the terms of competition. Seemingly, it can be observed that markets develop a process of oligopoly concentration of power and another relation with regard to the public administration and actors reconfiguring their role as customers, regulators and clients (Saxenian 1994). Patterns of flexible regionalization depend on a highly mobile workforce with a strong back hold of "social capital" and especially with above average skills (Angel 1989). Related to this flexibilization of economic ties and of the "work" factor, are consequences concerning the overall societal organization which has to cope with an accelerated economic insecurity and social inequalities on a regional scale (Leitner/ Sheppard 1998).

Paradigmatic Regions

The processes of regionalization have been described as following different paths of development. Nevertheless, the mode of "new industrial districts" is often linked to a certain image which goes back to the early analysis of "Marshallian areas" (Marshall 1987). These regions have been regarded as paradigmatic for a long time and they still occupy the imagination of many scholars and the public debate. The identification of certain regions as following this stereotype spatial entity has been of great significance. Underlying the debate about "Silicon Valleys" is the assumption that with the new types of regional morphologies, the new development of socio-political spaces is unavoidable and, from a political point of view, the special conditions for supporting or initiating processes for a regional growth process à la Silicon Valley have become popular and wide-spread. Linked to the debate is the concept of "innovative milieux", which has been the starting point to research the required prerogatives in establishing this new form of region. Considerable research has been undertaken to develop a broader understanding of the communalities of these new industrial regions (Florida/Kennedy 1990). Nevertheless, the generalization of certain cases of the "New Marshallian Districts" has been proved to be critical. Especially within the European context, only the north Italian regionalization seems to fit into the US-led imagination on these typical forms of regional restructuring and seems to have a reasonable amount of common indicators (Best 1990).

Recent debates on this form of new districts suppose that regionalization is increasingly developing probably more important and common forms of regional-urban structures. As Markusen (1999a) has pointed out, as an outcome of international comparative studies, three other forms of regionalization have to be taken into account: (1) The further existence of mono-structured regions which are dominated by one major economical actor or branch. (2) Regions which primarily function as satellite areas for globally operating industrial complexes or single multinational firms. Here, arenas of high-tech industries and low wage-service industries are often to be found. In many cases, public money has been pumped into these areas to foster the settlement of these firms. (3) For some regions, these financial investments by government bodies are a predominant factor. This can be seen in the obvious case of military-industrial areas and those mega city-regions which host capital city functions and thereby produce some kind of chain investment flows from the private market. This typology might be helpful to discuss the significance of what has been called the "endogenous growth" of regions and the influence of the exterior world. Furthermore, the possible opportunities to influence regional growth by local, regional and national politics are becoming visible. To sum up the discussion, the overwhelming influence of certain regional and global players in three of four types of regionalization becomes obvious; so that certain scholars question the ability of political steering in the face of existing negative dependence patterns (Howes 1993), while others have been neglecting those effects (Hellmer/Friese/Kollros/Krumbein 1999). It is presupposed that regions have, in any case, some kind of capacity of their own that only needs to be developed and strengthened with regard to its global competitiveness and compatibility. Many scholars have been critical about the issue of public intervention in general. It has been argued that these temptations lead to a kind of cultural conservatism, which is due to overshadowing positive short term effects in the long run. The politically wishful transformation from one type of region to another - especially towards the creation of self sustaining new industrial districts - needs some kind of liberal atmosphere. Although research on this issue has not yet reached a satisfying state of art, it seems that some prerogatives can be pointed to. Universities and other educational and cultural institutions deliver a more flexible and innovative work force to regional labour markets. Elaborated producer-consumer relationships, a high quality work force, networks between competing firms and a strongly engaged political culture locally are often mentioned as necessary prerogatives (Markussen 1999a, 40).

Regionalization as Regime

Apart from defining categorical approaches to forms of regionalization, the question that remains most significant is that in which way the obviously increasing importance of regions in a global and national economy can be explained and analysed. Changes in the regional production structure are often debated in a broader theoretical framework which circulates around more general ideas about the architecture of society as such. We have to reconsider the relationship between endogenous and external influences on regions. It has become common to identify certain aspects as expressing a new style of economic order. Regime theories are considering political governance of these processes as of having lesser control and impact. To a certain degree, the evidence of crisis in planning has fostered many different approaches to elaborate new forms of planning. Those often remain weak in the sense that they do not consider the planning incapacity of public administration as a consequence of broader societal changes and thus propose models like those of the so-called "third generation" (Heidemann 1992) which limit the view on the internal reform of planning authorities (Schönwandt 2002) .

While there is considerable evidence to the assumption of some kind of new regime of the regions, the description of those changes can be assumed rather as a sort of principal way of restructuring than as a clear picture of how regions (already) function. Stough describes these changes as the appearance of a neo-fordist economic structure of the regions, characterized by horizontal networks operating in volatile markets of global scope where the competition between sub-national companies and the geographic mobility of business is high. The organization of the new economy leads to a challenged form of production based on information and knowledge resources, where innovation, quality, time to market and costs are the sources of competitive advantages and the growth driver. Life long learning, collaborative labour-management relations and linked power grid are consequently the effects on the inner structures of firms (Stough 1998). Regions have become a field for the so-called *école de la régulation* which researches the modes of societal rearrangements and their relationship with different regimes of accumulation. It is the very basic assumption of this theoretical concept that there is an ongoing transition from an economy dominated by mass-production (fordist) to a new economy based on the politics of flexible production (post-fordist) (Lipietz 1986). The central point of interest in the regulation research is the anchorage of regional firms and branches within the region (Cox/Mair 1988).

As the usage of the vocabulary of "fordism" and "post-fordism" is intended to shape an integrative framework, few new insights can be possibly concluded from this starting point of research. It remains unclear, in how far the basic question of the regions, as a motor or as an expression of the emerging new economy, can be traced down in particular cases. It is certainly true that the "signs" of these neo-fordist regimes of regionalization can be found everywhere. It is another matter, however, to understand why this is the case. It can be said that the regulation theory does not really explain why there are differences in regions compared on a global scale without taking into account the already existing global division of labour. The "new economy" regions – more as an exception than as a rule, at least in the full sense of their definition – do not shape the appearance of most world city regions. Fordist space production, on the contrary, is still the most powerful regime (Markusen/Lee/DiGiovanna 1999). It is more fruitful then to understand these overwhelming forms of regionalization as necessary movements to meet the requirements of a restructured global economy (Storper/Walker 1989).

Theorists on post-fordist regionalization are delivering rich literature on the description of new regionalization patterns, in which they direct research for the remaining space for political steering as the main concern (Keim 2002). It relates the concept of policies for regional arenas to the theories of neo-institutional economies, which defines and analyses institutions in relation to their effects on transaction costs (North 1990). It then becomes interesting to see that on a micro-level, the understanding of political actors is integrated into these analyses in a rather classical way which pronounces the abilities of choices. As a consequence, leadership becomes a crucial point of research (Johansson/Karlsson/ Stóugh 2000). This leads to another widespread assumption derived from the pronounced significance of institutional settings and framings. Led by the focus on institutions, the basic assumptions about their functioning are generalized and considered as key elements for understanding the process of regionalization. Mostly, mutual trust and the capacity to mobilize all forms of resources are seen as the overall principles to understand steering processes in the region. It appears that those characteristics which explain leadership and the internal hierarchy are not compatible with the organizational form of the new economy, being described through "flexible" and collaborative labour-management forms. In this way, we have to imagine an old fashioned leadership operating on the basis of resources and trust and, at the same time, functioning in an economic milieu where innovation and knowledge are most important. In the light of books such as "The Flexible Man" by Richard Sennett (1998), the contradiction between a flexible work force and organizational steering does not seem to be impossible. But especially in those prototypes of flexible organization, the construction of "trust" seems to be more eroded than upgraded.

Regionalization as a Global Pattern of Urbanization

While the cities in the non-OECD world - like Mexico City, Sao Paulo, Mumbai, Cairo and others - had long been discussed as not fitting in the analytical scheme for the modern city any longer; the phenomena of "regional cities" has become an issue for the western urban scholars only recently. It is one of the main achievements of the debate about the so called "L.A. School" (Soja 2000) that the issue has been given a new priority. A lot has to be taken into account, if one wants to look at the morphological similarities all over the world. What might obviously be the same pattern of urban development in the OECD and the non-OECD world can be traced down to different, if not antagonist, reasons for processes leading to comparable urban morphological forms. A central issue has been the enduring significance and socio-political role of the city centre. When geographical space is interlinked with areas not included so far into the political reach of urban governance, the territorial organization of the city loses its ability to direct and govern the spatial development in total. "Regionalization" therefore goes beyond the debate on how to cope with a multiplication of interests and the immense growth of stake-holders. Politically, it is a quantum leap into an area where the definition of political territory within the nation state regains crucial importance. Whereas globalization generates, with the same challenge, the definition of the economic, social and political "local" in the face of an ever growing attendance, influence and power of the "global"; the relationship between the city and the region asks the same question with regard to the remaining territorialization of the "city". Both processes of regionalization and globalization confront the existent urban structures and established forms of governance with the challenge of increasing interconnectedness. The global comes near via new communication and transport systems; the regional unbinds the limitations between cities, cities and their back-yard and even national borders. At the heart of this development, the redefinition of functional borders becomes most evident for planning and living within the new emerging spatial constructs. The discourse on how to plan regions in a global area has just begun and is often framed by theories of sustainability. Using terms like city, country-side, suburbia, and now region implies ipso facto that fixed linkages are assumed between spatial development modes and phases of societal arrangements. No-body will question that a suburb is and looks different in every two cases, but this does not imply–a concept of urban development wherein sub-urbanization is seen as some kind of natural (if not ecological) part of a given scheme of phases as such. When the focus now turns onto the phenomena of the regionalized urban landscape, the research intrinsically looks for new patterns of same quality. One could argue that their is either no general way of developing a world-wide spread mode of regiona-lization or describe as many types of regionalization as evident in their case studies. Here, the history of researching the industrial or the modern, the fordist or the post-modern city seems to be repeated. Learning from the Global City-debate, we could conclude that future urban research should not end up in classifications and hierarchies ("Which city is a global one?"), but in understanding the processes of globalization, and here, regionalization as putting urban space onto a scale where it can be placed according to the intensity of these processes. From identifying the modes of regionalization in each case, the focal point of research would lie on the task of identifying the circumstances that sustain or hinder the melting of cities into the region.

Regionalization after Urban Sprawl

Suburbanization has been a guiding model to analyse the city-region-relationship for a long period. With the term "suburban," the debate holds a connotation of hierarchy between the city and its surrounding. While this might be considered as being of theoretical relevance, the development of the regionalized space shows that there is evidence to reject a simple domination of the city over suburbia. The formerly detached and depen-dent urban areas are evolving as more autonomously functioning spaces. As a consequence of this discursive development regarding regionali-zation, the focus of research shifts from a merely suburbanization of housing (Aring 1999) to a more holistic approach which includes in-creasingly other important features of post-suburbia. As a first reflex, this morphological phenomenon was analysed in a normative perspective with a clearly negative estimation. Publications such as "The Disappearance of the city" (Krämer-Badoni 1997) or the "Dissolution of the City into the Sur-rounding" (Bose 1997) influenced political programmes which were more or less dedicated to fight suburbanization. An important argument was that suburban life is less sustainable. In the second phase, some scholars questioned the conception of suburbanization from historical, sociological and spatial planning aspects. Then came a certain reflection on the regionalized city with a more positive attitude towards its aesthetical, ecological and other functions (Sieverts 1997). The observation of a growing independence of these outer town areas found an international audience and a broader theoretical framework (Prigge 1998). Recent debates consider the "Region City" as a given fact but also include counter-developments "after sprawl" (Calthorpe/Fulton 2001).
While the shrinkage of distances and the re-evaluation of nearness might lie at the heart of the global city discourse, the new debate regarding the growth of cities has been another important feature in urban studies for

the last decade. This topic has been expressed in a wide range of specific terminologies. Urban sprawl, edge cities, peripherization, mega cities, networking cities, regionalization or post-suburbanization are some key words often used in studies to point mostly at the same phenomenon. Although significant differences have to be taken care of, most scholars working on the analysis of these processes of new spatial forms are motivated by the observation of appearances which are neither urban nor rural at first sight. In particular, the fast growth of those areas regularly called "mega cities" brings into consciousness that our understanding of social processes evolving in these "regions" with many million inhabitants is limited. After more than a century of institutionalized research on the modern city, it seems that the established forms of researching social life cannot simply be applied in these hyper growth areas. Pitfalls await those scholars who ignore the fact that size does matter. While there has always been an awareness that urban life needs to have a considerable number of fellow citizens necessary to develop "urban mindedness", to-day, the question comes up whether there is also a maximum limit of inhabitants for calling a place a "city." It has to be seriously reconsidered if the functional integration of social organizations is due to the scope of spatial capacities. Until now, the term "city" implies the image of intensive and widely interconnected parts of different actors on behalf of a common good. While the different spheres of functionalism have their own logic of development, control and communication; all major functional areas of urban life such as transport, housing, consumption, production, com-munication, political decision making, public administration and social and cultural infrastructure are bound to and embedded into a spatial organization which is more or less transparent and with some kind of coherence.

Regionalization of Politics

Another point leads to a critical review of the concept of neo-fordist regionalization and the re-established analysis of leadership. It is the question of scale and distance. Although it might be easier to travel and communicate in those regions which are most restructured by the new economy, the pure fact that we have to deal with ever growing and increasingly interfering spaces provokes the idea that the concept of "mutual trust," deriving from intra-organizational and personal interaction, cannot be simultaneously applied with regard to socio-political areas as large as regions. Reconsidering the assumptions of Giddens (1990) about the transformation of trust as a consequence of modernity, it could be said that regionalized trust might be the product of some kind organizational form not especially linked to those actors, firms and organizations that are meant to be the primary source of restructuring the region. Moreover, it seems unlikely that a flexible economy structure, wherein the workforce is lesser supported by public institutions and capturing a lesser secured social position, develops a "trustworthy" attitude of their employees towards their place of momentary stay.

The issue of leadership thus leads to the debate on mechanisms ensuring political support for regional governance. A first assumption could be that a support system is produced by abstract feedback lines. As found in much politic rhetoric to advocate a more flexible regime, positive effects on the outcome of those processes give legitimacy to the political system. To achieve these confirming results, (real or imagined) achievements have to be recognized by the most relevant voter groups and network actors. The latter can be regarded as decisive in some cases, as they create an image or a public atmosphere in the media. The significance of new roles for public actors and politicians can be explained exactly from this point of view towards regionalized politics. There is an increasing loss of interference between policy outcome and positive social impact which leads to a regeneration of support mechanism in the public arena. Network policies and structures have regained importance and, in this regard, "institutional thickness" has been identified to be most relevant to transform a local culture and thereby guarantee support for the economic restructuring (Amin/Thrift 1994). Regionalization requires a sort of "deeper" (Clarke1996) politics which is based on a colourful "tiger pattern" of institutional networks (Hirst 1994). The term "institution" is stretched in these analyses so as to also cover informal and social arrangements which are capable of producing a regional quality (Krtätke/Heeg/Stein 1998, 134-143). The literature, therefore, has extended the research on networks and regions with regard to the redefinition of regional politics. How to stimulate and foster regional networks to contribute to the wealth of the region has been an issue for many politicians already (Hollbach-Grömig 2001, 5). During initial research studies, the focus on regional networks broadened up by including regional milieus and the "soft ties". The question that became crucial was that in which way regional networking could be seen as a means to produce a "creative milieu" (Adrian 2003).

Planning Regionalization?

With regard to German regional planning, the introduction of "Regional Development Concepts," mostly alongside the Christaller's classical "Theory of Central Places," has been evaluated to produce positive side-effects especially in non-planning areas like "learning processes" and as a means to increase the capacity of regional governance (Keim/Kühn

2002). Networks in regional policies are often placed into a theoretical consideration where "tacit knowledge" and "weak ties" are crucial (Genosko 1999). It remains critical at this point that there still is not a satisfying definition for regional networks; since political, economical or social forms of interaction can all be labelled as "networks" or described with other terms like "institutions". Here, different approaches; either from sociology, economy or political theory; have led to an unclear picture on what regional networks might be.

It is worth recalling that it was once considered an achievement that in (fordist) times the influence of networks on public decision making was reduced and made transparent. Now, the leadership-approach, guided by many network theories in urban governance debates, links the issue of networks to the positively co-notated enlargement of public involvement. In the debate on governance, these forms of network policies are considered to be part of a new form of participation and direct democracy. While initial research has shown that these networks are increasingly organized in an informal way, the relationship with the existing ad-ministrative and formal planning procedures remains unclear (Gorsler 2002). Many authors (Scheer 1993; Selle 1996) have argued here with a normative concept of governance which enlarges the scope of public involvement in administrative activities and decision making-processes. By doing so, the challenged perception of the role of networks in organizing the region leaves the question open as to how these new forms of cooperation are different from those having been regarded critical in fordist times. Since the administrative bodies and local political institutions have been under public criticism as insufficiently reflecting the interests of the concerned citizens and reducing them to the role of per-ceiving decisions by abstract and incommunicative officials, the opening up of the administrative "closed shop" certainly has to be analysed in the framework of participative democracy. While this is obvious in cases with a direct link to inhabitants' interests, it seems to be difficult to place many new networks under the same heading. Networks between political re-presentatives and strong economic players, especially when they do not take the shape of institutionalized private-public partnerships, bring-up the issue of political exclusion of those social groups not able to participate. Control of networks and political legitimacy of decisions taken or influenced by those exclusive forums are of major concern here (Priebs 2004). Returning to the basic concept of a leadership-style political regionalization, "trust" becomes an even more critical concept; as long as the issue of power relations within interest/"growth" and advocacy co-alitions is left unrewarded. The experience of debates around networks related analysis leaves back a research agenda which should primarily include a neutral analysis of changed political settings by focusing on the outcome of both political regimes: who gains, and who loses influence on decision making processes if the political system evolves from a fordist bureaucracy towards a jungle of flexible post-fordist networks?

The way this question is formulated allows polarizing the two different approaches one could have with regard to the examination of changes in political representation. In reality, this alternative is not available and the political landscape of regions is often characterized by the co-existence of both institutional duration and emergence of new political and social arrangements. Thus, the issue of evaluating the outcome of the regime has to be traced back to the analysis of relationships of the whole regional political landscape and the single institutions. It has to be considered, in which way the neo-institutional framework views the external field of institutions as part of a historical, regional and local particularity. In this regard, this framework has to be extended by including a closer look at the origins of the so-called fordist bureaucracy and its link to the particular form of modernity it expresses. If modernity is taken as the common history of currently existing forms of governance and those are considered as being fordist, the differences of regionalization would be embedded into a wider research on different modes of modernization. To follow this road of research would not simply mean that there is a historization of analysis for its own sake; but understanding the roots of societal power hierarchies and social conflicts embedded in the spatial dimension of fordism/ post-fordism would lead to an explanation of the different paths of regional and urban development.

Regional Governance and Democracy

As a starting point, the debate on the political dimension of the new regional research has taken a theoretical embedding where a broader consideration of state restructuring is regarded to be the overarching issue. This has to do with those tendencies visible in contemporary re-forms of the welfare state where, at the same time, the state is reduced to its basic functions; the philosophy of self-containment of the population and the growth of new demands regarding environmental problems, for example, has shaped a new form of understanding what political organization is meant to be (Benz et al. 1999, 22). In this perspective, the term "regional governance" has been introduced in many discourses to underpin a qualitative difference with regard to those forms of regional institutionalization mostly concerned with functional steering tasks taken over from the state (Fürst 2003). A major change in the political architecture of regions has been found in inter-communal cooperation. International comparison leads to the conclusion that since the late eighties, policies have underlined the necessity to increase cooperation between the cities and the surrounding region. Fragmentation of the political and administrative structure at the local level, a dynamic development of the functional interferences, changed tasks of the political administration, financial disputes between the city and the region, and other factors have been reflected in political discourses all over Europe in such a way that cooperation has been fostered by some (central policy actors, political representatives of the core cities, economical players, media and advisory institutions) and refused by others (existing cooperative organizations, cities outside of the core, certain social groups, some scientists). In practice, increased cooperation leads to a project bound, either task or theme specific, renaissance of regional cooperation (Heinz 2000).

Regionalization and Culture

The issue of regionalization processes not directly linked to economic restructuring or derived from them has been embedded in discourses that operate more or less in great autonomy. While it is certainly true that the cultural aspect of regionalization has to be fitted within a broader perspective on societal developments, the very significance of regions as places of cultural activities and processes is of doubtless importance. Although this consideration might lead to a more fundamental discussion about culture and society in general (Hannerz 1996), with regard to the research on regions and processes of regionalization, the issue of "culture" cannot be left out. On the contrary, many apparent characteristics of regions, especially the process of transformation of the old industrial areas into the so-called new industrial zones, are related to one or the other aspect of cultural life. Culture has been used as a concept within the regulationist approach to define some kind of institutional prerogatives. The degree of interference of institutions within a region could then indicate the value of economical restructuring. Within this framework, regional cultures are more or less a product of an institutional landscape that is linked and interacting with the economical restructuring process. While "culture," here, as such remains a narrowed analytical concept, at the same time it remains unclear as to how the mechanism of regional culture and economy functions. It can be supposed that, within the predominant economic theory of regions, the relationship between both terms of analysis is constructed as a top-down hierarchy, leaving little or no autonomous sphere for local and regional cultures.

Surprisingly, in the wider debate on the restructuring of regions, many scholars end up with a notion of culture within a policy analysis. Here, terms such as identity politics, symbolic intervention, festivalization of politics and others count up to outline new ways of political steering. This is all the more true with regard to the political attempts to use culture as a means of urban regeneration (Bianchini/Parkinson 1993). As far as regions are concerned, only a few cases are already internationally discussed as being of presumably paradigmatic significance. One example mentioned quite often is the International Building Exhibition in the Rhine-Ruhr Region (Prossek 2004). Many others have not received as much attention or are linked to cities which are heads of regions. While there is a considerable debate already on the consequences of this "culturalization" of urban politics, which often is a simple instrumentalization of culture, the same cannot yet be said with regard to research in regional studies. Probably, the lacking research mirrors the nonexistence of regional cultural policies. This, however, can only be considered to be true as long as one keeps to the framework of the predominant theory of economical restructuring elaborated above. From a socio-psychological point of departure, the region has had a significant role for many inhabitants in defining their spatial basis of personal identity. This might especially be true in nation states with a weak or critical national identity. According to many surveys, the recognition of some regional particularity important to the interviewed person is evident. In most cases, regions here are not considered in terms of morphological-functional entities but as some kind of historical construct. Examples can be found all over Europe like Bavaria in Germany, Breton in France or Castile in Spain. Conflicts about the relation between these regions and the respective nation states have been a major issue for the reshaping of Europe after the end of the cold war. With the process of European integration, the regions have not only gained political status but they are also considered as an essential basis for the realization of European governance. Many accessing countries had to change their state constitution to introduce or adapt the EU defined concept of regions.

Regionalization and Identity Politics

Until now, it has not been discussed whether both forms of socio-psychological processes of identity building (the historical and the morphological) are to be analysed in the same way. It is worth debating whether regionalization will produce mechanisms which are capable of developing a socio-psychological function comparable with those cases of historical regionalism. As this might be easy to answer at first sight, there are some indications that an intensified research on this issue might be worth the effort. Firstly, the references to historical sources as the basis for certain forms of regionalism has to be understood as a construct of changes in political steering regimes as they obviously also happen in those regionalizing city areas (Elsner 2000). Secondly, many regionalized urban areas are emerging not just within the last decade but they do have some social and cultural notion of their belonging together which can be traced to a longer period of tradition. Thirdly, in many cases, European regionalism is constructed with vague borders and the spatial basis for those politically motivated entities is related to some urban-regional centre. Barcelona in Castile, the city-states Berlin, Hamburg and Bremen in Germany, Edinburgh and Glasgow in Scotland, Rennes in Breton and other places are not just another place within their regions but they have been regarded as their centres and have been overloaded with symbolic significance for regionalism. Finally, the effects of macro-societal trends, such as globalization and medialization, have influenced the spatial element of both mechanisms to create a personal identity.

Seriously taking into account the concept of identity in regional studies would require a theoretical framework that needs to reflect, in the first place, the effects of key changes in society and an understanding of the role "identity" would be able to play. In many contributions on this issue, the term "identity politics" remains vague and reflects the critical assumption of identity as a social construct rather than as a personal one. In the tradition of sociological considerations stemming out of Weber's neglecting of collective actors, it is nothing but self-evident to declare the existence of those collective identities. On the contrary, there are important arguments to reject this way of analysis. Not only must a scientific debate on "collective identity" beware of a distance to the political instrumentalization, but also the analysis of a personal and a regional identity obviously needs different methodologies. It has become common to understand the construction of personal identity in two ways. Firstly, a person integrates and out-balances biographical development and change of social roles within his identity (Habermas 1984-89). What then is described as one's own identity is thus, and secondly, not only the result of self-interpretation but also a consequence of external attribution of characteristics (Goffman 1999). In the light of the overall reshaping of society, where flexible life styles are observed to be replacing the traditional milieus, it has been argued that the influences of external settings are either of to a lesser extent or reshaped in new forms of socialization. According to scholars following the idea that in post-modern times the individual is no longer embedded in social arenas with fixed settings of norms and values, the construction of identity takes place in direct relation to the macro-structures of society (Beck 2003). In the light of this consideration, the individual is forced to look for new ways of redefining his identity framing and his very place. Re-territorialization could then be one consequence of the disembedded man and the form of this "re-search" of one's own place could be the city or the region. Identity politics would offer to put his feet back on the ground.

Regionalized Life-Styles

Another position is the possibility that the process of shaping more flexible life-styles produces a nearly endless offer of identity models, some more applicable for certain social groups than others. In the end, only a few life-styles are clearly distinguishable and others are left to be of minor importance. Spaces here never vanish and are a factor for narrowing or enlarging the opportunities to choose or link up to certain life style-groups. The personal biography needs to integrate this differences and the external "backing" of becoming a member of a different life style-group, which has to provide the external attribution. The process of urbanization has shaped various forms of spatial entities. Significant differences have been the outcome of specific historical and societal circumstances of the morphologies of space. In the first place, the founding of cities and the migration flow from the countryside to them has been regarded as a major development in both society and space. In the analysis of these pro-cesses, many scholars have found evidence to build up theories of a wider range. The phenomena of the European city have influenced Max Weber in his thoughts about modern society as such. Especially, the growth of the industrial city at the end of the 19th century brought up the question of the specific relationship between space and society. Migrants only recently arriving in the new cities of the second industrial revolution have had another habitus as the classical citoyen. The difference between a rural attitude towards community (Gemeinschaft) and an urban minded person embedded in an abstract social system (Gesellschaft) remained to be of importance. Whether these primary assumptions hold ground on the basis of empirical research, has been the issue for decades of research. The basic line of analysis was always the idea that the composition and framework of space has a significant influence on the conceptualization of social interaction and personal prepositions.

Empirical research has shown that it is still reasonable to consider so-cialization processes as the basis for identification building, but also that it is no longer the direct surroundings in early childhood which create the "natural resource" for personal identities. Instead, the significance of normatively perceived relevant "others" and their relationship to spatial entities, especially the region, is most evident. Secondly, identification processes are linked in a negative way to stereotypization and solidarity organization of those affected. Finally, identification with a region is more rational as considered in theories which supposedly work with images and other emotional aspects of communication. Images are regarded to con-tribute to the social construction of regional knowledge (Buttimer 1999). It is still the functional outcome of the region which allows the development of a positive view on the living conditions. In other words, I feel at home when the region is offering work, education, housing and other qualities The mobility is generally lower, if people identify more with the region. But in general, however, one should not trust the effects of identification with the region too much (Mühler/Opp 2004).

Space, probably, has even more functions in the new arrangement of the individual identity. Cities are considered to be of importance in this way, as they provide a kind of playground for experiencing the process of external and auto-definition of identity. Within this theoretical observation, regional identity politics would have to deal with a multitude of identities and would be nearly incapable of defining a common denominator for all socially and individually practiced identity strategies. Looking at the home pages of regions and cities and into documents attempting to describe what is it like to be a citizen of this particular place, the slogans are ridiculous, vague or pumped up with catchy terms which already express the predominance of certain lifestyle groups in the local discourse or administration. But there are other factors which underline that the de- and re-territorialization, assumed by Beck and others, only reflects the particular construction of one single life-style group. Nevertheless, the example of this group gives us insights into the general logic on how the mechanism of de- and reterritorialization works and points at the necessity to have a closer look at the medialization of society. Not only do the new communication and information technologies, along with the effects of the old television (now in global scope), transmit possible forms of role patterns including acceptable norms and values (returning to Mc Luhan's wisdom that the media is also the message) but they also frame our understanding of fundamental socio-psychological concepts of space and time. Socio-spatial references to key points of personal identity like distance, difference, nearness, and home are reshaped by medial deliverance of new models. As identities are not solely shaped in interest aware and rationally steered processes, the emotional side of these processes becomes especially covered by globally connected media. "Spaces" as cities or regions and their perception in that sense is also an emotional experience which needs to be brought into a form that goes along with the media life of each inhabitant and traveller. Cities and regions therefore reproduce globally spread "emotion pictures" as a romantized and exoticized establishment of ethnic cuisines and the Parisian or Italian-style reshaping of public spaces with the obligatory table-on-the-sidewalk cafés.

Socio-Psychological Regionalization

While it might become somewhat clearer as to how the processes of spatialization of personal identities work, the relation between dis-embedding and rearrangement in life style-groups has to be regarded against a societal horizon that indicates the historical and particular regional constraints of their development. In this aspect, the difference be-tween the so-called regionalism and the regionalization of urban space becomes significant once again. Regional identity politics can thus have different points of departure and build up various considerations about the reinvention of traditions and self-images attractive to the outside world – particular tourists, investors, and visitors – as well. The encounter with the external view, however, is a crucial point to analyse identity politics. The region as "home," and in particular the German notion of "Heimat," has been merely constructed with the endogenous definition of regional particularity and has been, to a certain degree, a product or the basis of ethnocentricity (Lindner 1994, 9). Identity politics for a world city region is of another kind and, here, the comparison with personal identity pro-cesses might be useful: Regions are composing a specific way to inte-grate the non-local, the flexible, and the flow of people, products, service-es, images and concepts. It is appropriate to debate whether the region could take over this primarily emotional function which has long been fulfilled by the social geography of cities. The regionalization of life has let their users, inhabitants, clients and actors operate on another scale. While the city has been built up by a shared view on its socio-geographic di-vision into centre-suburbia-periphery; which is meant to be an integrative concept directed towards an evolving "inner part" and other parts as of being "transition" (compare the Chicago School tradition of urban re-search); limits are becoming the main characteristic of the socio-psycho-logical imagination of the region (Schilling 2000, 11). The remaining significance of the urban centrality and its socio-psychological significance as a fixed point of orientation seem to be replaced by regional images integrating other spaces relevant for the organization of individual emo-tions (Hübern/Brinckmann 1995).

To research the significance of regionalization in everyday life, the ethno-graphy of regionalized life needs to overcome essentialist approaches which (re-)construct authenticity. It is a well observed process that those characteristics often attributed to a regional identity are intended to fulfil other means. With the re-lecture of Webers concept of "ethnic com-munities", Lindner proposes to research those activities in a new form of European ethnography which begins with the observation of activities be-yond and outside religious and language based communities. In this sense, the analysis of the unspoken regionalization of our lives would give us clues about the transformed grammar of everyday culture (Lindner 1996).

Taking into consideration the change of definition, scope, theoretical outreach, and critical and empirical operationalization of the term "region", the conclusion one can draw from the recent debates is that (1) we have to tame the expectation that "regionalization" is a clearer concept than others in social science, geography, urban studies, economical theories and other space oriented disciplines (Miggelbrink 2002) and that (2) an enlarged understanding of regionalization as a social geography of everyday life is necessary. As a first step, the theoretical founding has to re-consider the ontological basis of societal-spatial relationships. So far, the considerations of Werlen have primarily linked the structuration theory Giddens' to the essentials of social geography (Werlen 1995). A major achievement of this approach is that it integrates a methodological dualism (means and media of activities) with a principal analysis of society as such. The letter describes certain forms of social geography of regionalization with regard to different stages of modernity. Time and space are differently incorporated in the constitution of traditional societies and the ones in the period of late modernity. For Werlen, an ontological difference can be pointed out in both periods of societal development in the sense that the pre-modern ontology is based on subjective, heuristic and a naturalistic conception of space wherein the perception of inorganic features of the cosmos is extended to the mapping of every soul. The body of the earth not only incorporates the physical character of the animated world but also the areas of consciousness (202). In a modern society, space is not "behind" or "next to" other objects but is anchored in a reflexive and relational conception of space and society. Space becomes an abbreviation for problems and opportunities in the realization of intentions for activities and social communication. Theories of new regionalism have to be radicalized so as to allow the "making of geography" to include an analysis of the constitution of society within a globalized world. The "region" endangers the ontological view on the late-modern society as it is still bound to a concept of absolute and not relative spaces (Werlen 1997, 209). Following an acceptance of the social construction of the "region", a phenomenological perspective can avoid this pitfall of seeing the region as an already given fact. Globalization leads to a re-embedding of the construction and constitution in everyday regionalization as a productive-consumptive linkage, in a normative-political form and as an informative-significant mode (283).

Refocusing Regional Studies

Particularity of the urban and regional case study on the one hand and the search for a general mode of socio-spatial development on the other has not yet been brought together. The region has developed to be an object of separate interests and "Regional Science" can as well be regarded as a field of many specialists who do not necessarily integrate an urban perspective in their work. At the same time, most urban scholars use the term "the city," as if there still is a clear definition to where New York, Frankfurt, Paris, Rio or Shanghai end. If the challenge placed by "regionalization" would be taken up seriously, the integration of both regional and urban studies must be reinforced in a way that the analytical framework for research is redirected to analyse the basic assumptions about the relationship between territory and society. Does regionalization produce – framed by particular historical settings – a new fixation of spatial and social organization? It is of the highest significance to link this question to an analysis of the macro tendencies of societal changes, foremost of those within the nation state, and with regard to the shaping of new globalization processes of socialization and governance. In other words, the issue of space in a world where places are playing new roles in the social and political order must be more strongly linked to the analysis of globalization and the processes linked to it. Asking for such a redirection of urban and regional research seems to be a complicated and confusing perspective. But if urban studies should avoid losing its relevance, because space and society are no longer only interlinked by the "urban" but by the "global" and the "regional", the analysis of those phenomena has to be globalized and regionalized first. Comparative studies, which are always difficult, have to become the major approach for a translocal perspective on the regionalization of space and society (Eckardt 2004).

As this book samples some case studies which are written in the light of an intensified study on the principle characteristics of regionalization, there is no major discourse in any related discipline about how to read the socio-political signs deriving from the emerging regional landscape. Instead, the varying use and understanding of the term "region" (Weichhart 1996) leads to link research findings only to questions relevant in the own discipline. It remains difficult to organize a fruitful cross-over without having a new platform for discourse. Nevertheless, it might be more fruitful to keep the term in its verity, as it allows us to discuss the embedding of the city and the new form of urban organization into a broader context of spatial and societal development. In this way, the region signifies an entity that encaptures, prolongs or frames the city on a sub-national level.

References:

Adrian, L. (2003) Regionale Netzwerke als Handlungskonzept. Erfolg versprechender Weg einer innovationsorientierten Regionalentwicklung? Berlin: Difu.

Amin, A. /Thirft, N. (1994) Neo-Marshallin Nodes in Global Networks. In: Krumbein, W.(ed.) Ökonomische und politische Netzwerke in der Region. Münster: LIT, 115-140.

Aring, J. (1999) Suburbia- Postsuburbia – Zwischenstadt. Die jüngere Wohnsiedlungsentwicklung im Umland der großen Städte Westdeutschlands und Folgerungen für die Regionale Planung und Steuerung. Hannover: ARL.

Balchin, P. /Sýkora, L. /Bull, G. (1999) Regional Policy and Planning in Europe. London/New York: Routledge.

Beck, U. (2003) Individualization: Institutionalized Individualism and its Social And Political Consequences. London: Sage.

Benz, A. Fürst, D. /Kilper, H. /Rehfeld, S. (1999) Regionalisierung: Theorie, Praxis, Perspektiven. Opladen: Leske+Budrich.

Bianchini, F. /Parkinson, M. (eds.) (1993) Cultural Policy and Urban Regeneration: the West-European Experience. Manchester University Press.

Boland, P. (1996) Regional Development Strategies in Europe: A Summary of Key Issues. In: Alden, J. /Boland, P. (eds.) Regional Development Strategies. A European Perspective. London/Bristol: Jessica Kingsley.

Bose, M. (ed.) (1997) Die unaufhaltsame Auflösung der Stadt in die Region? Kritische Betrachtungen neuer Leitbilder, Konzepte, Kooperationsstrategien und Verwaltungsstrukturen für Stadtregionen. Dortmund: Dortmunder Vertrieb für Bau- und Planungsliteratur.

Buttimer, A. (1999) Text and Image: Social Construction of Regional Knowledge. Leipzig: Institut für Länderkunde.

Calthorpe, P. /Fulton, W. (2001) The Regional City. Planning for the End of Sprawl. Washington: Island Press.

Castells, M. (1996) The Rise of Network Society. Oxford: Blackwell.

Clarke, P. B. (1996) Deep Citizenship. London: Pluto.

Costa, F. J.et al. (1998) Currents of Change: Urban Planning and Regional Development. In: Noble, A. G. (ed.) Regional Development and Planning for the 21st Century. New Priorities, New Philosophies. Aldershot: Ashgate.

Danielzyk, R./Müller, B./Wirth, P. (2000) Regionale Entwicklungsansätze in Ostdeutschland – Eine Zwischenbilanz. In: Danielzyk, R. et al. (eds.) Sanierung und Entwicklung in Ostdeutschland – regionale Strategien auf dem Prüfstand. Dresden: IÖR.

DiGiovanna, S. (1996) Industrial Districts from a Regulation Perspective. In: Regional Studies, No. 4, pp. 373-386.

Drèze, J. (ed.) (2001) Advances in macroeconomic theory. Basingstoke: Palgrave.

Eckardt, F. (2004) Soziologie der Stadt. Bielefeld: transcript.

Elsner, W. (2000) "Regionalisierung und neuer Regionalismus. The Big Divide: Neoliberalismus oder Proaktive Regionalpolitik. In: Informationen zur Raumentwicklung, 9/10, Bonn: BBR.

Frey, Bruno S. /Eichenberger, R. (2001) Federalism with Overlapping Jursidictions and Variable Levels of Integration: The Concept of FOCI. In: Hagen, J.v./Widgren, M. (eds.) Regionalism in Europe. Geometrics and Strategies After 2000. Boston/ Dordrecht/ London: Kluwer.

Fürst, D. (2003) Steuerung auf regionaler Ebene versus Regional Governance. In: Informationen zur Raumentwicklung, Nr. 8/9., pp. 441-450.

Gawron, T./Jähnke, P. (2000) Kooperation in der Region – Einführung und Problemstellung. In: Jähnke, P./ Gawron, T. (eds.) Regionale Kooperation – Notwendigkeit und Herausforderung kommunaler Politik. Erkner: IRS.

Genosko, J. (1999) Netzwerke in der Regionalpolitik. Marburg: Schüren.

Giddens, A. (1990) Consequences of Modernity. Cambridge University Press.

Goffman, E. (1999) Frame Analysis: An Essay on the Organization of Experience.Boston: Northeastern University Press.

Gorsler, D: (2002) Informelle räumliche Planung. Stand der aktuellen Forschung und Forschungsbedarf. Hannover: ARL.

Habermas, J. (1984-1989) The theory of Communicative Action. Boston: Beacon.

Hannerz, U. (1996) Transnational Connections. Culture, People, Places. London: Routledge.

Heidemann, C. (1992) Regional Planning Methodology. Discussion Paper. University of Karlsruhe.

Hellmer, F./Friese, C./Kollros, H./Krumbein, W. (1999) Mythos Netwerke. Regionale Innovationsprozesse zwischen Kontinuität und Wandel. Berlin: edition sigma.

Herrschel, T./Newman, P. (2002) Governance of Europe's City Regions. Planning, Policy and Politics. London/New York: Routledge.

Hirst, (1994) Associative Democracy: New Forms of Economic and Social Governance. Cambridge University Press.

Hollbach-Grömig, B. (2001) Kommunale Wirtschaftsförderung in der Bundesrepublik Deutschland. Aktuelle Informationen des Difu.

Johansson, B./Karlson, C./Stough, R. (2000) Theories of Endogenous Regional,Growth – Lessons for Regional Policies. In: Johansson, B. /Karlsson, C. /Stough, R.R. (eds.) Theories of Endogenous Regional Growth. Berlin: Springer.

Keim, K.-D. (2002) Steuerungstheoretische Grundlagen für regionale Entwicklungskonzepte. In: Keim, K.-D./Kühn, M. (eds.) Regionale Entwicklungskonzepte. Strategien und Steuerungswirkungen. Hannover: ARL, pp 1-9.

Keim, K.-D./Kühn, M. (2002) Strategien und Steuerungswirkungen regionaler Entwicklungskonzepte – Ergebnisse und Schlussfolgerungen. In: Keim, K.-D./Kühn, M. (eds.) Regionale Entwicklungskonzepte. Strategien und Steuerungswirkungen. Hannover: ARL.

Krätke, S./Heeg, S./Stein, R (1997) Regionen im Umbruch : Probleme der Regionalentwicklung an den Grenzen zwischen "Ost" und "West". Frankfurt. Campus.

Lindner, R. (1996) Region als Forschungsgegenstand der Europäischen Ethnologie. In: Brunn, G. (ed) Region und Regionsbildung in Europa. Konzeptionen der Forschungen und empirische Befunde. Baden-Baden: Nomos, pp.94-99.

Maillat, D./Kebir, L. (2000) The Learning Region and Territorial Production Systems. In: Johansson, B. /Karlsson, C. /Stough, R.R. (eds.) Theories of Endogenous Regional Growth. Berlin: Springer.

Markusen, A. /DiGiovanna, S. (1999) Comprehending Fast Growing Regions. In: Markusen, A. /Lee, Y.-S. (eds.) Second Tier Cities, Rapid Growth beyond the Metropolis. Mineapolis: University of Minnesota Press.

Massey, D. /Meegan, R. (1978) Industrial Restructuring versus the Cities. In: US, No.15, pp. 273-288.

Miggelbrink, J. (2002) Der gezähmte Blick: zum Wandel des Diskurses über „Raum" und „Region" in humangeographischen Forschungsansätzen des ausgehenden 20. Jahrhunderts. Leipzig: Institut für Länderkunde.

Mühler, K./Opp, K.-D. (2004) Region und Nation. Zu den Ursachen und Wirkungen regionaler und überregionaler Identifikation. Wiesbaden: VS Verlag.

Newman, P./Thornley, Y. (2001) Globalization, World Cities, and Urban Planning. In: Thornley, A. /Rydin, Y. (eds.) Planning in a Global Era. Aldershot :Ashgate.

North, D. (1990) Institutions, Institutional Change, and Economic Performance. Cambridge University Press.

Pfaffenholz, N. (2002) Raumordnung und Regional- und Strukturförderung. Universität Münster.

Priebs, A. (2004) Vom Stadt-Umland-Gegensatz zur vernetzten Stadtregion. In: Gestring, N. et. Al. (eds.) Jahrbuch StadtRegion 2003. Schwerpunkt: Urbane Regionen. Opladen: Leske+Budrich, pp.17-42.

Prigge, W. (1998) (ed.) Peripherie ist überall. Frankfurt: Campus.

Rolle, C. (2000) Europäische Regionalpolitik zwischen ökonomischer Rationalität und politischer Macht. Eine förderalismustheoretische und politökonomische Analyse. Universität Münster.

Scheer, G. (1993) Erfahrungen mit der Organization Eigenständiger Regionalentwicklung. In: Schaffer, F. (ed.) Innovative Regionalentwicklung – Von der Planungsphilosophie zur Umsetzung. University of Augsburg.

Schönwandt, W. (2002) Planung in der Krise? Theoretische Orientierungen für Architektur, Stadt- und Raumplanung. Stuttgart: Kohlhammer.

Selle, K. (1996) Qualifikation für Planerinnen und Planer. In: Zentrale Einrichtung für Weiterbildung (ed.) Zukunftsaufgabe Moderation – Herausforderungen in der Raum- und Umweltplanung. Hannover: University Press.

Sennett, R. (1998) The Corrosion of Character: the Personal Consequences of Work in the New Capitalism. New York: Norton.

Soja, E. (2000) Postmetropolis: Critical Studies of Cities and Regions. Oxford: Blackwell.

Storper, M. (1997a) The Regional World: Territorial Development in a Globalized Economy. New York: Guilford Press.

-, /Walker, R. (1989) The capitalist Imperative: Territory, Technology, and Industrial Growth. London: Blackwell.

Stough, R.R. (1998) Learning and Learning Capability in the Fordist and Post Fordist Age: an Integrative Framework. In: Environment and Planning A, V40, 1255-1278.

Thornley, A. /Rydin, Y. (2002) Planning in a Global Era. In: Thornley, A. /Rydin, Y.(eds.) Planning in a Global Era. Aldershot: Ashgate.

Weichhart, P. (1996) Die Region – Chimäre, Artefakt oder Strukturprinzip sozialer Systeme? In: Brunn, G. (ed.) Region und Regionsbildung in Europa. Konzeptionen der Forschungen und empirische Befunde. Baden-Baden: Nomos, pp.25-43.

Werlen, B. (1995) Sozialgeographie alltäglicher Regionalisierungen. Band 1: Zur Ontologie von Gesellschaft und Raum. Stuttgart: Franz Steiner.

-, (1997) Sozialgeographie alltäglicher Regionalisierungen. Band 2: Globalisierung, Region und Regionalisierung. Stuttgart: Franz Steiner.

The Rise of the Urban Network Region; Characteristics, Conditions and Policies

Sako Musterd

Introduction

Many European cities have transformed from a situation in which they could be regarded as major compact historical centres, towards new urban formations at regional or metropolitan level. The rise of the new regional city or urban region is a complex process, in which the relationship between urban form and function is continuously re-constructed. The changes that occurred over the past decades are not to be regarded as an enlargement of the old compact city or city-region, but are the formation of a substantially different polycentric urban con-stellation in which new complementary links are being developed between cities; cities which formerly were related to the dominant core only.

This transformation process can be shown for many cities, across the world. Yet, at the same time there appear to be significant differences between urban development processes in various contexts. The dif-ferences seem to be due to different urban histories, different paths the cities have followed, but also due to different attitudes towards urban life, differences between the institutional structures that have been developed, and differences in actual governance of cities.

In this contribution it is my intention to add to the knowledge of that difference. I will focus on the emergence and internal differentiation of the regional city in the Dutch context, the Amsterdam region in particular, while referring, from time to time, to selected experiences elsewhere, mainly in the Western world. This contribution is partly based on a book: 'Amsterdam Human Capital' (Musterd and Salet 2003). The focus of the book is on the integral (social, economical, political, cultural, historical and contemporary) process of urban transformation of and in the Amsterdam region.

I will start with a very brief introduction of some of the geographical de-bates on changing urban forms and functions, both outside the Nether-lands and inside. Then I will present some research information, which helps to construct my own view of the emerging urban regions in the Dutch (Amsterdam) context. The internal variation of the newly developed urban regions will subsequently be dealt with, showing the rise of characteristic economic and residential milieus in a regional setting. Since the Netherlands is characterised by extensive state and local govern-mental interventions, which is often regarded to have major impacts on the urban economic and residential development processes it makes sense to briefly evaluate these interventions in the light of the changing urban fabric. The paper will be finished with some reflections and conclusions.

Cities without boundaries or compact polycentric urban network regions?

In the international debates on urban form and function we can find a fairly strong voice stating that the new urban realities may better be compared to star-spangled skies or even galaxies of urban space, than with compact settlements. Some believe that almost unlimited cities have developed or are about to develop. Friedman and Miller (1965) introduced the concept of 'urban field' to label the new urban zones, areas of low-density occupation, thin spaces and therefore highly dependent on car-traffic, but realities because of the economic and social networks that exist on that scale. Characteristic is the large scale and the polycentric structure, as well as the inclusion of large rural areas and recreation space. The new urban realities have many faces, but in all of them expansion processes beyond suburban sprawl have taken the lead. Due to the large size of the new urban fields, also new so-called edge cities have developed (Garreau 1991). These are peripheral cities, in which more or less complete packages of work, services and residential space are put together. This makes them more independent of the old core city centres. The suburb is not simply a space anymore that is an appendix of the old economic core area, but is one of the many cities in a new urban region. According to Fishman (1987) the 'new city' is truly multi-centred, consisting of a series of 'technoburbs'; the former core of the metropolitan area has lost its dominance. His work can in fact be presented as an extension of the ideas of Frank Lloyd Wright, who as early as in 1935 predicted that the suburb would make the city redundant Wright 1935).

However, there seems to be reason to question the view that cities would inevitably transform to vast urban spaces. Comments can be given which are of a general character and more specific if we focus the attention to Europe. As far as the general comments are concerned I have the impression that the references to super-regions in the American context insufficiently take into account the insights, which were put forward by Torsten Hägerstrand, already in the early 1970s. Stressing the link between time and space he showed that people's daily behaviour is highly structured and bounded by a variety of constraints. All sorts of capability constraints (the capacity of people, the speed of the car, traffic jams, access to resources, etc.) limit the activity spaces of individuals; coupling constraints (individuals will have to meet others on a certain location at a certain moment, for a certain time-period) reduce the time-space framework even further; finally authority constraints (rules, regulations, opening hours of institutions, etc.) imply additional limits to the behaviour of individuals (Hägerstrand 1970). These constraints limit the size of the daily urban system that can be covered during a day. On top of these comments there are specific European factors, which may affect the form and function of European cities in particular. In many European cities urban life has been much more deeply ingrained in societies than elsewhere. Part of the bourgeois elite always seems to have expressed a preference for urban living in inner cities. Examples can be found in thirteenth-century Italy (see Benevolo 1993) and from the Renaissance onwards, when many efforts were made to construct 'ideal cities' (Eaton 2001). Over the history of European cities, elites have shown their preference for urban living, already in the fortified cities where they lived together with, but separated from other social classes. Sjoberg's (1960) model of the pre-capitalist city reveals that especially the political, religious, administrative and social elite used to live in the centre of the city in a high-status core. This city centre orientation was reconfirmed in later times, for example in the middle of the 19th century, when the famous restructuring activities of Haussmann took place, in Paris, but also elsewhere. Again, this successful effort to create more space for the bourgeois expressed the value that was given to living in inner cities. Moreover, during the 20st century most inner cities in Europe – as opposed to American cities – did not suffer from the development of extreme sharp racial or class segregation. European welfare states may have played a crucial role in preventing such sharp patterns to develop (Musterd and Ostendorf 1998). As a result European fewer inner cities experienced serious social crisis.

This picture of urban life in continental Europe contrasts to the urban histories of Britain and the United States. There, major sections of the urban elites turned their backs on the noise and other negative aspects of the city. They preferred to live and defend their lives in homogeneous and later on in modern fortified (gated) neighbourhoods in suburban settings (Fishman 1987). The centres of many cities in these contexts are almost entirely dominated by commercial functions; living there has traditionally been a marginal activity. I am not arguing, though, that there is no variation within the Anglo Saxon world at all. American east coast cities and various medium sized cities in the UK can be found, which show parallels with continental European types of cities.

All in all continental European society is much more based in firmly established urban histories and urban value systems than many other places in the Western world. The historic inner city centres, which have functioned as real centres for ages, did appear to lose part of their function during the 20th century, but many of them seem to have survived the attacks and were able to recover. Over the past four decades, extensive gentrification and upgrading processes have taken place in many central cities and today many of them still play a fairly big role in daily life of European citizens. The upgrading of cities has been partly driven by economic restructuring processes that produced new economic activities. Some of these fit well in the sometimes extremely old urban structures; also demographic changes have helped a lot. The rise of the share of small households, who predominantly show an urban orientation, has put pressure on many inner city residential districts. The urban orientation of many Europeans has also been reinforced through the parallel development of private and public institutions. The relatively strong public transport network in many European cities – clearly associated with higher density urban space – is an example of that.

As a result, the development of widespread and large-scale urban fields and cities that are left behind probably will not parallel the American examples. European suburbs still tend to be connected much tighter to the central cities compared to American suburbs and middle and upper class residential mobility directed to the suburbs was much less dramatic in European cities than in the US. Having said that, this does not imply that European cities do not expand. They certainly do, and large-scale suburbanisation processes can also be found. The historical urban paths how-ever, seem to have had major impact on the shape of the present transition from city to regional city at the same time. Network cities will have developed, and polycentric cities have appeared, but the scale seems to be much more compact than many want us to believe. In many European contexts, housing markets, labour markets, transport markets and various other markets may operate more at the level of the city region than at the level of the urban field. The development of the Amsterdam urban region may serve as an example.

The Amsterdam urban region
Dutch cities were hardly influenced by Haussmann's ideas. The absence of restructuring of the core of the city, however, did not result in an early and rigorous destruction of those city areas, neither did it lead to the development of pure Central Business Districts in the 20th century, as happened in many other cities. There were attempts to push Dutch cities in that direction, but these were almost all prevented. As a result, the city remained a fairly mixed entity in physical and social terms, and not only mixed, but also compact.

If we now turn our attention to the spatial reach of all sorts of 'markets', we also have to conclude that urban development in the Dutch context has been rather compact. The housing market, for example, reveals strong links between the large cities and their surrounding municipalities, including growth centres, which are located nearby the central city. Figures about residential mobility reveal fairly compact urban networks. In the year 2000 75 per cent of all people who moved from within Amsterdam found another place within the core city of Amsterdam and half of those who left the city settled in a directly adjacent municipality not far from the city. The labour markets also function at a regional scale. This can be illustrated with home-to-work interactions, for example:

Area of departure	Area of arrival			
	Amsterdam Agglomeration		Rest of the daily urban System	Rest of the Netherlands
Amsterdam	53	13	17	17
Agglomeration	29	39	17	15
Rest of the daily urban system	15	7	65	13

Table 1   Percentage distribution of home-to-work trips between sub-milieus of the urban region of Amsterdam, 1997 Source: Statistics Netherlands; Bontje, 2001

Clearly, the majority of home-to-work relations in the Amsterdam urban region stay within the urban region. However, it is also obvious that the interaction between non-core-city areas is highly significant. This is reflected in criss-cross relations in compact urban networks (cf. Bontje 2001). In other markets we can find similar compactness. The education market and even the higher education market, for example, are showing similar local orientations. Perhaps the only market, which is really becoming large-scale, is the 'recreational market'.

In short, the majority of interactions between parts of urban areas still take place within relatively compact urban regions. For the case of the Netherlands, that would imply that the level of the Randstad, or Delta Metropolis, as it is sometimes called, would not be the appropriate level to look at, if urban form and function are discussed. However, it is very important to consider that the compact urban regions are not simply the enlargement of the old city or urban district. It is not a further expansion of the mono-centric city or the mono-centric urban district, in which the hierarchy of places is strictly indicated, the largest core also being the entity with the most urban functions and having the highest level of each function. This pattern fits in with classic hierarchical urban models, which in effect date from the time when agriculture was still the dominant economic sector. Today's urban region is developing to a polycentric entity. The cores are less hierarchically related to one another than they used to be. The patterns of interaction in the two models differ considerably: whereas the mono-centric city had a mainly radial pattern of interaction, with the main and most dense flows to and from the core city, in the non-hierarchical polycentric model we find far more criss-cross and tangential movements between the local centres of the urban region. Even in Amsterdam, with its radial history par excellence, the dominance of the central core is reduced substantially (see e.g. Bontje 2001).

Variation within the Amsterdam urban region
The question then is, how does the new compact polycentric urban region look like. Clearly, the regionalisation process did not result in a flat and similar space; various geographical selections can be shown. Both in economic terms and in residential terms, specialised districts and domains have developed. As far as the economy is concerned, it is demand and supply, which show uneven geographies: the regional economic structure and the geographical distribution of types of employment and levels of education differs within the region. The regionalisation of the labour market implies that people changing jobs within the region do not generally see this as a reason to move house, as the demand for accessibility has also become regionalized. Similarly, the housing markets have become regionalised. However, here too, this does not imply that there is a balanced housing distribution across the areas. The subsidised rented sector, for example, is still largely concentrated in the old central cities, whereas the owner-occupied sector is spread throughout the region.

The process of regionalisation entails a large number of geographical selections. Musterd and Salet (2003) recently stated that these selections are sometimes promoted in a considered, deliberate manner, but often also based on unintentional and more or less coincidental results of the play of forces within the geographical domain in question. In the remaining part of this section some indications of the internal differentiation of the economic structure and the spatial orientation of different households will be elaborated upon for the Amsterdam urban region, to show the variety of spaces, which have developed and may develop in the near future. The development of varied spaces in the economic and in the residential spheres coincides the rise of the polycentric urban region.

The urban region typically consists of several distinguished economic centres. The geographies of these centres tell their own story. We find clusters of cultural industries in the centre of Amsterdam. Specialised sections of the media industries can be found in the classic media clusters in Hilversum, southeast of the city (Dutch radio and TV broadcasting started there), in the new town of Almere (large studios) and in the centre of Amsterdam (diverse); information, communication and technology clusters, as well as the business services sectors, have shown a preference for location along the most important highway corridors (A2, A6, A10 in particular), well connected to the rest of Europe and to the airport. Various new internationally oriented economic focal points are developing around the economic magnet of Schiphol Airport. Flower exports are concentrated around the international auction centres nearby, in Aalsmeer (south of Amsterdam). The financial sector is regrouping along Amsterdam's South Axis, an area that will be connected to the old core of the city with a new subway (which will bring people to the heart of the old city in a five minutes trip).

The various urban residential areas too are now to be found throughout the region, the largest and most striking example is the new town of Almere, which is set to grow into a town with a population of 400,000 over the next thirty years. As said before, the majority of new towns have been developed not too far from the old core areas. The few exceptions, such as Lelystad, at a distance of 60 km from Amsterdam, turned out to be a failure (high vacancy rates and low demand).

The regional urban development has resulted in a clear division between small and indeed urban oriented households in the city of Amsterdam on one side and larger family oriented households in areas with a less urban character on the other side; many immigrant households settled in the post-war urban residential districts, and many other family households moved to new towns and adjacent suburban areas. However, former immigrant households who were labelled 'non-Dutch' increasingly find housing in the rest of the urban region as well.

In socio-economic terms a certain division between the city of Amsterdam and its surrounding area developed in the early 1970s. Before that time the core city used to be richer than the surrounding environment. However, with the explosion of suburbanisation in the Netherlands, around that time higher income households left the city. There is a general feeling that the old cities have become poorer since, but this is not true. A dynamic balance developed with few fluctuations over time. Indeed, in most recent years the old core areas slowly seem to regain their former social position somewhat. In Amsterdam and Utrecht, this process goes along with an income increase in their environments as well. This is not the case for Rotterdam and The Hague (Figure 1).

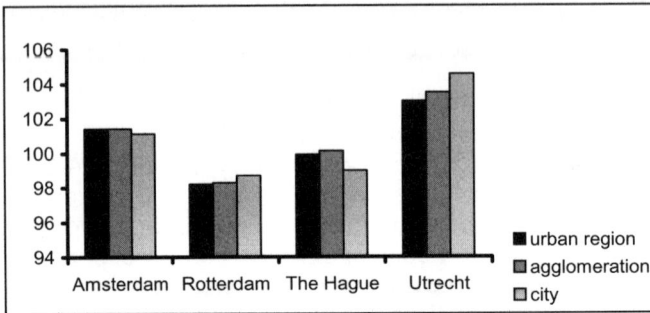

Fig.1: Development of the average income per earner, 1989-2000 (1989=100)

Within the central cities there are clear divisions too. The inner city appears to be the area, which is upgrading fastest; post-war residential districts with large shares of social housing tend to show a downgrading process. A closer inspection of these socio-spatial patterns reveals that there is a tendency for specific residential territories to develop. These territories should not be seen as tight local communities; instead most of them are more or less homogeneous communities of limited liability; in extreme cases even gated communities can be found.

Another way of understanding the socio-spatial differentiation of Dutch cities is to look at the residential orientations of various categories of the workforce. Recently, we have carried out a research project in which we looked at the residential orientation of so-called knowledge workers, who worked in Amsterdam, in selected economic sectors (Arnoldus and Musterd 2002; Musterd 2002). The selection was aimed at sectors of which many insiders think they hold prospects for the future of the urban economies in the Netherlands. We selected middle and higher income workers in the creative sector: science, design; in the (perhaps also creative) business professionals sector: business services, financial sector, ICT; in the so-called soft information sector workers: advertising, media; and in local government: civil servants. We could get access to postcode work and residence addresses of workers in firms and institutions, which were settled in Amsterdam. The sample we could get is representative for architects, accountants and workers in higher education, since we got access to their complete registers; the sample is indicative for the financial sector (where we got the home addresses of workers of only one of the large banks), and for advertising, media and the ICT sector, where we received the required information of many firms, but not of all of them.

Category	%
Architects	71
Local government	60
Advertising	52
Higher education social sciences	52
Higher education humanities	50
Media	48
Higher education law	47
Higher education medical sciences	37
Higher education sciences	35
Higher education economic sciences	33
Accountants	19
Financial sector (bank)	19
ICT	17

Tab. 2. Percentage of knowledge workers working in Amsterdam who also live in Amsterdam, 2002. Source:ABF Strategie 2002; Musterd 2002

Table 2 shows some results of the orientations of various workers. The results allow for a grouping of the sectors in a few logical classes: first, people working in the creative sector, in local government and in higher education in social sciences, law and humanities; secondly those who are working in higher education in medicine, sciences or economics; thirdly the financial and business services sector (finance, accountants, bank employees, ict-workers). It will be clear that workers in the creative sector (architects, advertising, media) and workers in higher education who are active in cultural and social sciences are more than proportionally living in Amsterdam and within Amsterdam they tend to settle in the most urbanised parts of the city (mainly the central areas and adjacent south-west sector) (Figure 2);

Legend text within image:
kenniswerkers in reclame-, media- en
overheidssector, architecten, staf
HBO/WO rechtsgeleerdheid, geestes-
en maatschappijwetenschappen,

locatiequotiënt
kleiner dan 1
tussen 1 en 5
tussen 5 en 10
tussen 10 en 20
groter dan 20

Fig. 2: Residential orientation of workers in government, social sciences, humanities, law, advertising, architects and media

those who represent the financial sector (accountants, bank employees), and those who are active in information, communication and technology, tend to be oriented on suburban domains, yet predominantly not too far from the economic key areas, and certainly within the so-called Northern Wing of the Randstad area (Musterd 2002).

It should be noticed that the creative sector and the workers in the cultural industries seem to be attracted to the old and functionally varied urban districts in particular. Perhaps these environments provide the inspiration they require to do their jobs properly (also Helbrecht 1998). Or these areas can show the right mix of 'diversity'; 'tolerance' and attractive living, with the required cultural and other amenities to attract the so-called talent pool (Florida and Gates 2001). These factors may thus be crucial conditions for innovations and economic growth. This is not new, nor unique. It is of importance, though, since the sectors I mentioned are often regarded to be the key sectors in the future economies. The most urban sections of the urban region could get new impulses through these sectors. They may be able to renew their functions as centres of innovation of all kinds of products (new financial products, new services, new methods to sell products, etceteras) and as centres of culture in their widest form. Cities like Amsterdam seem to have promising settings in that respect. To my opinion the vital characteristics, which help to attract young and dynamic workers, are linked to the human scale, dynamism, vitality and public atmosphere, supported by the large and diverse populations and visitors. The fact that residential and economic functions have been mixed from the very start of the city in the early 13th century, and continues until today, is also of major importance. Currently just below 100,000 people are living in the historic centre, ranging from students and bohemians to affluent households who occupy the canal-side residences.

New major economic centres on the edge of the city complement this new position for the most classic urbanised part of the region. A crucial question related to these edges is what new identities will develop there? It is not only about how the physical patterns change (infrastructure, new sites of residential and working areas etc.) but also about how ideas on the significance of 'urban space' evolve. It is evidently a complicated business getting to know the new opportunities of local positions and interpreting them in today's global society. What existing qualities can we put in and strengthen in the competition to tie new economic activity to the region, and how can we get this to link up with other regional needs?
People used to identify strongly with their cities and other local communities; the question now is, are there new regional identities de-veloping? What new socio-geographical patterns are forming at regional level? Is it possible at all to develop new regional visions that can serve as a common framework for plans and other public and private initiatives? What specifically ties people and organizations to their regions if the considerations that motivate them are increasingly less purely territorial? So far there are more questions than answers.

Interventions and urban change
The discussions in sections 3 and 4 roughly allow for two preliminary conclusions. The first is that functional urban space in the Netherlands is still rather compact and focused on relatively small urban regions around each of the large cities in the country, while these regions are polycentric. The second is that specific residential orientations could be revealed. Specific households tend to settle (some have to settle somewhere due to lack of choice) in specific residential territories. In short, characteristic residential milieus or residential domains are developing.

In the introduction I referred to the strong Dutch welfare state, characterised by frequent interventions by the government, in spatial processes too. Two clear examples of effects of that intervention can be mentioned. One concerns the preservation of the so-called Green Heart, a more or less open space between the cities of Amsterdam, Utrecht, Rotterdam and The Hague, which would probably been filled with activities if the government would not have developed extensive policies to prevent that to happen. The second refers to the fast growth of growth centres and new towns, which were developed to control the urbanisation process. Perhaps the state level spatial policies of these kinds did contribute to keeping the urban patterns relatively compact.

However, recent policies are not very much supporting our two main findings anymore. The state wants to reduce its public interventionist policies, and also pleas for more privatisation and decentralised government. For a short while, and only a few years ago, the influential advisory board of the Ministry of the Environment even supported thinking about the development of the largest scale urban territories possible. Concepts such as urban field and edge city, and accompanying recommendations in terms of the type of infrastructure (for example), played a big role in those advices. However, within a year the board changed that view and supported the compact urban region again. But the non-intervention atmosphere did not change radically. One strong instrument, that played a big role in spatial planning over the past fifty years, the spatial allocation of new social housing, has now virtually vanished. The housing market has become much more privatised than before. Because of that the government has lost part of its grip upon the spatial development process.

Our second finding, the development of characteristic residential domains is even less supported by Dutch policies. Key concepts in Dutch policies today are related to the creation of so-called balanced communities, mixed housing neighbourhoods and mixed populations. These policies are completely opposite to the actual processes of developing homogeneous residential domains and opposite to the general policy of reduction of governmental intervention in the spheres of housing and detailed urban planning. Anyway, the basic assumption behind the political and policy efforts is that mixed housing policies would help the integration of weaker parts of society. Current political debates are highly focused on the integration of various immigrant categories, but also on improving the life chances of poor households. So, there is a double focus, on ethnic mix and on socio-economic mix. However, the assumptions behind that neighbourhood effect thinking are hardly tested. Research, which was focused on the evaluation of the neighbourhood effect theses, is inconclusive or at best, in the Dutch context, reveals that only marginal effects exist (Ellen and Turner 1997; Musterd et al. 2003).

As far as the development of the urban economy is concerned, there is a lot of attention to the so-called 'hard' sectors: accessibility and infrastructure, science, knowledge, communication and technology; however, there is less attention to the 'soft' sectors such as media, cultural industries, arts, and the conditions for the creative dimension that are related to the new firms in general. One example is again related to the residential sphere. In large and successful cities, such as Amsterdam, the housing market is functioning worse and worse due to a lack of sufficient dwellings for middle-income knowledge workers. Local government seems to frustrate housing opportunities for the talent pool.

Conclusions: conditions for the new urban region

The Amsterdam region shows interaction patterns that reveal the development of compact polycentric urban regional networks. The city of Amsterdam is not the centre for all activities anymore; other centres have developed and reveal new opportunities. Home-to-work relations have, therefore, also become much more varied and criss-cross; a series of specialised economic centres has developed, but still on a fairly compact spatial scale. Overall the cities have expanded in urban regions with characteristic milieus, but this has not resulted in doughnut cities, in the loss of the central city and the rise of almost independent edge cities. The occupation patterns of urbanization and the associated movements take place over relatively short distances in threaded chains of urbanization. The historical centres that have maintained their residential and physical qualities appear to be a valuable asset to attract specialised firms and young talented people who want to live there. The impact this has on public space is still very large. These inner city potentials, the more compact urban regions, and moderate development of remote suburbs, has given this and several other European regions strong own stakes.

However, critical thing is that many (local) politicians still have old modernist city models in their head; they tend to focus investments too heavily on accessibility and often the spatial level at which intervention is aimed at is oversized; and occasionally on types of workers who are not there anymore. Smaller cities still try to copy the largest city when they have the ambition to become an important city (a strategy that fits the old idea of hierarchical cities). The idea of developing complementary urban milieus in a compact regional setting is not yet fully understood everywhere. Finally, politicians do not want to distance themselves from policies aimed at balanced, mixed communities, even though this is completely opposite the actual residential sorting processes.

Particularly crucial for regional Amsterdam is its relatively favourable position at the international sub-top level of the financial and business network economy, its international role in aviation and the striking position of its subculture in the international networks of the 'creative economy'. The importance of being sited in economic networks of this kind is grossly exaggerated, however, if this is to suggest that businesses and people no longer have any regional ties, that they have become footloose, indifferent to specific regional qualities. The qualities of the city and other milieus in the urban region have considerable significance for the development of residents and companies. Or even stronger: if some qualities, e.g. ICT and physical infrastructure, are available in virtually all urban regions, other qualities, such as a climate that is attractive to creative knowledge workers, take on more distinguishing power. It is exactly that, which gives European cities a potentially strong position.

References
Arnoldus, M. and Sako M. (2002) Wonen in de Regionale Kennisstad; Wonen in de Ambitieuze Stad – Verdieping. Amsterdam: AME.
Benevolo, L. (1993) De Europese Stad, Amsterdam, Agon.
Bontje, M. (2001) The Challenge of Planned Urbanization. Urbanization and national urbanization policy in the Netherlands in a Northwest-European perspective.Thesis AME Universiteit van Amsterdam. Amsterdam.
Eaton, R. (2001) Ideal Cities; Utopianism and the (Un)Built Environment. Antwerp: Mercatorfonds.
Ellen, I.G. and M.A. Turner (1997) Does Neighborhood Matter? Assessing Recent Evidence, Housing Policy Debate, vol. 8, nr. 4, pp. 833-866.
Fishman, R (1987) Bourgeois Utopias: The Rise and fall of suburbia. New York, Basic Books.
Florida, R. and G. Gates (2001) Technology and Tolerance: the importance of diversity to high-technology growth. Washington DC: The Brookings Institution.
Friedmann, J. and J. Miller (1965) The Urban Field. Journal of the American Institute of Planners, pp. 312-319.
Garreau, J. (1991) Edge City: Life on the New Frontier. New York, etc.: Doubleday.
Hägerstrand, T. (1970) 'What about people in Regional Science?' Papers of the Regional Sciences Association 24: 7-21.
Helbrecht, I. (1998) The Creative Metropolis; services, symbols and spaces. Paper presented at the yearly conference for the association of Canadastudies. Grainau.
Musterd, S. (2002) De Nieuwe Amsterdamse Kernvoorraad. Amsterdam: gemeente Amsterdam
-,   and Ostendorf, W. (1998) 'Segregation and Social Participation in the Welfare State. The case of Amsterdam', in: S. Musterd and W. Ostendorf (eds.) Urban Segregation and the Welfare State: Inequality and Exclusion in Western Cities, pp. 191-206. London: Routledge
-,   and W. Salet (2003) The Emergence of the Regional City. In: S. Musterd and W. Salet (Eds.) Amsterdam Human Capital, pp. 13-27. Amsterdam: Amsterdam University Press.

-;   Ostendorf, W. and de Vos, S. (2003) 'Neighbourhood Effects and Social
        Mobility; a Longitudinal Analysis', Housing Studies 18 (6): 877-92.
Sjoberg, W. (1960) The Pre-industrial City; Past and Present. Glencoe, Illinois:
        Free Press.
Wright, F. L. (1935) Broadacre City: A New Community Plan. In: R.T. Le Gates
        and F. Stout (Eds.) (1996) The City Reader, pp. 376-381.

Growth Management:
The Europeanization of a US City Region?

Jefferey M. Sellers

Increasingly, European students of urban regions have pointed to the spread of residences, workplaces and spaces of consumption beyond established urban centers, and accompanying new patterns of social polarization along spatial lines. European observers, referring to the more dispersed, more segregated urban forms seen as typical of the United States, often discuss this process of metropolitan regionalization as "Americanization" (Ascher, 2000; Zjiderveld, 1998). On both continents, however, the evolution of city-regions has been and remains a contested process. From the days of Frederick Law Olmstead and John Nolen in the United States, countermovements within urban planning have aimed at more compact urban forms and more integrated urban development. Ideals that implicitly or explicitly draw on traditional European city forms have often served as a rallying point for these movements. The latest versions of these movements, adopting such names as "smart growth", "growth management" and the "new urbanism," follow their predecessors in what might be termed an effort to "Europeanize" U.S. urban forms (cf. Calthorpe 1993, p. 15; Beatley 2000; Duany and Plater-Zyberk 2000; Zoyani 2001). In various guises, these movements now wield considerable influence over new development in a significant portion of the United States.

This paper addresses the seldom-considered question that follows inevitably from the reverse mirror that these developments in the United States hold up to the reputed Americanization of European cities. Granted that growth management and new fashions for more compact urban development have increased currency in parts of the United States, have they succeeded in substituting European urban practices for North American and specifically U.S. ones? Are U.S. urban regions subject to these influences now taking on a more regulated, more centralized, less segregated, less polarized patterns reminiscent of European counter-parts? Alternatively, have the growing chorus of calls and accumulating local movements in favor of more controlled urban development failed to bring about significant changes in U.S. landscapes? Or is a new, hybrid form of urbanity emerged in the new space between traditional European and U.S. models?

My examination of this question focuses on the case in the United States that has undoubtedly attracted the most attention as a success story of smart growth and the new urbanism. As the setting for some of the most systematic policies and planning strategies associated with the management of urban growth and the new urbanism, Portland has emerged as a model for U.S. planners of the best of all possible urban outcomes. As such the Portland metropolitan area offers an instructive example of the possibilities within the U.S. for these strategies to bring about a form of urban development similar to those familiar in Europe. Through a combination of local and state-level initiatives that drew at least implicitly on European models, policymakers in Portland attempted to reproduce elements typical of European urban regions within the United States. The question posed here is how much the result actually resembles any kind of European city region, remains typically American, or belongs to an altogether distinctive type.

Growth Management in a United States City Region: An Instance of Europeanization?

Europeans faced with tendencies toward metropolitanzation and urban polarization often point to these trends as evidence of Americanization of urban landscapes. At the same time, however, a significant number of states and urban regions in the United States have sought to regulate these processes in ways suggestive of European land use regulation. This tendency gives rise to the converse question to what has typically been asked. Are American urban regions in fact becoming Europeanized?

Portland stands at the center of a growing trend toward greater regulation of land use and urban form that has altered the traditional non-interventionist posture of state and local governments toward markets for land use. Even in the early and mid-twentieth centuries, when suburbanization and sprawl grew to dominate metropolitan development in the United States, it was not unusual to find localities that had adopted and strictly enforced zoning and other means of land use control. Since the 1960s, however, local governments and even state legislatures have in turning more and more to various forms of land use control, have increasingly imposed regulatory constraints on markets for housing, offices and residences outside dense urban centers.

State level regulation stands at the center of this shift. In the 1960s and 1970s, during what was at the time called a "silent revolution" in land use control, a total of four disparate state legislatures passed statewide schemes aimed largely at control over suburban expansion and sprawl. By 2002, a total of 14 states, or 28 percent of the total, had adopted legislation of this sort. All told, these states contained 37 percent of the national population (Sellers 2004). In a host of other states, such as California, growth controls that in some instances operated as even more stringent brakes on local metropolitan expansion were in place at the municipal and county levels. In a country with a population that was now predominantly suburban rather than either urban or rural, a large proportion if not the majority of suburban residents were becoming accustomed to substantial zoning and other forms of land use control. At the same time, not among public officials but in the world of architects and real estate professionals, the "new urbanist" movement increasingly influenced even fashions of development. A chorus of voices now extols the virtues of mixed residential, commercial and workplace uses, of denser and centralized settlement, of carefully cultivated public spaces, and of transit corridors (e.g., Calthorpe 1993; Beatley 2000).

Oregon in general, and Portland in particular as its capital, has emerged as the leading model for both growth management and the new urbanist practices that have accompanied it. Held out in textbooks and docu- mentaries throughout North America as the exemplary case of a sus- tainable city (See, e.g., United Nations Centre for Human Settlement 1996, pp. 319-320), Portland offers the best possible case to test how far the spread of these new practices has brought about convergence within North America toward the more centralized, more compact, less se- gregated patterns that remain more typical of European city regions.

Myriad aspects of the context in which these efforts have arisen have led many analysts to conclude otherwise. Such authors as Nivola (1999), Downs (1994), Massey and Denton (1993), Jackson (1986) and Fainstein and Fainstein (1982) have surveyed the many influences that have set urban development in the United States at large on a distinctive path from that of European cities. At the national level, property rights, tax in- centives, highway policies and other measures have long given home- owners, firms and local officials ample incentives to pursue sprawl and segregation. Cheap land, building materials and transportation have encouraged less concern to conserve space. Without the physical legacies and traditions of medieval and early modern old towns in Europe, U.S. central cities lack the cultural attraction of their counterparts for either residents or planners. Such accounts foster the impression that even a partial shift toward denser, less segregated forms in some U.S. metro- politan areas would contradict fundamental structural properties of U.S. urbanism. In the conclusion to his well-known book on the sub- urbanization of the United States, historian Kenneth Jackson marveled at how "truck farmers tend their crops within two thousand yards of the skyscrapers of Dusseldorf (sic), the richest city on the continent, not be- cause alternative land uses would not yield a higher return, but because the government rejects the very possibility of development" (1986, p. 295). Such a sight, he implied, would be unimaginable in the U.S.

Urban Centrality in Portland

Portland is one of the few U.S. metropolitan areas with a population over one million where one might in fact find the image that so struck Jackson outside Düsseldorf. State and local policies in clear contrast to those applied in other urban regions have contributed to this difference. Yet no one would mistake the downtown or the suburban configuration of this urban region as European. The elements of European urban centralization there remain tempered by typically American decentralization of much of workplaces and elite residences.

Growth management in Portland has a long history (Little 1974; Abbott 1983; Abbott, Howe and Adler 1994; Lewis 1995; Leo 1998), and several elements that set this metropolitan area apart from most others in the United States. Local planning and regulation of land use has been unusually extensive, ambitious and effective in shaping patterns of development. Since the 1970s, Oregon has led the country in statewide regulation of local land use. The centerpiece of this regulation, enforced by authorities at the state level, has been the Urban Growth Boundary required of all cities. Defined at the local level, the Boundary imposes a twenty-year limit on development outside urbanized area.

A second distinctive institutional element has also enabled Portland to overcome the fragmentation among municipal jurisdiction that might otherwise frustrate the formulation and implementation of a growth boundary around the city. In place of the county officials elsewhere around the state received the authority to determine the Urban Growth Boundary, a legislative compromise gave this authority to a special Metropolitan planning district that encompassed towns from the three counties in which the urbanized area of Portland was located. In 1978, building on a three county Metropolitan Planning Commission that had existed since 1957, an elected metropolitan government was created to oversee the regional planning scheme. In this way, Portland has overcome the fragmentation typical of most larger U.S. urban regions (cf. Lewis 1995).

In greater Portland, more or less the same Urban Growth Boundary remained in place from 1979, subject to only limited modifications in the early 1990s. As Figure 1 shows, the growth boundary extended well beyond the central city alone to circumscribe the ring of incorporated towns that surrounded it. Although a number of further outlying towns had separate Urban Growth Boundaries, the boundaries clearly had the effect of holding the line on new development. As Figure 1 depicts, settlement density in 2000 remains high in nearly all of the towns within the boundaries, at 800 persons per square mile or higher. Comparison of housing ages shows housing in the 1980s and 1990s concentrated largely in these areas, often taking the form of infill development in the areas between the urban core and boundary.

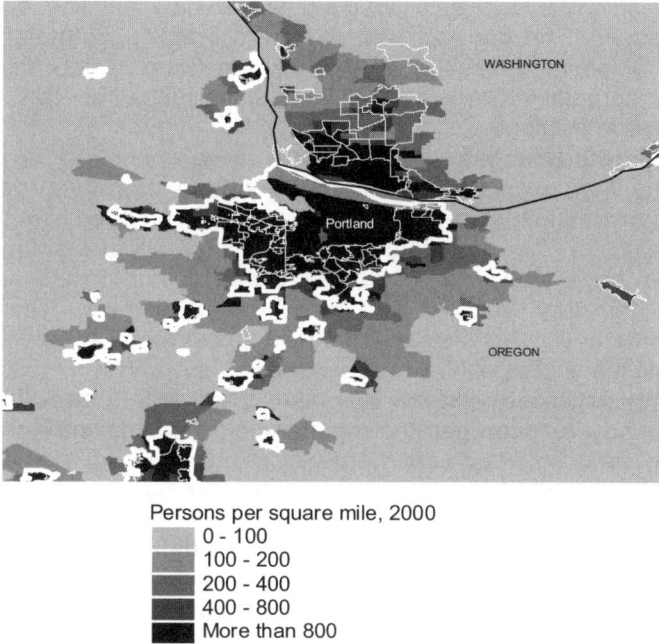

Persons per square mile, 2000
- 0 - 100
- 100 - 200
- 200 - 400
- 400 - 800
- More than 800

Fig. 1: Growth Boundaries as of 2000 indicated by bold white lines; municipal boundaries indicated by light white lines; state boundary indicated by black line. Source: U.S. Census 2000 STF1 Data.

Beyond the boundaries, especially the one that defines the central urban area, the density drops rapidly to 100-200 persons per square mile or even lower. The fall-off is especially dramatic on the west side, where intense neighborhood activism has helped hold the line against new development. The contrast with the more irregular patterns of density around adjacent Vancouver in Washington State, which has lacked a growth boundary, underscores the significance of the regulatory measures in Portland.

Urban Growth Boundary has been only one element in a full panoply of initiatives that began in Portland long before the statewide planning legislation was introduced, and since that time have complemented the constraints of the boundary. In promoting infill development, local planners have sought to place new housing and employment along transit corridors leading out from the downtown. The resulting arrangements have ultimately made it possible to supplement mass transit with a successful light rail system, a U.S. rarity.

Following practices evident in many other U.S. cities, planners in Portland have encouraged the regeneration of the downtown in order to bring in new entertainment and service businesses. Large-scale re-development projects have converted Pioneer Square in the downtown to an attractive shopping area, and the old port district on the Columbia River to a waterfront park. Indeed, more than in many other U.S. efforts to bring residents back into central cities, planners and policymakers in Portland have emphasized the creation and improved of green areas and public spaces. A regional network of parks now weaves throughout the metropolitan region.

More systematic comparisons with other U.S. cities point to Portland as one of a number of city regions that have limited the dispersal of metropolitan settlement. For Lopez and Hynes, who measure metro-politan sprawl by means of residential density, this metropolitan area ranks 76th out of 83 in the degree of this form of sprawl. For Galster et al (2000), who employ a multidimensional conception of sprawl, Portland remains reliably less sprawling than most of its U.S. counterparts. Other studies point to Oregon in general as the most successful instance of effective growth management at the state level (Burby and May 1997; Carruthers 2002).

As such commentators as Nelson (2002) have noted, individual towns or counties elsewhere, most notably in California, have often drawn the line at least as strictly on new development. Doing so without providing for alternative, higher density housing, however, can drive up prices for land and new housing. In greater Portland, the provision of infill housing has helped satisfy demand. As a result, except for a period in the early 1990s, a series of studies demonstrates that other forces have outweighed upward pressures from regulation on prices for housing and land (Knaap and Nelson 1985; Philipps and Goodstein 2000; Downs 2002).

Partly as a result of this control over suburban expansion, and partly as a consequence of the policies that have supported the growth and transformation of the downtown itself, Portland has also limited the central city hardship typical of most large U.S. city regions. In a recent analysis of all U.S. metropolitan areas with populations over 200,000, Sellers (2004) employed a "Central City Hardship" index applied by Nathan and Adams in the 1970s and 1980s to compare relative disadvantage in central cities and their suburbs. The index combined six distinct indicators of disadvantage: Per capita income, the proportion of housing units with more than one person per room, the percent of adults with only secondary education, rates of poverty and unemployment, and proportions of dependents (including persons over 65 as well as children under 18). Four of these six indicators remained at least in relative parity between the central city and suburbs, and one of these (dependency) ranged fifteen percent higher in the suburbs than in the central city.[1] Of the other two, although the poverty rate was 44% higher in the central city, the unemployment rate was only 15% higher.

Overall, based on a cumulative index that added up central city disadvantages on standardized versions of all six indicators yielded an overall rating much lower than the average for all U.S. metropolitan areas over 200,000 (Figure 2). As Nathan and Adams found in their earlier analysis of the largest 65 U.S. metropolitan areas, Portland fit clearly into the quartile with the least cumulative urban disadvantage.

---

[1] Rates of dependency were 32.6% in the central city and 37.6% in the suburbs; rates of low education were 11.0% in the central city and 10.7% in the suburbs (for a ratio of 1.04); rates of crowded housing were 5.3% in the central city and 5.2% in the suburbs (1.01); and rates of per capita income were $22,643 in the central city and $22,977 in the suburbs (1.01).

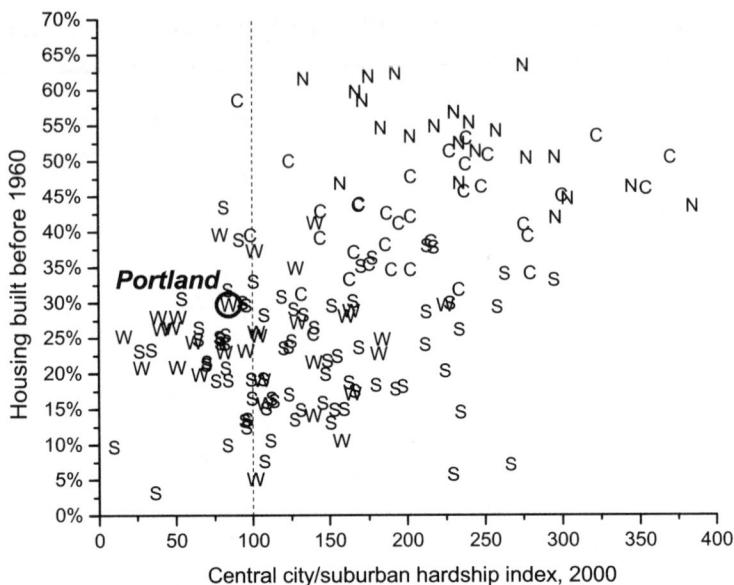

Fig. 2: Data symbols indicate regional location of metropolitan area (N=Northeast, C=North Central, S=South, W=West). Six-item hardship index calculated on the basis of differences between central city values and those for the rest of metropolitan area, with cumulative indices for all six items and normalization such that 100=parity between central city and suburban elements See Nathan and Adams (1976; 1984); Sellers 2004a

If Portland clearly deviates from the national average in both centralization of population and hardship, the city in neither sense represents a wholly isolated exception. Figure 2 makes this especially clear in the case of urban hardship. In general, the Sunbelt regions where more of the new construction and urban growth of the last several decades have gravitated have enjoyed less unequal relations between central cities and suburbs than the older metropolitan areas of the Northeast and North Central regions. Part of the reason for this clear contrast stems from the removal of an array of discriminatory policies that fostered segregation of inner city minority populations up to the 1960s (Massey and Denton 1993; Glaeser and Vigdor 2002). Cheaper land and local annexation and incorporation processes in the Sunbelt reinforced these advantages. Indeed, in comparison with Western metropolitan areas only, or those with percent or more of housing units constructed since 1960, Portland ranks closer to average.

At the same time, closer examination of Portland indicates how even a relatively centralized U.S. city region of this type continues to differ in important ways from the centralized patterns in much of Europe. Even overall urban hardship, as Hoffmann-Martinot (2004) shows in his application of the Nathan-Adams index to French metropolitan areas, remains generally lower in French metropolitan areas than it does in Portland. Although redevelopment in Portland has attracted a sizeable proportion of the region's highly educated workforce to neighborhoods within or surrounding the central city, suburban neighborhoods of single-family homes still largely dominate patterns of settlement. Local strategies for the location of new jobs have helped to reinforce this pattern. As the city attracted an array of high-tech employers during the boom of the 1990s, the largest firms (Intel, IBM, Epson) located their new facilities in the office parks of Beaverton or Hillsboro, both west side suburbs (cite atlas). Suburban housing along the growth boundaries stood closer than central city apartments to these "edge city" developments.

As Figure 3 shows, a ring of suburban and exurban census tracts along and outside the growth boundary also led local markets for housing with the highest prices in the metropolitan area. By comparison, with the exception of one area in the downtown, prices within the central city as well as further south in the Willamette Valley or across the river in the Washington suburbs remain low. Note that many of the highest values appear not outside the growth boundary but in the denser neigh-borhoods just inside it. Many of these same neighborhoods have been sources of the local activism that has helped maintain the growth boundary, and it seems clear that residents of these areas have reaped considerable benefits in terms of housing values. In a European city re-gion, one would also expect high values in the very center of the city, in the historic old town structures or others. Growth management by means of the boundary has operated quite differently, driving up prices more in the near suburbs around the boundary than in the central city.

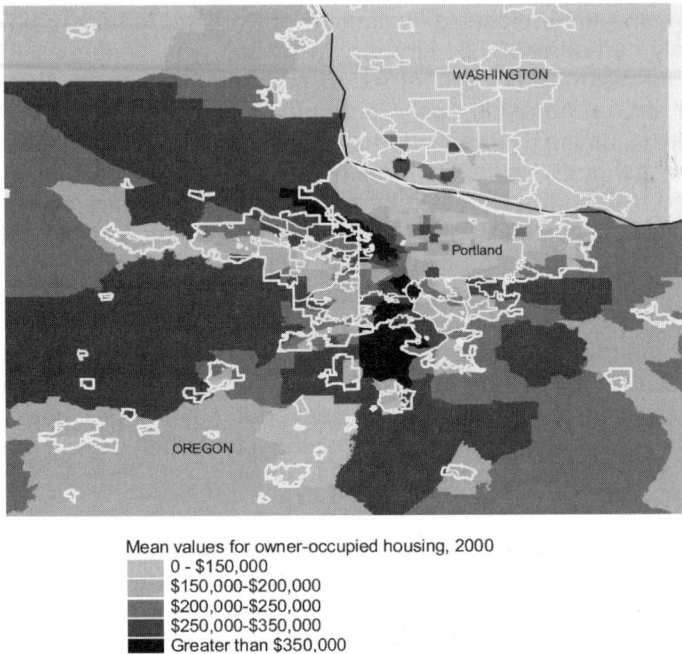

Mean values for owner-occupied housing, 2000
- 0 - $150,000
- $150,000-$200,000
- $200,000-$250,000
- $250,000-$350,000
- Greater than $350,000

Fig. 3: Growth Boundaries as of 2000 indicated by bold white lines; municipal boundaries indicated by light white lines; state boundary indicated by black line. Source: U.S. Census 2000 STF3 Data.

As a look at the class composition of neighborhoods shows, higher status professionals have moved downtown in Portland more than markets for single family homes alone would suggest (Figure 4). Like numerous other growing metropolitan areas in the United States in recent years, Portland has attracted large numbers of an expanding middle and upper-middle class associated with the growth of high-tech and professionalized services. One of the signal accomplishments of planning and urban development strategies in Portland, and an element that resembles the result of inner-city development in much of Europe, has been to draw large numbers of these residents to the downtown or adjacent neighborhoods. Although these groups make up half or more of the resident workforce in the suburban ring, they comprise sixty-five percent or more in a large portion of the central, southern and western neighborhoods of the central city itself. Rather than pay the higher housing costs of the suburban ring, many have chosen to rent or occupy the cheaper owner-occupied housing in many of these neighborhoods.

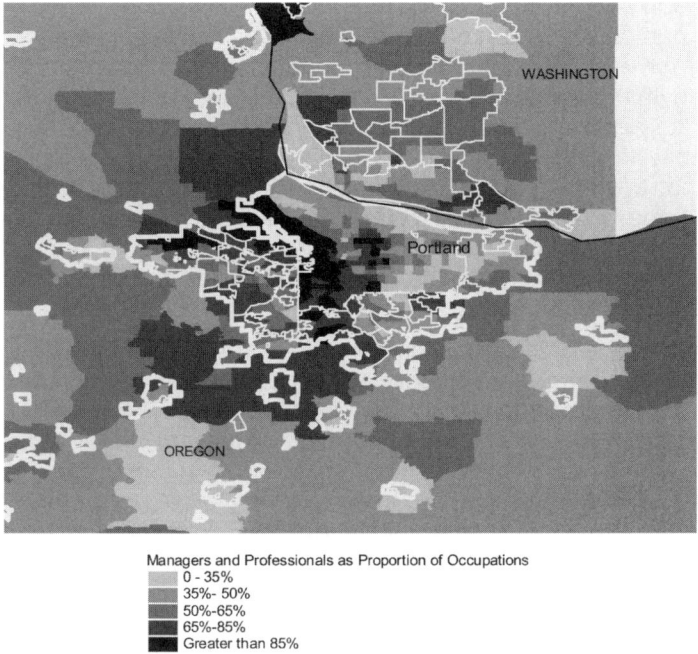

Managers and Professionals as Proportion of Occupations
  0 - 35%
  35%- 50%
  50%-65%
  65%-85%
  Greater than 85%

Fig. 4: Urban Growth Boundaries as of 2000 indicated by bold white lines; municipal boundaries indicated by light white lines; state boundary indicated by black line. Source: U.S. Census 2000 STF3 Data.

With its concentration of density within a central area, its attraction of middle-class professionals and managers to the downtown, and its comparative limitations on central city hardship, Portland stands at the forefront of a trend toward what amounts to a partial Europeanization of land use practices and urban form in parts of the United States. Yet however pleasant downtown Portland may have become by comparison with other U.S. downtowns, no one would confuse its auto-laden streets and central business district with the pedestrian malls of well-maintained European old town. Even within the growth boundary and along transit corridors, edge cities and privileged suburban areas of single-family homes predominate. The growth boundary as a tool has enabled only a more centralized version of the persistent suburban emphasis in U.S. urban development and policy.

Segregation and Spatial Polarization in Greater Portland
Like a portion of U.S. metropolitan areas, Portland also counts a considerably smaller proportion of its population as ethnic minorities than the cities that have typically served as the reference point for comparison between the U.S. and Europe. Portland has also succeeded significantly in reducing the worst patterns of racial and ethnic segregation that have historically distinguished U.S. metropolitan areas from many European counterparts. Yet several neighborhoods and schools in the city remain subject to major disadvantage. In both respects, the trends in this city region reflect broader tendencies across large portions of metropolitan America.

In recent decades, as Hispanics (or to use the more frequently applied contemporary term for people from Spanish-speaking countries, "Latinos") have grown to replace African-Americans as the largest ethnic or racial minority nationwide, and Asian-Americans have also grown rapidly in numbers, U.S. city regions have become increasingly diverse. At the same time, metropolitan areas still vary widely in the proportions and types of ethnic and racial minorities. Despite growing diversity, the Portland region remains relatively homogenously white and nonHispanic by comparison with the bulk of U.S. metropolitan areas. In 2000, non-Hispanic whites comprised some 81 percent of the metropolitan area population and 75.5 percent of the central city. These figures compared with 64 percent of the average metropolitan area over 200,000 and only 46.2 in central cities of these city regions.[2] The contrast is even more striking by comparison with a small number of metropolitan areas like Los Angeles or Miami, where nonHispanic whites now make up a minority of the metropolitan as well as the central city populations. Within Portland, however, both Hispanics and Asian Americans have recently replaced African Americans as the largest minorities in both the central city and the wider metropolitan region. By 2000 Latinos made up 6.8 percent in the central city and 8.6 percent of the metropolitan population, and Asian Americans comprised 6.8 percent of the central city and 4.1 percent of the metropolitan population. African-Americans still comprised 6.7 percent of the central city population, but only 2.4 percent of the metropolitan area. Although the Asian population in greater Portland approached the level in U.S. metropolitan areas over 200,000 more

---

[2] Central cities included here are only the largest incorporated place in a metropolitan area, along with any other places containing at least half the population of that city.

generally (4.5 percent), the Latino population remained just over half of the overall total (15 percent), and the black population was less than a fifth of this proportion (13 percent).

As a result of recent immigration concentrated mostly in the Latino population, the foreign-born population in the Portland metropolitan area rose to just under 11 percent by 2000, slightly below the total of 13 percent in all metropolitan areas over 200,000. But both figures stood in contrast with the 31 percent of greater Los Angeles and the 40 percent of greater Miami in this category. Noncitizens, generally a smaller proportion of the immigrants than in Europe due to birthright citizenship and easier naturalization rules, numbered 7 percent of the population in greater Portland and 8 percent in all larger metropolitan areas, but 19 percent in Los Angeles.

Whatever the differences between urban centralization in Portland and European settings, and despite the relatively low proportions of minorities for a U.S. city, evolving patterns of segregation in this region reflect more general U.S. patterns. On the one hand, the pockets of greatest urban disadvantage (in European terms, the neighborhoods of the greatest social exclusion) mirrored the continued disadvantages that African-Americans faced. On the other hand, African-Americans have increasingly moved to middle-class, more integrated neighborhoods outside of the neighborhoods where discrimination historically forced them to concentrate residences, and new ethnic and immigrant minorities have complicated patterns of ethnic and racial segregation. As a result, except in metropolitan areas of the Northeast and the very largest city regions, sociospatial segregation between blacks and whites has broadly declined (Glaeser and Vigdor 2002; Logan 2002).

In Portland, where local planners have sought sociospatial integration as one of the goals of planning, the decline has been especially dramatic. In 1980, when blacks comprised 2.5 of the population in the Primary Metropolitan Statistical (PMSA) Area,[3] the dissimilarity index between blacks and whites stood at 69, well above the threshold of 60 that Massey and Denton (1993) used to distinguish "hypersegregation". By 2000, as blacks grew to 3.2 percent of the population, the dissimilarity index fell by over 20 points to 48.

The attraction of white middle and upper middle class households to the inner city areas that had previously housed the biggest concentrations of African Americans played an important part in this trend. Yet even in 2000, the black population remained significantly more segregated in

---

[3] As distinguished from the wider Consolidated Metropolitan Statistical Area (CMSA), this area included only Portland and its immediately surrounding counties, and not the other PMSA of Salem (Marion County) to the south. Unless otherwise noted, the metropolitan statistics here draw upon CMSA rather than PMSA definitions.

these same areas than any other minority groups (Figure 5). As in other city regions around the country, segregation in some schools was especially pronounced. In the same year as the census, students at the high school in the heart of the African-American community remained 66 percent black, even as most high schools around the metropolitan area counted less than 4 percent of students as black (Loy et al, 2001, p. 43).

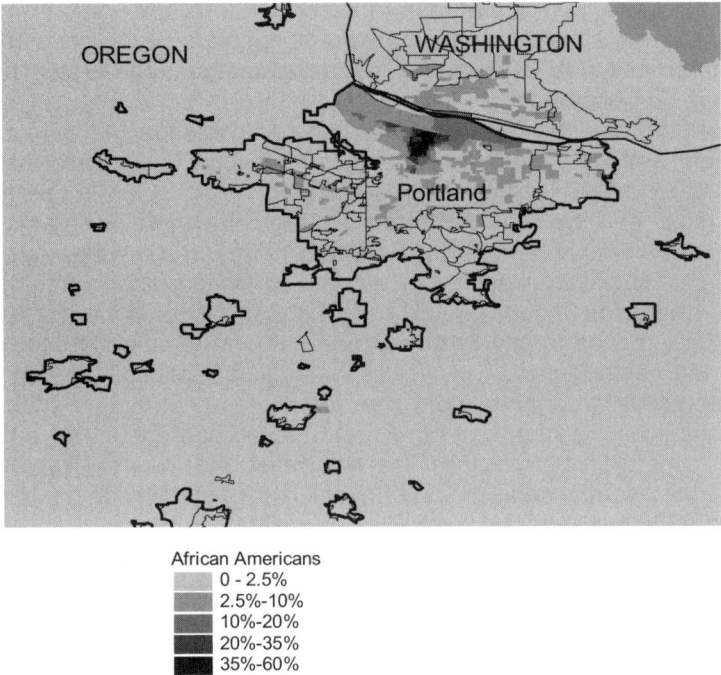

African Americans
0 - 2.5%
2.5%-10%
10%-20%
20%-35%
35%-60%

Fig. 5: Urban Growth Boundaries as of 2000 indicated by bold black lines; municipal and state boundaries indicated by light black lines. Source: U.S. Census 2000 STF1 Data.

At the same time the growth of the Latino population, spurred by recent immigrants who came mainly from Mexico, produced a largely cor-responding increase in segregation of this group. As the population ex-panded from 2 to 7.4 percent of the total, the dissimilarity index between Latinos and whites rose from 22 to 35. Yet for both this group and the Asian population, for whom the dissimilarity index stood at 32, settlement remained less concentrated than for blacks. Latinos also concentrated in the agricultural areas outside the suburban ring even more than in the central city. Largely agricultural workers, they settled in areas adjacent to jobs in the farms of the Willamette River Valley to the south.

These new patterns of immigration and resettlement produced an increasingly variegated pattern of economic stratification among neighborhoods across the metropolitan area (Figure 6). Gentrification in parts of the downtown accompanied continued impoverishment in other places, with alternative concentrations of whites and different minority groups. In comparison with the systematic segregation by race and income in most of the largest U.S. metropolitan areas, as variation in those below poverty level attests, the resulting diversity bore at least a passing resemblance to patterns in the downtowns of many European cities. At the same time, typical of metropolitan areas across much of the Southwest and the West, concentrations of poverty were also growing among the largely Latino concentrations on the outskirts of the metropolitan area. In Portland, rising housing prices in the ring immediately surrounding the growth boundary helped push these concentrations further out.

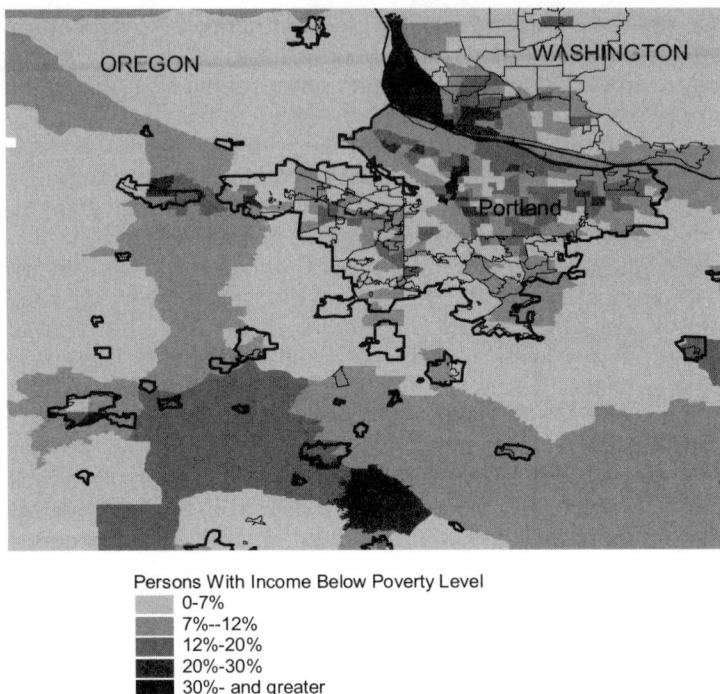

Persons With Income Below Poverty Level
- 0-7%
- 7%--12%
- 12%-20%
- 20%-30%
- 30%- and greater

Fig. 6: Urban Growth Boundaries as of 2000 indicated by bold black lines; municipal and state boundaries indicated by light black lines.Source: U.S. Census 2000 STF3 Data.

Policy and planning in Portland had thus limited U.S. tendencies toward comparatively high segregation and spatial polarization, but hardly eliminated these. Moreover, both the declining segregation of blacks and the expanding concentrations of disadvantaged Latino residents followed general trends that have been underway across the United States, and especially in the Western states. Although self-conscious local strategies made part of the difference for these trends, it remains difficult to sort out these influences from others.

The Political Vulnerability of Regional Growth Management
At the same time Portland manifests the potential of growth management in the U.S. context, the persistent political challenges to this regime demonstrate the vulnerability of the emergent new forms of regional regulation. Established opinion in the U.S. academic literature points to

opposition among suburban voters to the interests of the central city as the main obstacle to more integrated management of metropolitan regions (e.g., Dreier, Mollenkopf and Swanstrom 2001; Gainsborough 2001). In certain respects, voters in the Portland suburbs as well as the central city are less conservative than those outside the metropolitan area. Yet Portland suburbanites continue to draw the line where interests of homeowners there clash with that of renters and others in the downtown. Even here the metropolitan planning has remained vulnerable to local opposition to a degree that has seldom emerged so saliently under European planning systems.

Although suburban areas in the United States tend on the whole to vote more Republican, and more conservatively, than central cities, this tendency varies widely across the country. Portland, the suburbs as well as the central city have often voted Democratic in national elections. The entire metropolitan area often finds itself at odds politically with the conservative, rural areas that predominate over the remainder of Oregon (Loy et al 2001, pp. 48-47). Not only Multnomah County in the center, but the surrounding counties of Washington, Yamhill, Clackamas and Hood River voted consistently for Bill Clinton in 1992 and 1996, and all but Clackamas voted for Gore over Bush in 2000. This trend marked a departure from the pattern of the 1980s, when the same counties generally voted Republican. Results of ballot initiatives on specific issues reaffirm growing suburban propensities to side with the more left-leaning central city. Over the 1990s to 2000, these metropolitan counties sided against the rest of the state in support of medical use of marijuana and homosexual rights, and in opposition to hunting.

At the same time, the suburbs have emerged as a source of challenges to metropolitan growth management that ultimately highlights the political vulnerability of this regional scheme. From 1976-1982, support within the Portland suburbs proved crucial to defeat three successive challenges through this initiative process to the statewide planning legislation that undergirds metropolitan growth management in Portland. But in 2000, a new initiative was place on the ballot as part of a nationwide movement to reinforce property rights against local or state regulatory interventions. Initiative Measure 7, by requiring compensation to be paid to property owners for any regulatory action that diminished the profit from property, would have taken the teeth out of growth boundaries across the state. This time, the suburban counties broke from Multnomah to vote with the rural areas of the state in favor of a major constraint on growth manage-ment (Ibid.). Only a State Supreme Court decision that invalidated the

Initiative on procedural grounds spared the statewide legislative framework from this measure and its effects.[4]

Even in a state with the most successful instance of growth management, and with comparatively left-leaning suburbs, this result signaled how vulnerable regional growth management can be to political opposition from powerful interests based in the suburbs. Even in the European city regions that have increasingly dispersed, it would be difficult to imagine such an effective challenge to regional regulation or such strong suburban support for it.

Conclusion:
Global Trends, National Tendencies, Regional Divergences

Portland can hardly be taken as the typical U.S. metropolitan area. Yet neither can Los Angeles, New York, Peoria or indeed any other city region. Although it may be slightly more accurate to speak of a typical U.S. city region than of a typical European one, what is ultimately needed is a more disaggregated conceptualization that can take into account the wide variety of city regions within countries. For the U.S., any such account entails a recognition that entire class of cities, like Portland, Seattle, or Minneapolis, have faced conditions like greater ethnic and racial homogeneity and relatively modest size, and have been built out under different historical conditions of policy and technological development than the older and larger city regions that Europeans visit more regularly. Increasingly in recent decades, planners and policymakers in Portland and a growing number of metropolitan areas have also sought to counter sprawl and suburbanization with alternative public and private strategies that encourage denser, more integrated settlement forms. "Smart growth" and "new urbanist" movements follow local and state-level agendas that are as much a part of globalization as the sprawl and polarization they seek to counter. As applied in leading examples like Portland, these agendas have brought about what might be termed a partial Europeanization of U.S. planning and policy.

So far, however, in what may be the most advanced application of these strategies on a large scale, the city region that has resulted in greater Portland remains unmistakably American in character. Elements of suburban dominance and decentralization persist despite the success of the growth boundaries. Pockets of high poverty and disadvantaged minorities persist, and have taken new forms with the arrival of new minorities.

---

[4] League of Oregon Cities v. State of Oregon, 334 Or. 645, 56 P.3d 892 (Or. 2002), online at <http://www.abanet.org/rppt/committees/rp/c1/cases/League_ of_Oregon_Cities_v._State.pdf>. The decision held that the placement of two separate questions on the ballot in the same initiative for one vote violated the state constitution.

And political resistance to regulation of private property continues to press at the margins of planning and policy.

As in the case of European tendencies toward metropolitanization and polarization, a more fine-grained understanding that looks to influences at multiple levels affords the best analytical purchase on the processes apparent in Portland. Local and regional efforts need to be separated out from the national context of institutions, policies and culture. Directly or indirectly, these efforts also link to global trends, whether through communication among policy and planning professionals or in the dynamics of global capitalism. More systematic cross-national com-parative inquiry at the level of city regions themselves will be crucial to separate out the relations among these elements. Such efforts at data collection as the European Urban Audit or more recently the International Metropolitan Observatory are gradually making this kind of inquiry more attainable.[5] The picture of the city region that is likely to emerge from these endeavors, as the example of Portland highlights, will encompass local, national and global elements at the same time.

---

[5] Data from the European Urban Audit may be found online at the website <http://europa.eu.int/comm/regional_policy/urban2/urban/audit/>.   Information about the International Metropolitan Observatory, a global project with participants from sixteen countries, may be found at <http://www.usc.edu/dept/polsci/sellers/ IMO/IMOEnglish.htm>.

References:

Abbott, C. (1983) Portland: Planning, Politics and Growth in a Twentieth Century City. Lincoln, NE.

-, , Howe, D., Adler, S. (eds.) (1994) Planning the Oregon Way: A Twenty Year Evaluation, Corvallis, OR.

Ascher, F. (2000) Urban Homogenisation and Diversification in West Europe. In: Hambleton, R., Savitch, H., and Stewart, M., Globalism and Local Democracy. Houndsmills, Basingstroke, Hampshire.

Bollens, S. (1992). State Growth Management: Intergovernmental Frameworks and Policy Objectives. *APA* Journal 4: 454-465.

Burby, R. and May, P. (1997) Making Governments Plan: State Experiments in Managing Land Use. Baltimore, MD.

Calthorpe, P. (1993) The Next American Metropolis. Princeton.

Carruthers, J. (2002). The Impacts of State Growth Management Programmes: A Comparative Analysis. Urban Studies 39(11): 1959-1982.

Cobb, R. (1997). Toward Modern Local Statutes: A Survey of State Laws on Local Land-Use Planning.

Downs, A. (1994) New Visions for Metropolitan America. Washington.

-, (2002). Have Housing Princes Risen Faster in Portland Than Elsewhere? Housing Policy Debate 13(1): 7-31.

Dreier, P., Mollenkopf, J., and Swanstrom, T. (2001). Place Matters. Lawrence, KS.

Duany, A., Plater-Zyberk, E, and Speck, J. (2000) Suburban Nation. New York.

Fainstein, N. and Fainstein, N. (1982) Restructuring the American City: A Comparative Perspective, in N. Fainstein and S. Fainstein (eds.), Urban Policy under Capitalism. Beverly Hills.

Gainsborough, J. (2001). Fenced Off: The Suburbanization of American Politics. Washington.

Galster G, R Hanson, H Wolman, S Coleman & J Friebage (2000) Wrestling Sprawl to the Ground: Defining and Measuring an Elusive Concept Washington DC: Fannie Mae.

Glaeser, E. and Vigdor, Jacob. (2002). Racial Segregation: Promising News. In Katz, B. and Lang, R. (eds.), Redefining Urban and and Suburban America. Washington, DC.

Hero, Rodney E. and Tolbert, Caroline J. (1996). A Racial/Ethnic Diversity Interpretation of Politics and Policy in the States of the U.S. American Journal of Political Science, Vol. 40, No. 3., pp. 851-871.

Hoffmann-Martinot, V. (2004) Towards the Americanization of French Metropolitan Areas? Paper Presented to First Meeting of International Metropolitan Observatory, Bordeaux.

Jackson K. (1986) Crabgrass Frontier: The Suburbanization of the United States. New York.

Leo, Christopher, (1998) "Regional Growth Management Regime: The Case of Portland Oregon," Urban Affairs Quarterly, vol. 20, pp. 363-394.

Little, Charles. (1974). The New Oregon Trail. Washington, D.C.: The Conservation Foundation.

Lewis, P. (1995) Shaping Suburbia. Princeton, NJ.

Lopez R & H P Hynes (2003) Sprawl in the 1990s: Measurement, Distribution, and Trends Urban Affairs Review 38: 325-355

Logan, J. (2002). Ethnic Diversity Grows, Neighborhood Integration Lags. In: Katz, B. and Lang, R. (eds.), Redefining Urban and and Suburban America, pp. 235-256. Washington, DC: Brookings Institution.

Loy, W., et al. (2001). Atlas of Oregon. Second Edition. Eugene, OR.

Massey, D. and Denton, N. (1993). American Apartheid. Cambridge, MA.

Nathan R. and Adams, C. (1989) Four Perspectives on Urban Hardship. Political Science Quarterly 104(3): 483-508.

Nathan R. and Adams, C.. (1976). Understanding Central City Hardship. Political Science Quarterly 91(1): 47-62.

Nelson, A.C.. (2000). Does Growth Management Matter? The Effect of Growth Management on Economic Performance. Journal of Planning Education and Research 19:277-285.

Nivola, P. (1999). Laws of the Landscape. Washington, DC.

Orfield, M. (1997). Metropolitics. Washington, DC.

Philips, A. and Goodstein, B. (2000) Growth Management and Housing Prices: The Case of Portland, Oregon. Contemporary Economic Policy, 18(3):324-344.

Sellers, J. (2004a). The Suburbanization of Politics: Is There a U.S. Model? Paper presented at International Metropolitan Observatory Meeting. Bordeaux.

-, (2004b). The Suburbanization of State Growth Management. Washington.

-, (2002). Governing From Below: Urban Regions and the Global Economy. Cambridge.

United Nations Centre for Human Setttlements (HABITAT). (1996) An Urbanizing World: Global Report on Human Settlements 1996. Oxford.

Zjiderveld, A. C. (1998). The Theory of Urbanity: The Economic and Civic Culture of Cities. New Brunswick and London.

Zovanyi, G.. (2001). Growth Management for a Sustainable Future: Ecological Sustainability as the New Growth Management Focus for the 21st Century. Westport, CT.

H-City - Denmark as one urban system[1]

Tom Nielsen

Denmark is not an urban region, compared to urban regions like Randstad or Ruhr. Unlike those primary exponents for what we usually consider urban regions, Denmark does not have such massive concentration of people and 'program' in a very large geographical area. The urban consumption of landscape is not as critical in Denmark as in many other countries in Europe. The degree of 'Americanisation' and 'sprawl-ification' of the countryside, is relatively minimal due to rather rigorous planning, even though suburbs of single family housing make up the majority of the cities, both in terms of population and area.

In Denmark there is no merging of formerly separate metropolitan areas through permanent urban growth. Actually there are no real metropolis in Denmark, only an aspirant in the capital, Copenhagen, with its 1 mill inhabitants.

Nonetheless it seems reasonable to describe and perceive Denmark as one continuous urban system.

What François Ascher calls the 'metapolis' (Ascher 1995; Gausa et al. 2003: 430-1) in many ways seems to be a relevant framework for describing the way significant examples on urban development works in Denmark right now.

DE TRE AKSER I "DET STORE H"

Kilde: Landsplanredegørelse 1997

Fig. 1: Infrastructural H

---

[1]This article is a redeveloped version of an article originally co-written with Peter Hemmersam, and published in the anthology Urban Mutations – periodization, scale and mobility, Nielsen, T., N. Albertsen and P. Hemmersam (eds.) Aarhus: Arkitektskolens forlag, 2004The concept of H-City was originally invented and developed in the context of the architectural firm TRANSFORM architects, of which the author is a partner (see http://transform-architects.com).

H-City

This new urban system on a national scale that seems to be on the verge of existence in Denmark can be called H-City, after the layout and name of the primary infrastructural connections in the country. Build to connect the most important industrial cities from the 1950ies and on, the national highway system (that was planned in the 40ies), along with the primary railway-lines, makes up an H.

The national motorway system was originally conceptualised only as infrastructure, as a 'vessel of (economic) growth', but has as a consequence a new 'national meta-city'. This 'meta-city' is a result of what we could call a 'mutation' of the initial and planned role of the infrastructure into something much more comprehensive.

The H-City thus has been in the making since the 1950ies with the construction of the national motorway system and general development schemes in Denmark, but its potential only really became clear in June 1998 with the opening of the Great Belt Bridge. This 18 km's of infrastructure instantly more than doubled the amount of traffic travelling from East to West-Denmark.[2] Apart from a slight decrease in air traffic, this doubling was a result of the new possibilities the shortened travel time generated.

The Great Belt Bridge is a new national monument. Removing the one major hindrance in the communication between all major parts of the country, it unites two, according to the size of population, almost equally sized parts of the country.

In 2000, 2 years after the opening of the Great Beltfixed link, the Øresund Bridge linking East-Denmark and The Copenhagen area with Malmö and Southern Sweden opened.

The 'H' then includes the 5 biggest cities in Denmark, 2/3's of the population, and what is fast becoming the second biggest city in Sweden, Malmö.

Fig. 2: The Great Belt Bridge

---

[2] The amount of travels by train has more than doubled, and the car traffic has nearly tripled since the opening. (www.trm.dk)

H-city is based on accessibility, but as movement and information, and not as proximity and space as in the dense and centered historical town or city.

The basis or framework for this urban region or metapolis is not a giant metropolis that has started to expand in a new way by including new smaller urban enclaves, like the urban regions of for example London or Paris.

For H-City it is the national state itself that makes up an outer framework for the urban system to develop as a 'metapolic' system of mutually competing and collaborating urban enclaves.

This could be so because the country has an appropriate size for a region, and that it – even if the nation states are under pressure from globalization – still in many ways is an entity regarding language and political administration.

Fig. 3: H-City

The national state frames the urban development in a way that makes it perceivable as a region. It is important though, to note that like the national state whose borders have been fixed since 1920, H-City can easily expand beyond this initial framework. The emerging integration between Eastern Denmark and Southern Sweden is an example. But it is also an example that shows that this kind of development evolves much more slowly due to the (in fact rather minimal) differences in cultural and administrative practices. Compared to the instant doubling of the traffic over the Great Belt after the opening of the fixed link, the increase of traffic between Denmark and Sweden as a consequence of the Øresund-link was less dramatic. Whereas Denmark already worked as an integrated region culturally, economically and politically (with a bad connection between its major parts) before the construction of the Great Belt Bridge the integration between Eastern Denmark and Southern Sweden is stimulated 'artificially' by the adding of new infrastructure.[3]

If the national state makes up an outer frame, however weak or porous it might be, the internal framework for the region – that which makes it work and develop as a metapolis – is its infrastructure.
The infrastructural H with its high-speed connections makes Denmark work as an urban region where different districts or 'sub-cities' can emerge or develop more freely.
Freely in the way that they are not dependent of struggling to become 'fully equipped' cities that accommodates any thinkable need like the metropolis, and therefore has the potential to compete by enhancing specific local qualities or competences.

Life in H-City
H-City is an aspect of globalization. It is a (trans)national urban system, and represents a way to overcome the problems of isolation that doom small provincial towns to decline in the face of the general replacement of small-town community with metropolitan lifestyle in an urbanized society. Life in H-City is characterized by new forms of sociality and is no longer 'naturally' embedded in mono-centric urban form.
To introduce the image of H-City is to point towards the possibility of a new urban identity on a national level, an alternative to the former hierarchy of urban identities going from capital, over larger provincial centres, to smaller provincial towns and villages. H-City is a large open space - a platform - that creates a potential for each of its parts to develop more 'freely', but also for its citizens to be able to choose from a greater variety of neighbourhoods and local cultural and social enclaves.

---

[3] After 4 years the traffic over Øresund has steadily increased and is now near the double of what is was before the completion of the bridge. (www.trm.dk)

By describing and developing the integration of the smaller communities into a national urban system, there might be a possibility of a much more open and tolerant society for the individual, making it a place where personal experiences will be attainable across a variety of locations and social relations over a variety of communities no longer linked to local territory (provinciality).

Moving through H-City:

Towns and cities will continue to develop with many of the same elements as before, but may, as a result of infrastructure and the knowledge of the 'meta-city' it eventually constitutes, develop more powerful functions and unique identities, which on an overall scale may result in a far greater variation of programme and identities than any one city today. H-City consists of an excessive number of well-known, well-tested elements, sometimes brought together in new ways: housing, infrastructural monuments, windmills, high-tension cables, billboards, reforestation programs, tourist- and leisure landscapes, entropic industrial landscapes etc. The description of H-City does not mean excluding previous conceptions of the city, nor still existing or reproduced fragments of urban form build according to different ideals and perspectives. After modernism and the belief in the planning of an all new and better society, the notions of cultural heritage and identity seems to have been the dominating metaphors in planning as well as in populist politics. They have been so powerful that they have resulted in what we could call 're-traditionalization'- the active re-construction of local cultural historical identity as an attempt to re-generate a feeling of small-town community and security in the city.

On a local scale, proximity still matters. A consequence of that is perhaps the repetition of certain, typical and popular elements through out H-City: shopping-environments, entertainment venues and fast food-restaurants.

The different new or emerging 'landscapes' or 'cities' that make up significant parts of H-City, are all in a way condensations of some of the overall principles.

A 'drive' though H-City and some of its actual neighbourhoods will illustrate some of these principles:

Fig. 4: Transit City: Copenhagen airport

Transit City

The airport is an essential element in H-City, as in any other urban region. The primary quality of this 'city' is connectivity and transit in an environment dominated by the intersection of different kinds of infrastructure. The airport develops from being a purely technical in-stallation, into a city of its own, with thousands of workers, hotels, shop-ping, conference rooms etc., but the majority of its 'inhabitants' are in transit, no longer permanently fixed in space. But it is not just the airport that is an environment like this. All around in H-City other cross-points for the public traffic are being rebuild and re-programmed with shops, cinemas and other recreational facilities to become Transit Cities like this one.

The Transit City is in a way an icon for H-City, as mobility is the keyword.

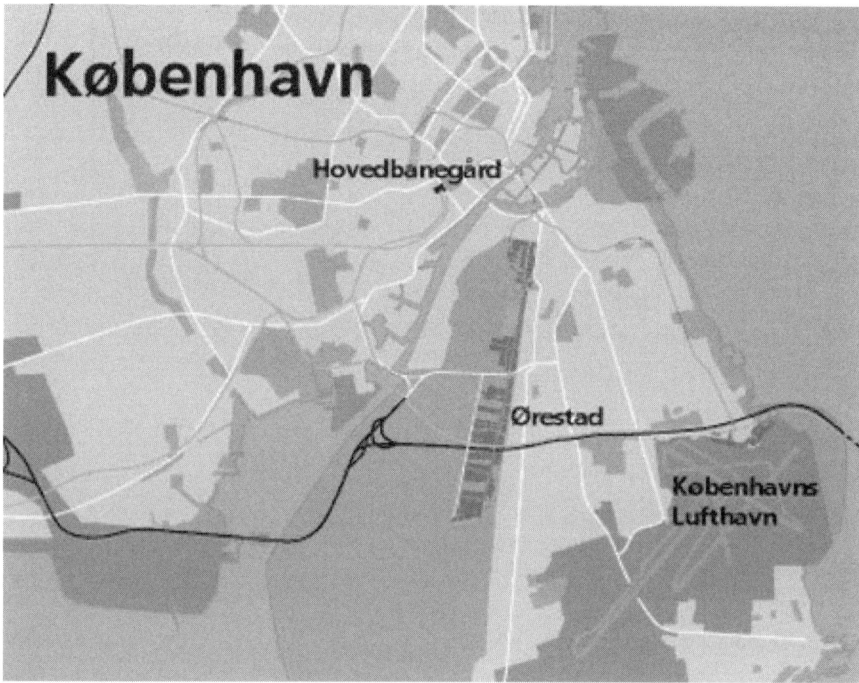

Fig. 5: Strip City: The Ørestad

Strip City

The Ørestad grows from the historical centre of Copenhagen towards the new infrastructural landscape of the airport and the Øresund Bridge connecting Denmark to Sweden and the rest of the world. It is developing around a light railway and is open to the landscape of Amager Fælled to one side. Ørestaden is a new district in H-City, where new big programmes of research, education, media, and commercial activities connect, and maximum interconnection to the landscape is aspired.

A major part of this new urban strip consists of buildings that because of their size or the character of the activity taking place within them does not fit in the center of Copenhagen. The University, The National Broadcasting Corporation, Scandinavia's largest shopping center (Fields), are examples of such urban 'spill-over'.

Even though this new strip is in close proximity of the existing urban centre, the determining thing about it is that it is built directly on and around the infrastructure, resulting in this urban enclave having a much larger hinterland, than many places in the central city.

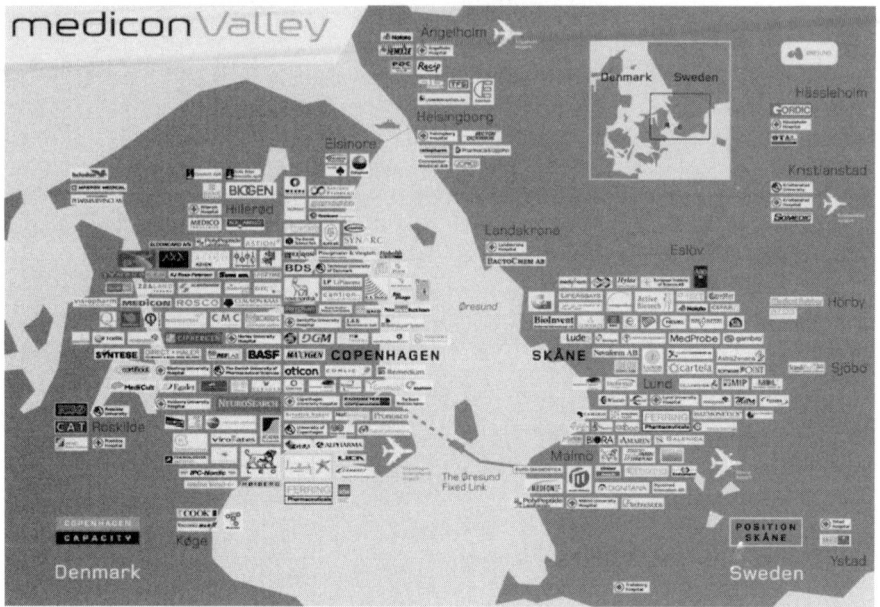

Fig. 6: Virtual City: Map of Medicon Valley

Virtual City

Medicon Valley owes its existence to Industrial Development Councils and coordinated effort by the Pharmaceutical Industry as a response to increased competition with other regions in a liberalized European marked.

Medicon Valley is a network of pharmaceutical and biotech-related companies and institutions in the Øresunds-region, with altogether 30.000 jobs. It has emerged overnight without being planned by any of the traditional public institutions. This is possible because the identity of the city to a large degree is independent of a concrete built realty, but primarily is promoted as a brand. That does not mean that it does not respond to actual qualities in the existing urban environment, as well as produce change in it: new laboratories and industrial complexes are constructed as well as housing and services. Medicon Valley is promoted as a city with distinct urban qualities that it 'borrows' from the rest of H-City. It has, for instance, 70 golf-courses, 12 universities, over 100 castles and churches and more than 20.000 nurses!

Apart from these attractive physical features, Medicon Valley and other types of Virtual Cities like it are promoted by diagrams showing the short traveltimes to other important virtual cities in the world.

Fig. 7: Instant City: Roskilde Festival

Instant City

'Instant Cities' are popping up in new 'Leisure-landscapes' the zones between the old and new cultural landscape, put-and-take ponds in abandoned gravel pits, golf courses on the edge of the agricultural land-scape, moto-cross tracks among industrial plots.

The Roskilde Festival is not characterized by traditional recreation, solitary recovery and reconstitution from urban bustle, but is a landscape of masses. One week each year it is the 5th largest city in Denmark with a population of approximately 100.000. Its identity, built up over the last 30 years, is based on a constantly returning state of emergency, creating a liminal space with rules and moral codes that differs from those follow-ed in the world outside.

It is located on areas adjacent to the motorway and is highly dependent on the infrastructure of H-City. Apart from the venues where music are performed, it also consists of many traditional urban elements, such as residential areas, commercial districts, public spaces, restaurants, banks, church, supermarket, laundrettes and movie theatres.

Instant Cities are being erected and taken down everywhere in cities to accommodate the celebration of special events. Any kind of urban festival, large scale conference or event will normally result in some kind of Instant City of tents and mobile elements.

Back to the countryside

BTTC's are new parts of the city with houses for city-workers and country-dwellers, in rural settings. We find it in proximity of all major centres in H-City. It houses mainly academics and well-off professionals in modernized farmhouses and new houses in 'modern rural style' with big plots. It relies on the motorway and other infrastructure to make com-muting to nearby occupational centres possible. It is a loosely knit field, incorporating historical elements, existing villages and topological features, with individual houses, windmills, industry and reforestation. It is also a modern ecological landscape, with extra emphasis on leisure activities in relation to large nearby residential areas. The relatively low density of these landscapes in H-City also contains small scale ecological farming and horse-riding centres.

Transport City

H-City develops its own enclaves focused entirely on infrastructure and mobility. The Danish Transport Center just north of the Vejle Bridge at the 'left leg' of the 'H' is an example. Around this transit-center new programs and new urban cultures develop. From being a place for truck drivers, the Transport Centre is developing into at leisure-landscape with car-related events and facilities: Drag-racing, car-dealers, hotel, bank, supermarket, tourist-information, conference-facilities, showroom for new homes and the nations best selling McDonalds.

This is the beginning of a whole new city, and this early urban form occurring in a 'natural' place in the completely manmade artificial landscape of the H, in a way echoes earlier versions of the larger cities of the H as they developed in the middle ages at naturally ideal locations: a certain crossing of a river, a natural harbour etc.

But as opposed to the cities of the middle ages the 'Transport city' will never become a 'whole' city with everything from town hall to commercial and residential districts.

Even though it occupies several acres, it will never become more than a district of the metapolis – of H-City.

Fig. 8: Shopping City: 'The Latin Quarters', Aarhus

Shopping City

The transformation of most historical urban centres to Shopping and Leisure Cities reflects the need for spatial and social intimacy, apparently greater than ever in the city characterised by mobility and tele-communication.

The general ban on new ex-urban shopping centres in Denmark, based on an idea of preserving the vitality and authenticity of historical centres, has paradoxically resulted in the conversion of the historic centres into fully equipped shopping-malls. In Aarhus a new commercial development near the railway station (Bruuns Galleri) – in itself an example of a new Transit City – is being conceived as the missing attraction or 'anchor' in the mall-like structure of the inner city retail district (Strøget), with the other attractor being the reinvented and 're-traditionalized' retail area of 'The Latin Quarters' (Latinerkvarteret). Aarhus is becoming a major shopping district in H-City.

Fig. 9: Season City: 'Authentic Skagen'

Season City

'Tourist landscapes' are emerging all over H-City. Tourism often has a dramatic restructuring effect on the natural landscape and historical centres that in the outset is the attraction. An example of the 'Tourist landscapes' is the advent of the season based city. Skagen, a small town at the outmost periphery of H-City, is an example of how a significant and 'authentic' urban situation mutates in the process of exploitation of identity, and how it even can be reproduced away from the original. Skagen was made famous by a group of painters who lived there 100 years ago, as 'original tourists'. By aestheticising the life of the old fishing village they paved the way for the mass tourism of today.

Skagen has developed into a double city. The original town is abandoned half the year as a consequence of staggering house prices that are a result of the influx of tourists. As a result of Skagens inclusion in H-City a new town housing the all-year inhabitants has developed, parallel to the 'authentic' environment.

H-City as part of a new urban revolution

In a recent article François Ascher describes what he understands as a new urban revolution to be compared with the one that took place from the last part of the 19th century, where new technology inspired the formulation of 'urbanism' as scientific practice and ideal (Ascher 2002). He characterises the new urban revolution as the emergence of a meta-urbanism.

The urban developments proposed in relation to H-City can be seen in the light of such a concept and be described through the concepts put forward by Ascher as characteristic aspects of this new urban revolution.

First of all there is the concept of 'meta-polisation' (Ascher 1995). This is characterised by the linking of several formerly autonomous urban centres into a heterogeneous but nonetheless coordinated urban field through the development of infrastructure. These new urban regions are not the result of expansive growth from a privileged centre like the great metropolis, but of the development of a coherent regional system of exchange. Metapolisation, like globalisation, results in a double process of homogenization (same type of economic actors in all countries and all cities) and differentiation (the actors adapt to the local circumstances and stimulates the enhancement of local 'intelligence' and regional and local identity.)

In H-City metapolisation can be seen in the simultaneous integration of provincial towns in overall regions and the development and enhancement of unique local identities.

The second factor put forward by Ascher is the transformation of urban mobility-systems. The development of communication and infrastructure networks not only facilitates the differentiation and coordinated urban growth within a region, it also changes the habits and practices of the urbanites within it. Both the possibility and the value of face to face meeting and of socially central collective experiences grow, resulting in the development of leisure- and shopping-landscapes in the city. The communal experience and the social 'event' become ever more central to both the economy and to the experience of the life within the new city. In H-City, along with the increase in trade and economic exchange, the Great Belt Bridge has resulted in a great increase in family-visits and cultural excursions across the country.

The third factor addresses the way urbanites improves their capacity to master personal time and space. With the development of communication technology and the easy access that most people have to these systems (cars, mobile-phones, internet-computers) we see an increase in the number of micro-events and entirely new 'time tables' for lives in the city. This again creates a demand for flexible and non-stop services and infrastructure that can accommodate a constant movement between domestic and collective spaces. As a result standardised office hours are becoming obsolete; rush hour traffic might be a thing of the past, as workers in Medicon Valley and other of the virtual cities within H-City work at home, or relate to business hours on the other side of the planet. A consequence of these developments might be a 'lighter' urban system, less dependent on industrial regulation of the life of the workers.

The fourth tendency is the development of an urban reflexive solidarity. Competition as well as local cooperation and consensus increases along with the establishment of physical and virtual connections between neighbourhoods and regions. The cooperation of institutions and companies in the Medicon Valley exemplifies this on a commercial scale. Operating and competing on a regional or even global scale means that every urban or commercial enclave has to be able to adjust continuously, to continuously be updated. This makes analysis of the role of the enclave within the network of the meta-city a necessity.

As a final factor Ascher suggests the concept of Risk society, introduced by Ulrich Beck (1992). The processes leading to a meta-urbanism is one of constant competition, uncertainty and demand for flexibility. In such a transformation of city and society, issues concerning security acquire importance. Globalization reveals limitations of the welfare systems and the shortcomings of national regulation and planning, that the system is based on. Growing uncertainty results in attempts to control and regulate events on a smaller scale, leading to a demand for controlled and 'safe' living environments, shopping centres with security guards and so on. In this way the new meta-urbanity is related to mechanisms of social and racial exclusion. This potential danger represents the dark side of H-City.

Imagineering[4]

Even though H-City is not fully grown as an urban region, like for instance Ruhr, Randstad, Los Angeles or other more prominent examples, it makes sense to perceive and discuss it as a region. Instead of just having to describe and try to improve a region already there, the current state of urban development in Denmark gives the opportunity to contribute to the development of it on a more basic level.

H-City should be understood as a very 'soft' and incomplete situation, with a very big potential.Focusing on it, describing it and 'branding' it, is a way to contribute to its development in a positive way.

Stuck with the left-over planning tools from modernism that still today constitutes the main instruments of planning, planners and politicians have been unable to act on the scale of cities for decades, making the invention of new tools and new concepts relating to the new urban condition necessary. Before any of that can take place, a change of view or perspective is necessary, a new way of looking based on observable changes in the environment.

H-City is a new image of Denmark and its cities, an image raising questions of urban identity and urban transformation on a large scale. 'H-City' represents the new Danish urban system in a way that makes it possible to act within it. H-City can be imagineered and designed through 'sampling' city and landscape, connecting specific and general characteristics, and through compressing and combining information. In this way it is possible to act in planning in a political sense. Political decisions depend on images and the ability to render a new situation imaginable and desirable.

Infrastructure determines the shape of H-City by determining lines of communication and fields of settlement. In a situation where cities seem difficult or even impossible to plan and control qualitatively, infrastructure seems to have at least some impact on urban form and structure. It

---

[4] Imagineering is the name of the department that designs the Walt Disney theme parks. It as an acronym put together words 'image' and 'engineering'. That means that 'imagineering' can be described as the art of establishing environments through the combination and resampling of images, fantasy references and actual constructions (see: Betsky, Adigard 2000: 1.7).

appears possible to apply this positively to determine certain qualities or aspects of the future urban development, using infrastructure to create both heterogeneity and homogeneity on different scales.

Within the context of H-City, infrastructure can be manipulated to point at new kinds of places, strategic regions, and new possible urban typologies. It can be used to open up and display whole new aspects of the meta-city, 'imageneering' it and exposing it in order to let the different institutions and powers of development and change recognize and 'get a hold' on it.

References:

Ascher, F. *(1995)* Métapolis, ou l'avenir des villes. Paris: Odile Jacob

-,   (2002) 'Urbanismen og den nye urbane revolution'. Distinktion, No.4,
      29-36.

Beck, U. (1992) Risk Society: Towards a New Modernity. Thousand Oaks: Sage
      Publications

Betsky, A., Adigard, E. (2000) Architecture Must Burn. London: Thames and Hudson
      Ltd.

Gausa, M. et al. (2003) The Metapolis Dictionary of Advanced Architecture
      Barcelona: Actar.

http://www.orestad.dk/

http://www.imagineering.org/

http://transform-architects.com

http://www.trm.dk

City and Region the Structurational Way
An Agency-based View of the City-Region

Ingo Dallgahs

Today's urban research as well as planning is confronted with the spreading interconnections between what was once called the city and its surrounding region. Concepts like "Postmetropolis", "Zwischenstadt" and "città reticolare" are reflecting this shift towards a tightly connected city-region. New approaches of what defines "urban research" are called for.

I.The Inventory
Before heading for the main issue we have to take a brief look at the standard approaches of urban geography and urban theory in general. In order to keep it short I will not attempt to discuss the following in depth; the focus is to recall the most important approaches, that form an almost taken-for-granted inventory of urban theory.

Structuralist views
Most prominent among the different approaches to urban and/or regional development are the macrostructure determined concepts, first of all the historic-materialistic approaches following for example David Harvey's *Social Justice and the City* (1973) or Henri Lefebvre's *La revolution urbaine* (1970)[1]. The idea behind these most influential works is that cities come into existence through the capitalistic logic underlying western societies. They are the expression of the capitalistic division of labor, of commodifying and exploiting *space* via creating an artificial environment that fits economic interests best. Projecting this analysis into the distant future, Lefebvre tends to predict a completely urbanized society in which the original counterpart of the urban – the rural – has ceased to exist.

Some more recent approaches to theorize urban space are the World and/or Global City hypotheses of John Friedmann (1986) and Saskia Sassen (1991). Despite important differences between them, they both consider capitalistic division of labor and therefore specialization and concentration of certain functions (e.g. headquarter economies) as the driving force behind urban development.

The same goes for the Regulation School following Alain Lipietz (1986). His argument is based on a macro-economic shift from a fordist to a post-fordist mode of regulation and production. Urban government, in

---

[1] Not to forget Manuel Castells' contribution in "The Urban Question" (1977) in which the city is seen as the place of collective consumption

order to survive and prosper, has to follow that shift which ultimately leads to the emergence of a post-fordist city, characterized for example by the use of public-private-partnerships in urban planning and the outsourcing of public services (in short: privatization).

The one thing in common is the top-down direction implicity used in these approaches. They claim that the state of or the change in the socioeconomic macro-structure determines the way human settlements look like, how they function, develop and decline. Along with that principally structuralist view there is a lack in considering the role and relevance of actors. I will return to that issue later on.

Individualistic views

Another very influential way of thinking about *the urban* is the individualistic tradition drawing from Louis Wirth's understanding of urbanity as a distinct way of life[2] (Wirth 1938; more recently: Sennett's *Civitas-trilogy* 1983; 1991; 1995; Bauman 1997), characterized through size, density and heterogeneity, visible for example in the opportunity to meet strangers and the ability to cope with uncertainty (which is thought to be created by strangers).

The problem with that view is that urbanity is tightly connected to **one** certain lifestyle which could be applied best to the small city-states as the greek and roman city or even the early industrial cities. But things changed. Today's cities are clearly marked by the simultaneous presence of a multitude of different lifestyles within an area. Furthermore, the rural settlements are no longer homogeneous, people don't know each other since childhood, are not relatives to each other. The point of getting in terms with strangers is not limited to the urban. It is a ubiquitous feature of contemporary life. Given that, one has to find another way to define *the urban*.

II. Structuration Theory revisited

An approach that attempts to match the intertwining and interdependent scales and processes of today's city-regions has to take account of structural elements **and** the actors' everyday experience. Anthony Giddens' *Theory of Structuration* serves as a point of departure here and it is necessary to recall some key elements and ideas.[3]

---

[2] Thereby echoing Georg Simmel's essay "Die Großstädte und das Geistesleben" of 1903 (quoted here as Simmel 1995)

[3] As (physical) space is limited here this can only be a rough sketch. For a more detailed elaboration see for example Dallgahs 2004.

The Structuration of Society

The center of Anthony Giddens' *Theory of Structuration* (1971; 1995; 1997) rests in the understanding of society as an inseparable entity of structural elements and human agency, which he call the *"duality of structure"*. Both are connected through the process of structuration, which means that there is no way of understanding the structure of a society without looking at the agencies that led to it and vice versa; agency can only be conceptualized via taking account of structural elements that enable or prevent change (which is agency). In acknowledging this it is obvious that the central field of research can neither be limited to the experiences of the individual nor to the existence of any determining entity (economics for example). It can only be found in the social practices situated in time and space (Giddens 1997: 52).

Structure in Giddens' view consists of rules and resources. Agency therefore is generated through relating to certain (commonly shared) rules and to certain (unevenly distributed) resources. In doing so the structure is constantly produced and reproduced, and effects the ongoing agencies (Giddens 1997: 75 ff.; Werlen 1995: 80). Structure as well as agency are medium and result of each other.

Rules are understood analogous to mathematic formulae; they are commonly known and regarded as true in a given context; they can be semantic as well as moral and regulate the use of resources. The disregard of rules is sanctioned.

Resources can be divided into authoritative and allocative resources. Their primary goal is the generation of power. Allocative resources comprise all material aspects of the environment – such as capital, soil, productive goods, produced goods etc. – that can easily be collected and stored. Authoritative resources refer to the ability to control the human aspects of the environment – such as the organization of labor, decision-making, access to information etc. The commonly used ways to store authoritative resources is through the use of writing and tradition (Giddens 1997: 86 f.; 315-320).

Power is the prerequisite of human agency in as far as it is understood as the possibility to cause – or to prevent – a change. This is possible through drawing at resources while obeying the necessary rules. Power can therefore be no resource; it exist only in the actual agency, is produced by the use of resources, it is the means through which agency is enabled (Giddens 1997: 67; 316).

Social Geography of Everyday Regionalization

As the focus of our attention lies in the question "What is urban space?" we have to take a short break and reconsider our understanding of space. One elaborated theoretical work on social theory and space is carried out by Benno Werlen (1995; 1997a; 1997b; 2000) by the title

"*Sozialgeographie alltäglicher Regionalisierungen*". Point of departure here is Giddens' *Theory of Structuration* which is modified in order to eliminate the contradictions based on Giddens' understanding of space as a physically defined area ("container-space"). This revised theory forms the foundation of a new social geography based on everday practices which are embodied in regionalizations.

The crucial point is that space in this conception is not understood as a constituting element but as a medium through which human agency is carried out, and which is constituted through human agency. It connects the human body and its material environment. One outcome of this structuring is called region.

Regions can analytically be divided into three main types, each relating to a certain type of agency, of everyday practice:

Productive and consumptive practices

⇒ geographies of production and consumption normative and political practices

⇒ geographies of normative acquisition and control informational and signifying practices

⇒ geographies of knowledge and symbolic appropriation

Regions in this conception are socially constructed realities, not an *a priori* category that is simply given, that is natural. Consequently it is only possible to look at regions (spaces) as *regions-in-construction*, as processes that lead to the genesis of a region. Not its ontology is the focus of attention but the way it is constructed and constituted by the actors.

Towards a structurational approach of the urban

As noted above most approaches to urban space lack either to account for the effects of human agency in the urban space or the aspects of structural elements that affect the individuals' perception and possibilities. One promising way to bridge the gap between structuralistic and individualistic positions is the consequent use of structurational propositions. That way it should be possible to overcome the structure-agency-disputes and to find a new access to *the urban*. That does not mean to discard the existing inventory of urban theory but to combine structuralistic and individualistic approaches in a less contradictory and fruitful way.

Agency is situated in the structure that is itself the intended and unintended result of former agency. So in order to take the above propositions seriously, one has to take account of both and, in a later stage, to connect both aspects of urban space to form a no longer reducing picture of what we call the city, or the region. And, furthermore, it seems possible to reformulate our understanding of the city-region.

The commonly used dichotomy *city* and *region* is in question. The city frontier is contested by urban sprawl making it hard if not impossible to distinguish the city and its surrounding region. City and region are tightly interwoven through commuting, intra-regional division of labor and functions, recreational traffic, administrational cooperation and many more. It is becoming more and more fragmented. While this is widely recognized, new concepts that try to bridge the old dichotomy are missing. There are new labels like "Zwischenstadt" (Sieverts 1997) or "Postmetropolis" (Soja 2000), containing great insights and descriptions, but the authors fail to attempt a synthetic view of *urban reality*. They still hold on to the city and the other (the surrounding, the region), as if there was still a city-wall clearly separating the inside from the outside, and homogenizing both internally. The city has to have certain features and lifestyles, that cannot be found elsewhere. The city is to be unique, clearly different from the region. Both seem to have some kind of own ontological status, and therefore can explain other aspects of social life.

From a structurational point of view that is not a valid assumption. Urban or regional space cannot represent an explanation, not a cause. City and region are to be constituted by social practices; their space is the sum of intended and unintended results of human agency (Werlen 2002: 212). Urban space is more than "urbanity" (as a distinct lifestyle or as a certain density of buildings, people and functions), more than the outcome of global capitalism. Urban space is formed in everyday practice and experience, in everyday perception and action. It is physical environment and symbolic content, remembrance of the past and anticipation of the future. And that way it has to be theorized.

One could think that that could easily be achieved by looking at Anthony Giddens' wide-ranging social theory, but that is not the case. He relates to it, especially in *A Contemporary Critique of Historical Materialism* (1995), but fails to apply his own hypothesis.
For Giddens (following in large parts Lewis Mumford) the origin of cities lies in the formation of a religious, ceremonial or commercial center that becomes the principal power container, implying a basic countryside (low power storage capacity) versus city (high power storage capacity) dichotomy (Giddens 1995: 10). It is merely a reprise of the commonly known story of the city, as developing from hunting and gathering nomads to first settlements of hydraulic civilizations and finally ending up in industrial cities, than a new approach. With each progression the capacity to store power generating resources is increased (1995: 97 ff). To Giddens the formation of cities lies in the very heart of societal organization:

"The city *in relation to the countryside* is the indispensable locus of the transformation/mediation relations (structural principles) involved in the differentiation of class-divided societies from tribal societies. Without cities, there are no classes and no state." (1995: 144)[4]

But he applies this only to capitalistic logic, not to a broader range of societal praxis. And together with that the city remains the expression of capitalistic logic, of macro-societal processes that 'happen' with literally no connection to human actors. In order to find a structurational approach to urban space we will have to find another point of departure.

III. City-Region the Structurational Way
To tell the story of the city-region from a structurational point of view it is essential to account equally for the structural elements and human agency, bond together by the structuration of urban space. Consequently I will not try to define what the city or the region is; my interest lies in the constituting processes that lead to what is called the city or the region.

Urban Structure
Structural elements of today's city-regions have been described and analyzed in manifold ways and with substantial depth. The most obvious common feature of these elements is that they originate from the macro-level of society, mostly from the economic realm. They are characterized by terms like globalization, post-fordist regulation and production, global city hierarchy and alike. They form the frame in which the cities and its inhabitants are able to act, by limiting as well as by expanding the range of possible action. Urban planning for example is urged to enable the city to compete and succeed in global, national and regional competition (e.g. through city marketing or non-bureaucratic handling of planning permissions). Urban planning is shaped by general trends (e.g. high rise buildings, redevelopment of the waterfront areas, loft living) as much as most inner cities look pretty similar because of the ever-the-same retail shops, and thus reminding of faceless, interchangeable shopping malls.
Structural elements imply a convergence of the cities: As the forces having impact on the single city are the same, the results tend to be similar as well. With every city applying the same strategies to face the same challenges, on the long run they will be the same (structurally).

---

[4] "A class-divided society" in Giddens' terms is not necessarily capitalistic (= "class society"). Though there are classes in capitalism, the actual division of classes is independent from it and occurred prior to capitalism. In class-divided societies the division "does not serve as the principal of organization" (1995: 108) which in class society is the main structural principle, visible first of all in the role of private property and the extraction of surplus value.

There may be some local color added, but basically the differences are leveled and vanish over time.

Urban Actors

The indispensable counterpart of structural elements of a structurational view of the city-region is human agency. Agency necessarily needs to be carried out by an actor, so the question rising with the aspect of agency is the question concerning the role and the constitution of actors. The term actors I'm referring to includes individual actors as well as collective actors. Technically speaking only human individuals are able to act, to use their body in order do make (or prevent) a difference. But in the context for example of urban planning, this view has to be revised. Nearly every actor represents some kind of collectivity (investors, city administration, political parties, civil interest groups etc.), is taking action because it is his/hers job or task. They are equipped with resources (and therefore power) belonging to the organization and are acting on behalf of it, pursuing primary the interests of it.[5] Contrasting with the original conception of methodological individualism (Werlen 1995) the term "actor" in the field of urban planning needs to be adapted to these requirements by extending it to institutional and collective actors (Colemann 1990; Esser 1993; MayntzandScharpf 1995).

Urban Agency

While actors in urban space are covering the whole range from the individual to institutions, the actual agency relating to and producing urban space is even more heterogeneous. Following Werlen's types of regionalization it is possible to identify at least three principal urban spaces:

- ♣ spaces of production and consumption (economy)
- ♣ spaces of normative acquisition and control (politics)
- ♣ spaces of knowledge and symbolic appropriation (culture).

The spaces of economic action deal with the side of production (supply) and the side of consumption (demand) by focusing primarily on allocative resources. To consider both sides is crucial, especially under contemporary conditions of an increasingly consumer-oriented market.

The spaces of politics are concerned with the use of authoritative resources in order to exercise control over subjects (via control over their bodies). Political power can thus not be conceptualized as control over a territory; rather political power rests on the ability to prescribe actors how

---

[5] There are indeed more personal interests involved into urban planning than one might think. In praxis the role of personal interests and relations can hardly be overestimated.

to act (and not to act), and only the range of that ability is possible to mark down cartographically.

The spaces of culture deal with the phenomenological dimensions of how (why, by whom) information and knowledge is spread and how (why, by whom) it is used to create symbolic contents of spaces, for example such as "Heimat" or "urbanity". The focus of attention lies in the generation and use of rules concerned with these symbolic contents.

All these spaces together form what is called urban, regional, rural space that is necessarily a combination of the different and often op-posing dimensions of the spatiality of human life. In that perspective the city or the region cannot constitute the subject of interest in its own right. Urban research can not take the city for granted and then analyze what is the difference for example to the region or other cities. City as well as region have to be defined in the everyday spatializing practices of actors. It can no longer hold that actors live different, have different experiences because they live here and not there. It is the actors' own constitution of his/hers everyday space that is the focus of interest, his/hers own view of his/hers space. Consequently the dichotomy city vs. region has to be discarded.

Urban Structuration: The Case of Urban Planning

The structuration of urban space consists of structural elements and human agency, both depending on and influencing each other. The re-quirements for a structurational view of today's city-regions are to over-come a one-sided view and account for both aspects equally. This is ev-en more important as urban planning is a multidimensional phenol-menon consisting of structural elements - such as demographic, political, social, economic, technological, cultural and ecological factors (Strat-mann 1999: 14 ff.) - and observable agency.

In order to get a grip on contemporary urban planning all the different spaces need to be covered in an analysis. One promising way to do so is to look at urban space as the product of complex network processes. Ur-ban planning for example was largely thought as a top-down appli-cation of urban policy. The underling bias is a structural-functionalistic one: In order to actually build the city, one has to take control of all con-cerned aspects (mostly technical) and merely engineer the city. Once this is achieved the task left is to calibrate the urban machine to keep it running. The manifold processes of the last decades like suburbanization, de-industrialization, deregulation and privatization on the structural side and for example individualization and fragmentation of lifestyles on the actors' side have led to new ways in planning. Planning no longer follows de-tailed, long term oriented master-plans but has become a multilateral negotiation and mediation between different interests. These processes are best described as networks[6].

Networks have been employed widely in recent economic analysis (for example Maillat 1998, Storper 1997, Batheltand Glückler 2002; Schamp 2000) as well as for policy analysis (for example Jansen and Schubert 1995; Kenis Schneider 1996); in planning theory they are mostly used in an implicit way (e.g. as "public-private-partnerships", "muddling through", "round table", "advocacy planning", "Perspektivischer Inkrementalismus", "Mediation"; Selle 1994; 1997; 2000; Schlusche 2000; Schönwandt 1999). The focus of network analysis rests first of all on the relations between actors and/or institutions. In these relations embedded are allocative and authoritative resources (that is: power relations) as well as individual orientations, preferences, interest and influences of the socio-economic macro-level. Furthermore, the general, accepted rules for the use of resources are obeyed by the actors.

The description of a network begins with question: What is a certain network about? In our case that is planning the city/the quarter/the building, and thereby considering all relevant aspects. The related aspects are embodied by the actors – private and public – participating in the planning process. In voicing the different (conflicting as well as matching) interest a negotiation process is started, in which certain relations are formed, ranging from coalitions to conflicts, both openly articulated as well as tacitly exercised. And as the relations can be that different, so can the results.

Results can – for the time being only in a preliminary, hypothetic draft – be classified analogous to the different spaces mentioned above; but one has to keep in mind to deal with both the intended and the unintended results.

The economic dimensions are pretty easy to identify, as they include mainly the outcomes of the use of allocative resources. Examples are all material results such as buildings, streets, parks etc. that are produced in the planning process and are consumed afterwards.[7]

The political dimension is less obvious. Spaces of normative acquisition and control are the result of the paramount use of authoritative resources. To identify them in an analysis one has to focus on the negotiation processes, both public and behind closed doors, and concentrate on the power relations, e.g. if a city administration is able to assert itself, or whose interests are balanced by other interests. That way

---

[6] For a more detailed account see Dallgahs 2004.
[7] There are of course reflexive interactions between supply and demand, for example to produce only the types of buildings that are demanded by the consumers.

it should be possible to reveal for example "power landscapes" within an administrative area.

The cultural dimensions of space are accessible only through a communication-theoretical approach. One has to track down the sources of knowledge, the use of semantic rules and the constitution of meaning. To analyze for example the creation of artificial names like "Euro-Quarter", "Harbor City" or "City West" and the intended emotional effects attached to them is a first step, but scratches (necessarily) only the surface.

As it is obvious in this short collection, it is hard to separate the analytical dimensions of space. All dimensions are tightly interconnected with each other, and the subdivision in primary resources and rules is not exclusive, as there are for example rules applied in the production process, and there are authoritative resources used in the symbolic appropriation of space. A detailed elaboration is truly needed.

Urban Structuration put to the test:
Other examples and perspectives

The Constitution of the Frankfurt/Rhein-Main-Region:
The discussion within the Frankfurt region on the possibilities to manage an intra-regional compensation between the core (Frankfurt) and its surrounding (the municipalities in the Rhein-Main area) goes on since the 1970s (e.g. Scheller 1998). The numerous proposals, ranging from lose cooperation over monetary compensation to incorporation into one regional-city, and the decades of debates have had hardly any countable results. Nevertheless there have been political rearrangements, economic changes and attempts to create a regional identity. A reliable assessment (in structurational perspective) of the created spaces of this decade-long discussion is still missing.

Cultures and Economies of Cities
Sharon Zukin (1995) is concerned with the cultural power generated by cities[8], driving the city's economic development through their images and symbolic contents.[9] Culture is used to regenerate run down areas, to improve the quality of public spaces and the look of retail stores, to separate ethic groups and social strata. Culture in her view is a powerful means to plan, build, promote and run a city. Culture serves as a mediating device between built environment and symbolic meaning,

---

[8] For a very detailed look on the economic power of cultural production see Scott 2000.
[9] And thereby generating conflicts on whose culture, aesthetic and interest is dominant

between global processes and local identities, between structure and agency.

Résumé?

As the end is pretty open, a résumé is hard to draw. A lot of research is to be done, and this article represents only the tip of the iceberg. Structurational approaches contain a high potential, but as they are claiming to cover social life in nearly all respects, the empirical work is hard to accomplish, especially when considering the manifold inter-connections and interdependencies between the analytical subdivisions. The work has just started, and this article should not be read as a final report but as a statement, but as a workshop-paper. All comments are welcome!

References:
Bathelt, H. and Glückler, J. (2002) Wirtschaftsgeographie: Ökonomische Beziehungen in räumlicher Perspektive. Stuttgart.
Bauman, Z. (1997):Flaneure, Spieler und Touristen. Hamburg.
Castells, M. (1977) The Urban Question. London.
Coleman, J. S. (1990) Handlungen und Handlungssysteme. München.
Dallgahs,I. (2004) Der Planungsprozess Europaviertel als Netzwerk: Stadtgeographische Forschung im Zeichen von Handlungstheorie, Strukturationstheorie und Spätmoderne. Frankfurt am Main (in print).
Esser, H. (1993) Soziologie. Frankfurt am Main.
Friedmann, J. (1986) The World City Hypothesis.- In: Development and Change 17, pp. 69-84.
Giddens, A. (1971) Capitalism and Modern Social Theory. Cambridge.
-, (1995) A Contemporary Critique of Historical Materialism. London (2nd edition).
-, (1997) Die Konstitution der Gesellschaft. Frankfurt am Main.
Harvey, D. (1973) Social Justice and the City. Baltimore.
Jansen, D. and Schubert, K. (Eds.) (1995) Netzwerke und Politikproduktion: Konzepte, Methoden, Perspektiven. Marburg.
Kenis, P. and Schneider, V. (Eds.) (1996) Organisation und Netzwerk: Institutionelle Steuerung in Wirtschaft und Politik. Frankfurt am Main, New York.
Levebvre, H. (1970) La revolution urbaine. Paris.
Lipietz, A. (1986) New Tendencies in the International Division of Labor: Regimes of Accumulation and Modes of Regulation. In: Scott, A. and Storper, M. (Eds.) (1986) Production, Work, Territory, pp. 16-40. Boston.
Mayntz, R. and Scharpf, F. W. (1999) Der Ansatz des akteurszentrierten Institutionalismus. In Mayntz, R. and Scharpf, F. W. (Eds.) (1999) Gesellschaftliche Selbstregelung und politische Steuerung, pp. 39-72. Frankfurt am Main, New York.
Maillat, D. (1998) Vom 'Industrial District' zum kreativen Milieu: Ein Beitrag zur Analyse delokalisierter Produktionssysteme. In: Geographische Zeitschrift 86 (1), pp. 1-15.
Sassen, S. (1991) The Global City. Princeton.
Schamp, E. W. (2000) Vernetzte Produktion: Industriegeographie aus institutioneller Perspektive. Darmstadt.
Schlusche, G. (2000) Neue Kooperationsformen: Planungsstrategien und

bürgerschaftliches Engagement. In: Wentz, M. (Ed.) (2000) Die kompakte Stadt, pp. 222-231. Frankfurt am Main, New York.

Schönwandt, W. (1999) Grundriß einer Planungstheorie der "dritten Generation". In: DISP 136/137, April 1999, 35. Jg., pp. 25-35.

Scott, A. J. (2000) The Cultural Economy of Cities: Essays on the Geography of Image Producing Industries. London, Thousand Oaks, New Delhi.

Scheller, J. (1998) Rhein-Main: Eine Region auf dem Weg zur politischen Existenz. Frankfurt am Main.

Selle, K. (1994) Was ist bloß mit der Planung los? Erkundungen auf dem Weg zum kooperativen Handeln: Ein Werkbuch. Dortmund.

-, (1997) Planung und Kommunikation: Anmerkungen zur Renaissance eines alten Themas. In: DISP 129 (1997), pp. 40-47.

-, (2000) Nachhaltige Kommunikation? Stadtentwicklung als Verständigungsarbeit: Entwicklungslinien, Stärken, Schwächen und Folgerungen. In: Informationen zur Raumentwicklung, 1/2000, pp. 9-19.

Sennett, R. (1983) Verfall und Ende des öffentlichen Lebens: Die Tyrannei der Intimität. Frankfurt am Main.

-, (1991) Civitas. Die Großstadt und die Kultur des Unterschieds. Frankfurt am Main.

-, (1995) Fleisch und Stein: Der Körper und die Stadt in der westlichen Zivilisation. Berlin.

Sieverts, T. (1997) Zwischenstadt: Zwischen Ort und Welt, Raum und Zeit, Stadt und Land. Braunschweig.

Simmel, G. (1995) Die Großstädte und das Geistesleben. Georg Simmel Gesamtausgabe Bd. 7, pp. 116-131. Frankfurt am Main.

Soja, E. W. (2000) Postmetropolis: Critical Studies of Cities and Regions. Oxford, Malden.

Storper, M. (1997) The Regional World: Territorial Development in a Global Economy. New York.

Werlen, B. (1995) Sozialgeographie alltäglicher Regionalisierungen: Bd. 1: Zur Ontologie von Gesellschaft und Raum. Stuttgart.

-, (1997a) Sozialgeographie alltäglicher Regionalisierungen: Bd. 2: Globalisierung, Region und Regionalisierung. Stuttgart.

-, (1997b) Gesellschaft, Handlung und Raum: Grundlagen handlungstheoretischer Sozialgeographie. Stuttgart (3rd edition).

-, (2000) Sozialgeographie: Eine Einführung. Bern.

-, (2002) Urbanität und Lebensstile: Einleitung. In: Stadt und Region: Dynamik von Lebenswelten, pp. 210-217. Leipzig.

Wirth, L. (1938) Urbanism as a Way of Life. In: American Journal of Sociology 44, pp. 1-24.

Zukin, S. (1995) The Cultures of Cities. Oxford, Ma.

Building an urban planning capacity at large scale.
Example of Nantes – Saint-Nazaire metropolitan area

Rémi Dormois

This contribution is based on a political science doctorate that I'm finishing at the Montpellier 's University. My research deals with the new forms of urban government in French cities which have appeared since the middle of the seventies. To study this evolution, we have chosen to follow urban planning dynamics during a long period since 1977 in the urban areas of Nantes and Rennes. Among research results, we propose here to describe how a decisional capacity in urban planning can be built on large scale with the example of Nantes / Saint-Nazaire metropolitan area. A building capacity has been obtained neither by the setting up of a political institution, a sort of metropolitan government institution, nor by the elaboration of a master plan but by the creation of a place where arrangements between elected leaders and private interests had been built.

What are the characteristics of this urban planning capacity? Why did the leaders accept to cooperate? Who are the winners, the followers and the losers of the institutionalisation of ACEL? Which limits can be noticed in that form of urban planning? Before trying to give some responses at these issues, we propose to make a presentation of Nantes / Saint-Nazaire metropolitan area in order to understand why urban planning has been set at agenda.

1. The setting up of the "Association Communautaire de l'estuaire de la Loire" and its role in urban planning of metropolitan area

1.1 An increasing pressure for a wider regulation in land use

The metropolitan area of Nantes / Saint-Nazaire is located in the north-west of France at 400 kilometres from Paris. This urban region had 845.000 habitants in 1999 which represents the fifth most populated of French urban areas after Paris, Lyon, Marseille and Lille (ACEL 1999). Population is mainly located in two urban areas: the urban area of Nantes (82 municipalities which represent 710.000 inhabitants in 1999) and the urban area of Saint-Nazaire (23 municipalities which represent 172.000 inhabitants). Between 1990 and 1999, demographic growth has been of + 8,6% which represents 67.300 new inhabitants. To compare, national demographic growth during the same period has been of + 3,2%. From an economic point of view, the Nantes / Saint-Nazaire metropolitan area concentrates 350.000 jobs in 1999 with an obvious economical speciality between the two main cities. Saint-Nazaire is characterised by manufactories especially in shipbuilding. A former industrial city, Nantes has succeeded to transform its economic basis with a fast increase of the service sector (Damette 1994).

This demographic and economic growth has had several consequences in land use. Like in most cities, large development areas were created around cities for the localisation of new households or new firms. This urban sprawl represents a consumption of 1,6 million of square meters each year. In the urban area of Nantes, urbanised areas have been multiplied by three since thirty years. Efficiency of public transportation system in Nantes is altered by a generalisation of individual dwellings. Intensity of urban sprawl tensions is accentuated by the presence of large spaces with a high environmental value (estuaire de la Loire, lac de Brière) and of an important harbour which has its own development projects. In this context, land use is subject to interest conflicts. Land use conflicts have started to find a political expression during the nineties. We assist to a generalisation of fights between ecological parties and harbour administration about decisions concerning new land develop-ments. A green municipality, Bouguenais located in the first ring of Nantes, used a legal way to obtain from harbour authority a modification of one of its development project concerning Bouguenais in the sense of a better natural areas protection.

A pressure for a more efficient governance was also existing from business interests. In 1989, a national study realized by DATAR about the place of French cities in European competition is published (Brunet 1989). This geographic work shows that French metropolitan areas, except Paris, haven't a demographic and an economic weight sufficient to be attractive for firms, for engineers who look for an implementation in the west of Europe. In particular, Nantes doesn't appear as a city with an European visibility. For private interests' organisation, the cooperation between Nantes and Saint-Nazaire seems to be the only way to find a solution to this situation.

1.2. The weakness of institutional and regulative responses leads to the settlement of a light structure

The necessity for a wider regulation concerning the development of the beginning of the river Loire's mouth. But traditional mechanisms of integration were inefficient. Concerning an institutional integration, none of the existing political institution had the legitimacy to act in urban planning field at this scale. Each effort from Nantes or Saint-Nazaire elected officials in this sense could have been perceived by other political leaders as a new attempt to accentuate their political domination on new areas. Thus an over-formalised co-operation was risked. The local state administrations can't play a role of coercive tiers providing the issues to cop with. The Decentralisation laws have dwindled the expertise and financial capacities of this administrations.

However, opportunities for the establishment of a co-operation between local authorities and private actors have existed. The region Pays de la Loire benefit from a political leadership factor which was an exceptionality because in France the most part of regions are traditionally faced to a crisis of their legitimacy (Pasquier 2004). From its creation in 1972 to 1998, Olivier Guichard, who was a prominent figure of the Gaullist movement, continuously chaired the Conseil régional des Pays-de-la Loire. At the local level, he outrageously dominated the right wing political networks, including the successive presidents of the Conseil Général de Loire-Atlantique. He got the power to influence the designation of préfets and used to work very closely with the State's field administrations. At the city level, things began to change with the election in 1989 of the Socialist Jean-Marc Ayrault and Joël Batteux as mayors of Nantes and Saint-Nazaire. The strong domination that Guichard exerts on the local right lead the mayor of the right wing mayors of the surrounding communes of Nantes to follow on the co-operative road, enabling thus the mayor of Nantes to reinforce the intercommunal co-operation. Even if the if the conseil général and the conseil regional were both controlled by rightwing parties until 2004, the mayor of Nantes was eager to preserve the co-operation links established by its rightwing predecessor. The presence of Olivier Guichard at the head of the regional council was favourable to this co-operation. The mayor of a seaside resort not far from Nantes, La Baule, Guichard has always proved favourable to the development of the regional capital, notwithstanding the colour of its political control. Jean-Marc Ayrault knew that and proved eager to preserve good relationships with him.

Taking account these opportunities, Jean-Joseph Regent president of the chamber of Commerce of Nantes, and former president of the harbour of Nantes / Saint-Nazaire decided to set up a light structure to build a decisional capacity at the metropolitan scale. In fact, ACEL born in an occasion that has nothing to see with the reasons that led to its "rebirth". It was first created as the ADEL (Association pour le Développement des Entreprises de l'Estuaire de la Loire) in the mid-1980's by the president of the Chamber of Commerce of Nantes, in order to attract inward investments and to enhance the industrial suppliers' system in the area. At the beginning, it was gathering the Chambers of Commerce of Nantes and Saint-Nazaire and the managers of the largest industrial plants in the area. Transformed in ACEL, it is then joined in the beginning of the 1990's by the city of Nantes and Saint-Nazaire and by the Conseil général de Loire-Atlantique and the Conseil régional des Pays-de-la-Loire. Concerning the management of ACEL, its president changes each year. He's chosen among its members. ACEL is an association with a limited staff: only two or three technicians and secretaries. ACEL is made of two main structures. A technical assembly which concern top administrators of all the organisations listed before. Meetings of this "comité technique" depend on the local agenda. A political assembly called "comité directeur" sets up only twice a year but use wants that political leaders concerned are required to be physically present at this meetings. Such public-private partnership don't occur often at large metropolitan scales in France. Public / private partnership was only present at a city scale in urban planning field. Local authorities and banks, firms used to share financial risks of urban projects inside specific societies which capital was made of public and private funds (the société d'économie mixte) (Le Galès and Caillosse 1994). This partnership has an operational aim and takes place in a legal public market system with large resources for the public (Lorrain 1998). Generalisation of public and private partnership in the definition of global urban planning orientations isn't generalized in France. Private actors meet difficulties to access to decisional arenas where urban planning policies are discussed. Conjoint actions can be noted around large cultural and sportive events (Lévine 1994) but experiences in urban planning are more limited.

Thus, the creation of ACEL appears as the result of a convergence of three dynamics already identified in urban governance literature (Borraz 1999) : dynamic of problems with conflict between development and protection, dynamic of organisation with a new use given to an existing co-operation's form between public and private interests and dynamic of politics change consecutive to local elections.

The action of ACEL concerning the organisation of metropolitan development has started in 1994. Local state representatives sign a contract with ACEL which defines an economical strategic program of actions (ACEL 1994). At this step, elected officials are the followers, they act in this structure because it's a way to give a visibility to their economical action in a context of industrial. Nantes and Saint-Nazaire must face to crises especially in shipbuilding. So the local public-private sector collaboration at metropolitan area has begun in a difficult economical context (Di Gaetano and Klemanski 1999). At the end of the nineties, political leaders increase their power in this organization. This evolution can explain why spatial orientations are more developed in a new document produced in 1997. In this second strategic document are formulated the main issues concerning urban planning. Members of ACEL express their priorities concerning new transport infrastructures with the creation of a new international airport, the building of a new bridge between the two main cities and the extension of harbour in its East part (Donges). The document also presents general orientations concerning new urbanisations with a polarisation of new residential areas in the cities (urban renewal), the preservation of agricultural and natural areas in order to keep clear limits between urbanized and non urbanized areas. Loire backs located in Nantes and Saint-Nazaire are identified also as urban renewal areas with two main urban projects: Nantes Island, City-Harbour in Saint-Nazaire. But neither a regulative master plan nor an urban planning agency are created. At this first level, ACEL plays a role of a locus for the production of common views shared by the different local authorities and the forging of common claims towards the State (Duran and Thoenig 1996). ACEL became the places where local leaders constructed common claims and prepare their common lobbying for the negotiation of the *Contrat de Plan Etat-Région*, the five years term negotiation between the State and local authorities where State's investments and policies on the territory are planned.

At a second level, ACEL has permitted a alignment of local political agendas. Its members have accepted to deploy their assets in order to achieve several urban development goals and to implement concrete projects. The Chamber of Commerce of Nantes has taken in charge the modernisation of Nantes Atlantique airport and the building of several engineers schools. The political institution of "Region des pays de la Loire" and the cities of Nantes and Saint-Nazaire have invested in rail public transport with an increase of relations and new materials. The *Conseil Général de Loire Atlantique* has modernised its road network between cities and towns of the metropolitan area. Organisation of sporting and cultural manifestations at metropolitan area scale has helped to increase its visibility for people, especially for elected re-presentatives. Public institutions give a budget to set up specific agencies charged to increase the capacity to convince new firms to implant themselves in the area.

After having described results examples of cooperation in ACEL, let's see why this type of light structure, or non formal political institution, has met a success.

2. Content and limits of cooperation in ACEL

2.1. The resorts of conjoint action
Why did the creation of ACEL make possible the building of an urban planning capacity on a large scale? Why did political and economical leaders accept to cooperate in ACEL? We propose to focuse upon three characteristics of this process.

The cooperation of elected leaders has been obtained because ACEL was clearly not settled as a new political institution. Its last director explained for example that's its budget, its organisational resources were limited in order to fight against the idea that ACEL would become a kind of metropolitan government institution with a large power concerning urban planning, public transportation or environment. In the same way, ACEL's limits aren't defined exactly. They change according the new actors integrated. The *Loire* estuary has a geographic reality but it doesn't correspond to an institutional territory. The distinction between ACEL and a classical political institution explains why political leaders gave up a biased attitude in their ACEL's action. Conflicts between multi-levels public institutions, which have for example stopped the creation of metropolitan governments in Italy at the beginning of the nineties (Jouve and Lefevre 2002), didn't appear in ACEL even if political leaders belong to different parties (the leaders of the cities are Socialists and the leaders of the department and the region are Conservators). The elected officials' interest in ACEL can be also explained by its pragmatism. By participating in ACEL, they know that they'll be informed of projects of other public bodies and maybe will be able to obtain modifications by bargaining. Concerning their own projects, they look for a general agreement of other political leaders and private interests. This arrangement increases their political and economical assets. Concerning economical resources, they try to obtain a mutual investment by other public institutions. Concerning political resources, they will insist on inter-institutional agreement in their executive to prevent from partisan conflicts. Indeed, the opposition can't criticize a project if members of the same political party has recognized in ACEL the well funded of this project. To obtain agreement of economics leaders is also important to legitimate the project. Elected leaders can refer to ACEL's private interest position in order to bring a testimony of its economics viability. This way of legitimating has increased with the generalisation of entre-preneurship mayor profile (Fontaine and Le Bart 1994).

The cooperation of interests groups in ACEL has been obtained because it has appeared for them as a way to talk about general subjects like transport infrastructures, environment policies. As an example, the

Chambers of Commerce had to face to a legitimacy crisis during the eighties. The number of their adherents was decreasing and its representative character was criticized concerning the new economical sector (Waters 1998). By participating at ACEL, the chambers of commerce of Nantes and Saint-Nazaire meet opportunities to present their economic context analysis and to ask for elected leaders and top administrators concrete programs. It's also a way for them to talk about harbour development even if since the seventies they have lost technical and political leadership on them since harbour authority is a public institution depending from the central state. The Chambers of Commerce of Nantes and Saint-Nazaire could mobilize specific resources to appear attractive for other partners. They have benefited of their historic expertise culture in urban planning fields. These Chambers of Commerce have kept an analysis capacity concerning economic and spatial dynamics, which isn't usual at a national level (Pinson 2002). The harbour authority has seen ACEL as an opportunity to obtain public budget participation concerning new infrastructures building and to have clear decisions about its projects of development. Beside, in a context of conflicts with environmental associations, its participation in ACEL's meetings helped to change its image. Instead of appearing as an actor acting according its own interest without bargaining with local government, the harbour authority became a local development agent like the Chambers of Commerce.

Then cooperation in ACEL can be explained by mutual self-interest achieving. But in the same time, ACEL has enhanced their collective governing capacity. Indeed, ACEL has represented an opportunity for local public bodies and private interests to be recognized by national government as partners. Local government, Chambers of Commerce didn't have the resources to start a cooperation with state representatives as equal partners. Partnership with the state was possible because they present themselves as a single collective actor: the ACEL. State representatives, by contracting with ACEL, has increased its legitimacy. From its part, the national government has supported ACEL. Without this association, state representatives would have faced to a lot of direct informal bargaining with all the members of ACEL. The ACEL brought a guarantee of success in discussions and limit risks of inter-institutional conflicts. Local political and economical leaders have received financial benefits of their cooperation with state representatives. Also, their symbolic resources stock has increased. Cooperating with state administrations gave them a new identity: they became representative of metropolitan area interests and only of their own interests. Then ACEL has benefited from a mutual support of national and local governments.

Cooperation in ACEL has been maintained also by the institutionalisation of norms. First, the metropolitan area of Nantes / Saint-Nazaire has been progressively integrated by them as their spatial horizon of development. As consequence, in 2002, a political agreement has been obtained by the mayors of Nantes and Saint-Nazaire to start the elaboration of a master plan at this large scale. The integration of this spatial representation by elected officials has permitted to prevent from political tensions between local authorities. Second, some political rules have set up in the ACEL's dynamic. The research of consensus became a common reference for members of ACEL. As example, the manager of the association is defining the agenda of meetings after face-to-face interviews in order to propose only consensual issues. This norms are built during interactions and debates. Their efficiency is linked to the way they are incrementally built. The imposition of a new formal structure of collaboration and of new formal norms for action could generate defensive behaviour among actors, and drives them to see in the new scale of action a threat to their institutional interests and identities.

2.2. The limits in the building of a urban planning capacity
ACEL's presentation could let think at an ideal form of organisation to build an urban planning capacity. Elements must be underlined to qualify this judgment.

First, creation of ACEL constraints democracy transparency of urban planning decision making. Visibility of ACEL's functioning isn't a priority for its members. The corridor bargaining within informal organisations, the informal mutual adjustment, the protection of the co-operative interactions from public scrutiny and marginalisation of inter-municipal assemblies seem as necessities to have successful exchanges. No public communication about debates, about decisions. Settlement of arena with a limited access and a functional finality seems to be general in urban governance. Political literature gives several examples of this evolution which limits the democratization process of new forms of urban government (Gaudin 1999). Contemporarily, the formal institutions which are politically responsible and which remain the most visible for citizens, like city councils, seem to be more and more marginalized in the territorial policy making. Formal councils seem to be reduced to powerless arenas where a pretence of "adversarial politics" comedy is still played but deals with secondary topics (Mansbridge 1980).

Second, the forms of inter-institutional co-operation that we observed in the Nantes/Saint-Nazaire metropolitan area tend to exclude some groups of the negotiation. Only few actors have access to this arena: public institutions, private interest representative organizations. Associations, trade unions, the most part of mayors or elected representatives can't express about urban planning decisions. Then, on the one side associations, firms play a new role in urban government and especially in urban planning processes (Le Galès 2003). But on the other side, the access to decisional arenas keeps limited to public institutions and private interest representative forms. Beside, organisations like ACEL participate to a sort of dilution of responsibilities. To attribute leadership on projects become difficult with the generalisation of contracts including several public institutions (Biarez 2000). This situation can be accentuated with the creation of coordination organisations which citizens meet difficulties to understand their function, the nature of their relations with classical institutions.

Third, as consensus is a political rule in ACEL, some issues disappear in debates even if they are important for urban planning. Urban planning agenda doesn't take care of issues like urban sprawl limitation, social housing localization, hypermarket development or social exclusion (Motte 1995). Metropolitan development, European competition, environmental protection benefit from a generalized adhesion so that this issues are relevant in ACEL's documents. Criterions to choose subjects aren't their intensity at a local level but the largest mobilisation they can cause. Urban planning agenda is shaped by members who keep the range of issues upon which they can agree. This bias is one of the reasons of the evolution of state representatives position concerning ACEL. We've noticed that a contract between ACEL and state administration was concluded in 1994. ACEL's members have tried to reproduce this process in 1997 but the state administration didn't accept. For state representatives, contracting with ACEL's members about urban planning orientations would have involved a difficulty to express its point of view about evolutions of Nantes / Saint-Nazaire metropolitan area concerning building of social housing, concerning land consumption, concerning choices contradictions in transport system. By bargaining, members of ACEL accede to a broader decision capacity in urban planning, but on the other hand, they loose their independence concerning main issues. ACEL participates to build a political capacity because a stock of resources can be connected with goals. But in the same time, each leader accepts to act by respecting collective rules and so to loose its independence.

Fourth, not any master plan has been adopted by ACEL. This element has limited implementation of orientations adopted in this arena concerning urban planning. But since last year, local governments of urban metropolitan area have decided to cooperate in a special public institution created to elaborate a master plan on this large scale. Does this decision mean a change in general principles elaborated in ACEL? More than a change, we propose to see it as an evolution. ACEL has convinced elected leaders that urban planning was different from a technocratic activity. They have seen how ACEL has helped the building of a collective capacity, with concrete decisions, and how the implementation of goals has produced financial, political and social resources for the members of ACEL. Political acceptability of a master plan has been obtained because ACEL has shown how concrete projects could emerge from a public and private partnership in urban planning.

3. Conclusion
Classical actions for urban planning on large urban scale are master plan elaboration or settlement of a metropolitan government with legal competence in this field. ACEL is an example of a different response at the fragmentation in the institutional structures of local government based on the settlement of a decision arena integrating public and private actors with a limited visibility. In ACEL, arrangements concerning concrete projects and global goals are built between political and economics leaders. Each institution or organisation keeps its power in the implementation of these decisions but we can observe a sort of collective regulation. Decisions are effectively implemented even if each actor keeps its control on its policies. Free rider or single ticket strategies are excluded because each partner understands that he needs the others to cooperate for the implementation of its own project. How can this cooperation be expected if he doesn't respect agreements? Temporal chains of exchanges (Marin 1990) are built between members of ACEL which introduces a political order in the cooperation.

Analysis of ACEL brings elements in the comprehension of public/private partnership. The exchanges of assets between members don't concern only material and financial ones. Resources exchanges concern identities, status and legitimacy. Similar conclusions have been dressed by authors of urban regime theory. C. Stone underlines that cognitive and symbolic resources have enhanced the stability of cooperation between members of an urban regime (Stone 2001).

References:
ACEL (1999) Nantes – Saint-Nazaire: le fait métropolitain. Nantes.
ACEL, Préfecture de la région des pays de la Loire (1994) Charte d'objectifs pour Nantes Saint-Nazaire. Nantes.
Balme, R. (1999) Les nouvelles politiques locales. Paris.
Biarez, S. (2000) Territoires et espaces politiques. Grenoble.
Bonneville, M. (1995) Le renouvellement du schéma directeur par le projet d'agglomération: réflexions à partir de l'exemple de Lyon. In Motte A. (1995) Schéma directeur et projet d'agglomération: l'expérimentation de nouvelles politiques urbaines spatialisées. Paris.
Borraz, O. (1999) Pour une sociologie des dynamiques de l'action publique locale. In Balme, R. (1999) Les nouvelles politiques locales. Paris.
Brunet, R. (1989) Les villes européennes. Montpellier.
Damette, F. (1994) La France en villes. Paris.
DiGaetano, A., Klemanski., J.S. (1999) Power and city governance: perspectives on urban development. University of Minnesota Press.
Duran, P.andThoenig, J.C. (1996) L'État et la gestion publique territoriale. In : Revue française de science politique, pp. 580-622.
Fontaine, J.and Le Bart, C. (1994) Le métier d'élu local. Paris.
Gaudin, J.P. (1999) Gouverner par contrat : l'action publique en question. Paris.
Jouve, B.and Lefevre, C. (2002) Métropoles ingouvernables. Montréal.
Le Galès, P.(2003) Le retour des villes européennes. Paris.
-,   . and Caillosse, J. (1994) SEML d'aménagement et d'urbanisme et gouvernance urbaine. Rennes.
Lévine, M.A. (1994) The transformation of urban politics in France. In: Urban affairs quarterly, 29(3), pp. 383-410.
Lorrain, D. (1998) Administrer, gouverner, réguler. In Annales de la recherche urbaine, 80-81, pp. 85-92.
Mansbridge, J. (1980) Beyond Adversary Democracy. Chicago.
Marin, B. (1990) Governance and generalized exchange : self-organizing policy networks in action, Frankfurt.
Motte, A. (1995) Schéma directeur et projet d'agglomération: l'expérimentation de nouvelles politiques urbaines spatialisées. Paris.
Pasquier, R. (2004) La capacité politique de régions. Une comparaison France-Espagne. Rennes.
Pinson, G. (2002) Projets et pouvoir dans les villes européennes. Une comparaison de Marseille, Venise, Nantes et Turin. Rennes.
Stone, C. (2001) The Atlanta's experience re-examined : the link between agenda and regime change. In: International Journal of Urban and Regional Research, 25(1), pp. 20-34.
Waters, S. (1998) Chambers of commerce and local development in France. In: Government and Policy, vol.16, pp. 591-604.

The Greek urban system: concentration or deconcentration, and estimation of metropolitan concentration

Petrakos George/Sotiris Pavleas/Angela Anagnostou

1. Introduction

During the last years, a large number of scientific studies have been concerned with the characteristics of urban and metropolitan development. The process of structural changes has not only influenced and helped develop the metropolitan regions, but it has also caused many urban problems in the metropolitan regions and more generally in the urban systems as a whole. These particular changes are considered to be part of the spatial evolution and have the ability to shape the urban and regional socio-economic structures even in non-reversible ways (Suarez-Villa 1988).

In Greece, it is important to examine the establishment of the spatial model of the domineering city (Athens), investigate the relations between the core and periphery, and further, analyze the structure of the Greek urban system. In terms of economic growth and quality of life, it is evident that Athens in the last decades was not able to adopt a balanced metropolitan plan so as to keep up with the other European capital cities (Prevelakis 2002). Consequently, such an investigation would give us the possibility to examine whether the Greek urban system is led to deconcentration, thus, aiding the small and intermediate cities to develop, or it is led to further concentration, that is to say, further enlargement of the metropolitan center of Athens. Given however the fact that statistical data at the urban level is unavailable for most Greek cities, and more generally for most cities of South Europe, apart from some cities of Italy, such an investigation becomes difficult, and thus, Greece has not been included in the relative scientific studies and analysis (Leondidou 1994).

The purpose of this study is to investigate the development of the Greek cities, and outline a metropolitan and urban policy at the national level. Thus, the paper is presented as follows: In the next section, we review the relative literature on the basic theoretical views, and further, we present some of the most important empirical studies on the metropolitan concentration and the development of the urban systems. Consisting of two parts, in section three we present our empirical analysis. In the first part, we estimate the rank-size distribution of the Greek cities with a population of 5.000 and 10.000 for the period of 1951-2001; while in the second section, we estimate the degree of the metropolitan concentration in Greece during the period 1961-2001, so as to examine the evolution of the metropolitan concentration. Finally, in the last section we conclude of our study by presenting our results and suggested policies.

2. Metropolitan Concentration: Theoretical and Empirical Approaches

The rapid growth of metropolitan centers in the developed and mainly in the developing countries has been widely attracting the interest of the scientists, i.e. economists, geographers, and city and urban planners. In the USA, the current studies, have either been concerned with the urban restructuring and development (Schafer 1978, Norton 1979, Peterson 1985, McDonald 1997), or with the development of suburbs and metropolitan regions (Isserman and Brown 1985, Baldassare 1986, Moomaw 1988, Mills and Hamilton 1989, Mills and Labuele 1995, Williamson 1992, Moomaw and Shatter 1996, Simon 1998, Ingram 1998, Moomaw 1998, Ding 2001, McMillen and Smith, 2003, Smith and Zenou, 2003). Yet, the last decades, there has been an increasing interest in Europe concerning the process of metropolitan development, resulting into a respectable number of theoretical and empirical studies analyzing and comparing different countries (Berg et al 1982, Hall and Hay 1980, Cheshire et al. 1986, Cheshire 1987, Cheshire 1990, Berry and McGreal 1995, Cheshire 1995, Batten 1995, Cheshire and Carbonaro 1996, Hall 1997, Hall 1997, Harris 1997, Ciccone 2000).

Worldwide, it has been shown that the metropolitan distribution is proportional to that of the spatial structure of the central places. Having this in mind, the relation between the process of metropolitan changes and the development of distribution of urban centers can be considered as an important factor for configuring the world metropolitan hierarchy and its effects on national urban systems. Over the last years, a large part of the literature on the urban and regional development has supported the idea that the long-run changes in the urban systems are influenced, to a large degree, by the changes that happen in the biggest or in the first in the hierarchy metropolitan center.

More specifically, the phenomenon of urban polarization has been approached in three different and contradicting ways. The first approach, the neoclassical one, supports the changes in spatial links via a mechanism of flowing factors of production from regions of high cost or low efficiency, to regions of low cost or high efficiency. This mechanism establishes a balanced environment in the spatial system, thus, decreasing the inequalities between the developed and non-developed regions (Siebert 1969, Armstrong and Taylor 1985). It should be pointed out however, that the mentioned approach assumes that the market is perfect and freely adjustable, while it does not take into consideration the utilities of scale that are created by the coexistence of productive active-ties in the big urban concentrations (Petrakos and Tsoukalas 1999, McCann 1995).

A contrary approach is adopted by the theory of accumulative causality (Myrdal, 1957), the theory of pole-growth (Perroux, 1950) and the theory of core-periphery relationship (Friedmann, 1969 and 1972) that investigate the factors for which growth and development lead to spatial polarization and not to spatial balance. Some significant empirical studies have elaborated by El-Shaks (1972).

In more recent studies, the economic factor - external economies of agglomeration - has been included in the research area, and it is considered to be the main reason for the pull of productive activities and resources in the metropolitan centers and the main factor of spatial polarization (Wheaton and Shishido 1981, Henderson 1986, Petrakos and Brada 1989). Nevertheless, and despite the fact that external economies of agglomeration are important and strengthen the metropolitan sovereignty, at last, they weaken and get diminished due to the increasing presence of the external diseconomies of agglomeration, which consist of high costs of land and transports and communications, low levels of quality of life and environmental degrading (Petrakos and Tsoukalas, 1999).

The trend of disurbanization-deconcentration that was observed during the decade of the 1970s first in US and afterwards in Europe[1] has caused the growth rates of the metropolitan centers to fall below the national average growth rate. On the contrary, the rates of demographic growth of the rural regions and small cities reached for the first time, or even passed, the national average (Lichtenberger 1976). This phenomenon described the majority of metropolitan centers internationally and it was attributed to the weakness of the metropolitan centers to create new jobs. The inability to create jobs was connected with the crisis in the industrial sector and the structural changes (Vining and Kontuly 1978, Fielding 1982, Vining and Pallone 1982). At this point, of great interest are the three different explanations that Frey (1988) offered on the phenomenon of counterurbanization: the explanation of periodicity, the explanation of regional restructuring, and the explanation of deconcentration.

An extension of the metropolitan concentration theory has been offered by Petrakos and Brada (1989) and takes into consideration additional parameters that influence the metropolitan development, especially in the developing countries. More specifically, in their study, they point out that the metropolitan regions in the developing countries participate in a

---

[1] According to Petrakos and Economou (1999) the phenomenon of disurbanization is the third phase of the urban cycle

process of international specialization and distribution of labor; thus, the degree of the national integration in the international process of production does not only influence the level of growth, but also the hierarchy of the cities within the country. Moreover, the rate of development of metropolitan centers depends also on two political factors: the democracy and the stability of political regime. In the conservative regimes or in the dictatorships, the power is assembled in the administrative center, as a result, the capital is assembled in the metropolis since the administrative departments need to be closer to those centers so as to exploit them more effectively and have more political influence.

In terms of empirical studies on the European cities and the metropolitan models, Hall and Hay (1980) have presented some important findings for fourteen countries considering the period 1950-1975. In their study, they described metropolitan growth as a process of four stages: a) that of fundamental period of concentration, b) the stage of deconcentration via the growth of suburban regions, c) the stage of maturity through the dissemination to the non metropolitan regions, and d) the stage of consequent metropolitan recession. Furthermore, Cheshire (1987), Cheshire and Hay (1989), Cheshire (1990) and Cheshire (1995) employed the concept of Functional Urban Regions (FURs)[8] and investigated in a synopsis of report and empirical study the performance and the problems of the most important urban centers of Western Europe for the decades 1970 and 1980. Regarding the FURs, they mainly concluded that the increasing tendency for deconcentration seems to be congested and reversed, while in a smaller scale and more rural regions especially in Northern Europe, their population continued to increase. According to their study, the deconcentration (for the FURs) was prevented in North-western Europe (Great Britain, countries Benelux: Belgium, Holland, Luxembourg). In France and Italy, the tendency to deconcentration has been prevented but has not been reversed. The deconcentration is persisting only in Southern Europe, especially in the urban regions that showed a major increase, while the urban regions of North-western Europe were in the phase of deconcentration.

At the level of metropolitan economic growth, the tendencies that prevailed regarding the effect of employment on metropolitan population are ambiguous (Mills and Labuele 1995). More specifically, in the US prevails the idea that labor mobility between the regions (regions regarded as significant spatial subdivisions of national economies) are so

---

[8] In the US the corresponding metropolitan regions have been termed as MSAs (Metropolitan Statistical Areas), (Simon, 1998)

intense, so as the differences in employment[2] and in income are equated on average (Cheshire and Carbonaro, 1996). In Europe, the researchers and academics claim that due to the restrictions that exist in the mobility of labor between the regions of a country and especially between the regions of different countries, the above equation abstains a lot from reality (Gordon 1985, Evans 1990). The particular perception of the weakness of diachronic convergence of levels of employment between the countries (in Europe) is reversed considerably in interregional level. Income and employment differentiations are balanced on average, where urban regions are considered to be nationally and socio-economically homogeneous. During the last years, after the lifting of restrictions (1992) and the adoption of common currency (Euro), a euphoria of industry services is observed. The employment in the sector of services tends to be relatively assembled in the urban centers and is expected to increase further. This will become particularly evident in the cities, economically in favor by the European economic integration. Simultaneously however, the above development is possible to be also accompanied by losses in the sector of services of the metropolis in the European periphery (like Athens).

Concluding this section, the increasing interest, for the processes of urban changes is related to a large extent with the process of metropolitan development. It is not impossible, however, with the byway of time and the maintenance of existing international trends, to become witnesses of functional transformation of bigger metropolitan regions to real 'cities-states', particularly in smaller countries with open economies. Recently however, a series of studies report indications of recentralization of population and activities in the big metropolitan centers (Cohrane and Vining, 1988 - Cheshire, 1990 - Petrakos and Kotzamanis 1994, Cheshire and Carbonaro, 1996 - Ingram, 1998), and show evidence of economic recovery. Thus, taking into account a series of realignments that take place in the structure of national productive systems, the interest on the way of affecting the evolution and the distribution of the urban centers emerges once again, particularly in Greece.

---

[2] Simon (1998) proved the existence of intense positive cross-correlation between the growth in the employment and in the mean of level of human capital in the American metropolitan regions (MSAs) for the period 1940-1986

3. The Evolution of the Greek Urban System
3.1 Introduction
Metropolitan economic changes can possibly produce transformations in the inter-urban spatial structure via the concentration, or the deconcentration of the population and economic activities. Interactions between the two factors, the metropolitan economic change and the evolution of spatial structure, have constituted an important challenge in the academic area. (Moore 1958, Simon 1968, Beckmann and McPherson 1970, Evans 1972, Parr 1979, White 1974, Pumain 1982, Parr and Jones 1983, Guerin-Pace 1995).

In the case of Greece, with the sovereignty of the Urban Complex of the Capital City (UCCC) over the remainder urban population, and in terms of the scientific literature, two main arguments prevail concerning the inequalities in international urban systems (Petrakos and Mardakis, 1999). The first argument is that metropolitan concentration is in recession as the population of UCCC stabilizes and the population of smaller cities rapidly increases (Katochianou and Markogiannaki, 1989, Katochianou 1992). On the other hand, it is believed that growth of the tertiary sector, the internationalization of economy and the consequent need of upgrading the capital city in the European Metropolitan hierarchy will contribute to further concentration of the Greek urban system (Petrakos and Kotzamanis 1994, Petrakos and Tsoukalas 1999).

The purpose of this section is to examine the recent changes in the constitution of Greek urban system, employing additional recent data from the population census of 2001, and relate them with the evolution of metropolitan concentration in Greece.

3.2 The Evolution of Rank-Size Distribution in the Greek Urban System
Every national economy includes an urban system, which is comprised by cities with different productive activities and different type and degree of economies of concentration. These cities follow an internal hierarchy such that serves to meet on the one hand the needs of internal market demand and on the other hand the total one. Theoretical and empirical studies (Beckmann 1958, Parr 1985, Rossen and Resnick 1981) have shown that this hierarchic structure of a closed urban system can be described more generally by the function of rank-size distribution:

$$S = A R^{-a}$$

(1) where S is the population of an urban center and R is its position in the hierarchy (e.g.. 1st, 2nd,..... 27th, e.t.c). The **a** power is a positive parameter (Pareto coefficient), close to one (bigger or equal or smaller to one) and it expresses the degree of concentration or deconcentration of

the population in upper part of hierarchy. The parameter A represents the expected size of the largest urban center (Petrakos and Mardakis, 1999). Therefore, based on the rank-size distribution, the first and biggest in the hierarchy urban center will have population $S_1=A$, the second, $S_2=A/2^a$, the third $S_3=A/3^a$, and so on. Obviously, when a = 1, each city in the hierarchy of system has population equal with the population of the largest city divided by the position in the hierarchy; that is to say the second city has population $S_2 = A / 2 = S_1 / 2$, the third city has population $S_3 = A / 3 = S_1 / 3$, while the nth city in the hierarchy has population equal to $Sn = A / n = S_1 / n$. Also, one can realize that when the Pareto parameter a takes values greater than one (a > 1), then the population distribution tends to more concentrated patterns. When a takes values smaller to one, the proportion of big cities grows in the national urban system. Consequently, **a** parameter could be considered as an indicator of the metropolitan concentration degree that could quantify the cross-correlation between the biggest and the smaller cities.

TABLE 1: *Estimation of the rank-size distribution for Greek cities over 5.000 residents for the years 1951.1961,1971,1981,1991 and 2001*

	$\ln(\hat{S}) = \ln(\hat{A}) + \hat{a} \ln(R)$			
Year	ln (Â)	â	R^2	N
1951	12,927	-0,947	0.955	106
(t)	(56,272)	(-16,394)		
1961	13,132	-0,980	0,954	112
(t)	(55,634)	(-16,694)		
1971	13,378	-1,029	0,954	112
(t)	(52,806)	(-16,347)		
1981	13,648	-1,070	0,963	128
(t)	(60,916)	(-19,846)		
1991	13,633	-1,029	0,973	156
(t)	(68,965)	(-22,522)		
2001	13,795	-1,024	0,974	184
(t)	(81,457)	(-27,189)		

Transforming equation (1) into a stochastic relationship, we add an error term ε, where ε is normally distributed and ($\varepsilon \sim N (0, \sigma_\varepsilon)$) and represents the not systematic or accidental factors that influence the size of urban center. At the same time, the equation is expressed in logarithmic terms and the equation (2) derives:
$$\ln(S_t) = \ln(A) - a \ln(R_t) + e_t$$

(2) where $e_t = \ln\varepsilon_t$. Estimating equation (2) using ordinary least squares method, we are able to estimate the A και a parameters for the years 1951, 1961, 1971, 1981, 1991 και 2001 concerning the Greek cities over 5.000 residents. The estimated results are given in Table 1, while the depiction of the data is given in Diagram 1:

DIAGRAM 1: Hierarchy of Greek cities (over 5.000 residents) using rank-size (1951, 1961, 1971, 1981, 1991 and 2001)

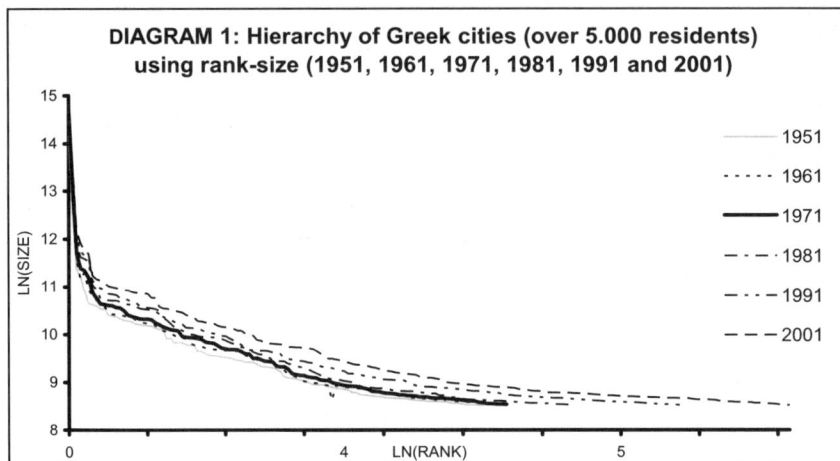

Source: Authors' elaboration

The estimated results have been corrected for heteroskedasticity[9]. The values in the parentheses present the t-statistics, which indicate of their high value and that the estimated coefficients are statistically significant. Furthermore, the reported values of R^3 show high explanatory power in the estimated econometric model. The choice for cities (urban and semi-urban centers) with population over 5000 residents at the day of the census was not random. Having as a fact the division of the semi-urban population into a big number of small cities (Petrakos and Mardakis, 1999), the estimates of Table 1 seek to record same tendencies as we take into consideration important number of small cities, which, even though they do not fall into the official definition of urban centers in Greece (over 10.000 residents), they include important urban operations and activities, powerful connections with the larger urban centers of their broader area and they are not considered to be non-urban agglomerations.

The estimation of rank-size distribution in different time periods allows us to record the trends of concentration or deconcentration in the Greek ur-ban system by studying the changes in the parameter â (Pareto

---

[3] The problem of heteroskedasticity was detected using the White Test

coefficient). Examining the evolution of the estimated parameter in Table 1, we observe that the diachronic behavior of the parameter â presents an increasing trend up to 1981, then it presents an explicit decline at the levels of the year 1971 and decreases even further until 2001. Thus, we can conclude, that the Greek urban system shows some trends of concentration for most of the postwar period up to the beginning of 1980s and during the next two decades there is a light tendency for deconcentration, providing a new element of interest in the scientific and research area. This last evidence of deconcentration of the Greek urban system is also supported in some of the relevant literature.

The question, however, of whether the increase of a number of small and intermediate cities is accompanied by real reduction of the degree of concentration of the Greek urban system and reduction of metropolitan sovereignty, still remains. In order to answer the above question, it is important to know the geographic location of the small and intermediate cities, which show an intense rate of demographic growth. In Diagrams 2(a, b) and 2(c, d, e) we present diachronically the percentage changes of population of urban centers at declining order of size for the periods 1951-1961, 1961-1971, 1971-1981, 1981-1991 and 1991-2001. For the last two periods, there have prevailed balanced trends in the Greek ur-ban system. In this particular Diagram, as the distance from the be-ginning of axes is extended we locate cities of smaller size and in all time periods. Also, the cities that are located within the Prefectures of Attica and Thessalonica are presented with an (x), while the remainder with a small line (-).

Diagram 2(a, b): Percentage changes of the population of cities over 5.000 residents distributed by their size and their place in the hierarchy over the period 1951-2001.

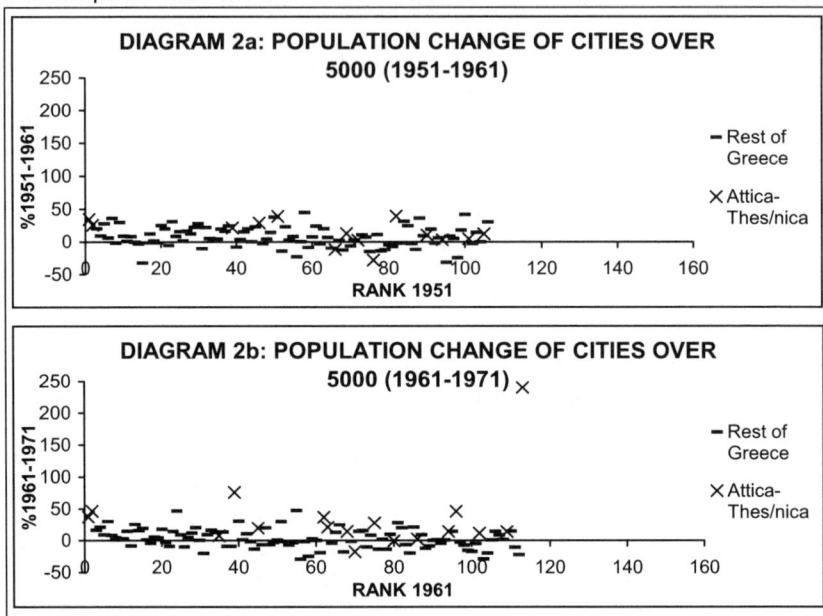

DIAGRAM 2a: POPULATION CHANGE OF CITIES OVER 5000 (1951-1961)

DIAGRAM 2b: POPULATION CHANGE OF CITIES OVER 5000 (1961-1971)

Source: Authors' elaboration

After observing the demographic changes of the cities over the time periods (Petrakos and Mardakis, 1999), it is realized, firstly, that during the first two periods (1951-1961, 1961-1971), a large number of cities suffered negative changes, independent of their place in the hierarchy. In the period of 1971-1981, a smaller number of cities appears with negative population changes, but they belong henceforth only in the relatively small cities with less than 10.000 residents (below the 50th place in the hierarchy).

Examining successively the five diagrams, it is observed that diachronically the dissemination becomes more intense. At the first decade, the spread of the observations was dense, leading henceforth in the next decades to patterns with higher variance and finally to the explicit differentiation of the last decade (at the lower limit of the distribution).

Diagram2 (c-e): Percentage changes of the population of cities over 5.000 residents 5.000 residents distributed by their size and their place in the hierarchy over the period 1951-2001.

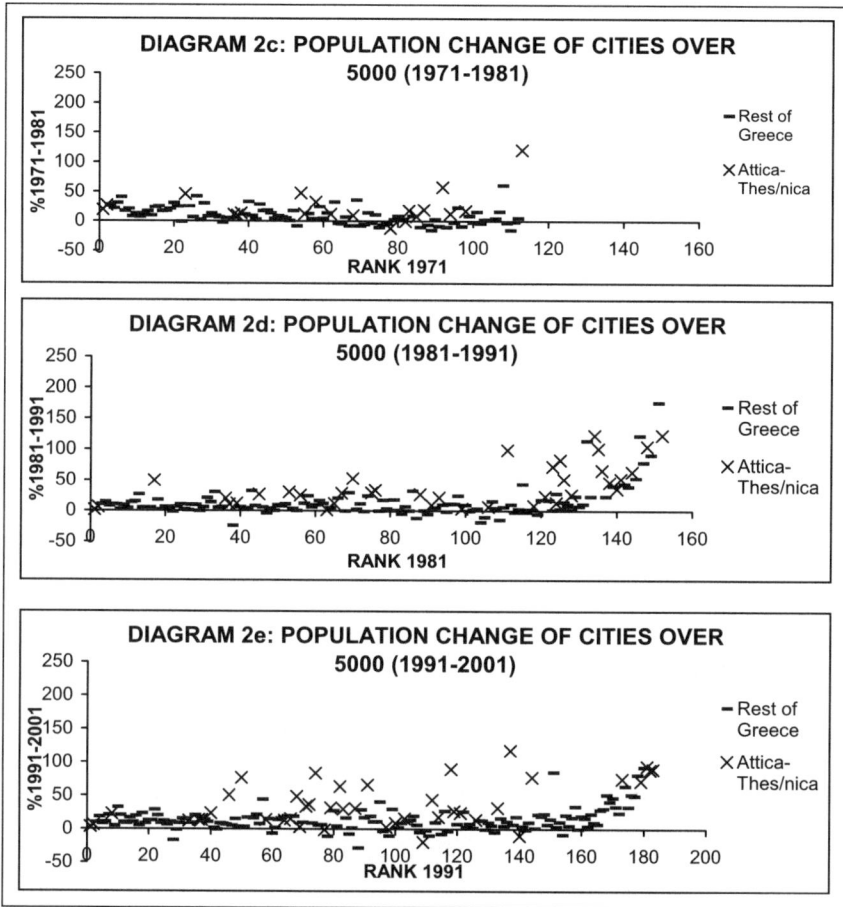

DIAGRAM 2c: POPULATION CHANGE OF CITIES OVER 5000 (1971-1981)

DIAGRAM 2d: POPULATION CHANGE OF CITIES OVER 5000 (1981-1991)

DIAGRAM 2e: POPULATION CHANGE OF CITIES OVER 5000 (1991-2001)

Source: Authors' elaboration

Finally, the number of cities over 5.000 residents has increased over time, however, the number of cities found within the administrative limits of Prefectures Attica and Thessalonica is increasing with greater growth rates. The majority of the remaining new cities (over 5.000 residents) is located in the tourist regions and has demonstrated during the last decade increased rates of economic growth (e.g. the islands of Crete and Cyclades).

The impressive, however, increase of the small cities is not possible to be accompanied with the argument that the metropolitan sovereignty is undermined in the Greek urban space. On the one hand, the majority of small cities is found within the Prefectures of Attica and Thessalonica, and on the other hand, even though there is tendency of ceasing the creation of new small cities (over 5.000 residents) within the magnitude of the two Prefectures, the existing ones show the greater positive changes in general. In short, the rate of appearance of small cities (over 5.000) in the Prefectures of Attica and Thessalonica has been decreased, however the existing ones are enlarging impressively. Taking into consideration the above conclusions, it becomes obvious that the thing that has changed during the two last decades in the Greek urban system, it is not so much the relative sovereignty of the two big metropolitan centers, but their geographic boundaries and their internal structure (Petrakos and Mardakis, 1999).

As it was also reported in the second section of the paper, this scientific analysis and discussion should not only concern the urban centers. It should also consider a new group of spatial division, which is the functional urban regions (FURs) according to the European terminology (Cheshire and Hay, 1980 – Cheshire, 1990 – Cheshire, 1995) and the metropolitan statistical areas (MSAs) according to the American one (Moomaw and Shatter 1996, Inrgam 1998, Simon 1998). Urban or semi-urban groups, such as Eleusina, Aharnes, Ano Liosia, Nea Makri, Agios Stefanos etc. constitute functional parts of the metropolitan cluster of the Capital and their demographic changes are due not to self-existent dynamics, but due to a wider internal restructuring of the metropolitan region.

To conclude, the rapid growth of small cities – with certain exceptions – does not constitute strong evidence of deconcentration of the Greek urban system but it is an element of internal decentralization of the two biggest urban complexes. The two Prefectures of Thessalonica and Attica, are basically evolving in wider multi-nodal metropolitan regions, each constituted by a connecting network of a central urban core with multiple urban concentrations (sub-centers) (picture 1), in the frame of their restructuring and their adaptation to the requirements of the new economic conditions and technological changes in the sectors of transports and communications.

3.3 The estimation of the degree of metropolitan concentration in Greece

The phenomenon of the high degree of metropolitan concentration is evident in the developing but also in the developed countries, while the factors of configuration and the stages of development are different

Picture 1: *Network of urban core (UCCC) and urban subcenters of metropolitan region of Athens*

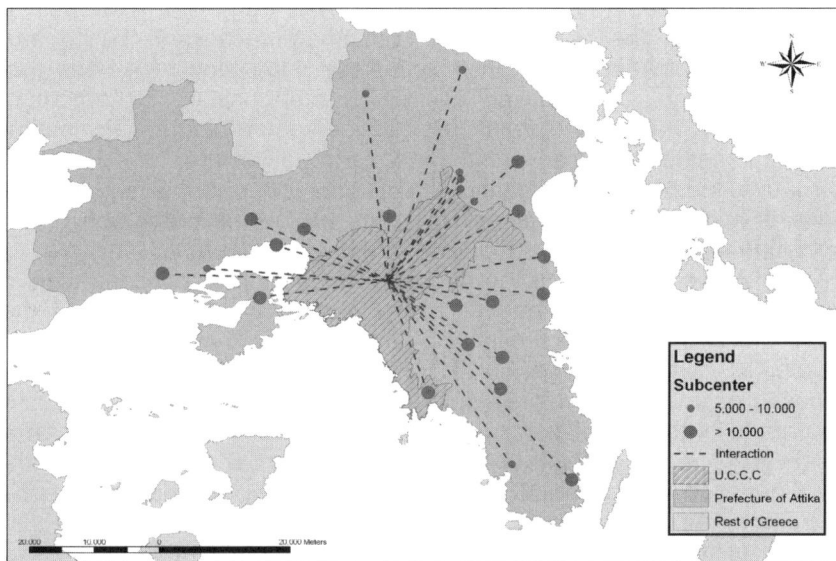

Source: Authors' elaboration

in every case. However, in many of these countries this phenomenon is accompanied by important urban problems that are related with the absolute size of the urban center, so it results to disproportionate development in each country's urban system.

During the last 40 years, a consequence of the rapid increase of world population and the urbanization was also the fast increase of the metropolises' number. According to Fuchs et al. (1994), up to 1950, only New York and London could be considered mega-cities, while up to 1990, 20 urban centers had exceeded the limit of 8.000.000 residents.

In the case of Greece, the phenomenon of high degree of metropolitan concentration has received important consideration, on the one hand, due to the big absolute size of the urban complex of Athens and on the other hand because of the degrading quality of life. This degrading refers to the environmental tax, the circulatory congestion and high built-up densities.

In the same framework, it is wide believed that the rapid growth of Capital and the continuous attracting of productive activities, overload and slow down the growth of the rest of the country's regions. At the same time, there are insufficient strategy and capable policies from the central governmental institutions aiming at stopping the demographic concentration in Athens and as a result the balancing of the Greek urban system. Therefore, a close investigation of the degree of metropolitan concentration in the Greek system becomes necessary, taking into consideration however the right size of the population of Athens that shapes the high comparatively degree of metropolitan concentration. Consequently, having shown in the previous section that the Prefecture of Attica constitutes a wider multi-nodal metropolitan area of Athens, an alternative method of estimating the degree of metropolitan concentration is suggested, that will not depend only on the proportion of the population of Athens to the population of the whole country.

In Table 2, the evolution of the degree of metropolitan concentration in Greece is presented, taking into consideration the population of the UCCC, according to data provided by the National Statistical Agency of Greece (NSAGr) for the period of 1951 until 2001. The method that is proposed estimates the degree of Metropolitan Concentration (MC) as a percentage of the population of the Prefecture Attica over the total Greece (PAt/PGr), with base fraction of the Number of Students of Elementary Education of Attica (NSEEAt) over the total number of Greece (NSEEGr). The category of students of elementary education is selected because of the obligatory character of Municipal Education in Greece; therefore a close relationship is expected between the fraction of the population and that of the students.

TABLE 2: *Evolution of the Degree of Metropolitan Concentration (DMC) in Greece, base on the population of UCCC*

YEARS	POPULATION OF UCCC	POPULATION OF GREECE	Degree of Metropolitan Concentration
1951	1.378.586	7.632.801	18,06%
1961	1.852.709	8.388.553	22,08%
1971	2.540.241	8.768.641	28,96%
1981	3.027.331	9.740.417	31,08%
1991	3.096.775	10.256.464	30,19%
2001	3.172.006	10.964.020	28,93%

Source: NSAG Population Census 1951,1961,1971,1981,1991, 2001

The above fraction is multiplied with a parameter K in order to adjust the estimated differences, firstly, to the degree of the students' integration in the education system, and secondly, to the populations' structure of the Prefecture of Attica and that of Greece. Thus, it will be possible to equate it with the fraction of the population and be used in the estimation of the degree of Metropolitan Concentration:

$$MC = [NSEEAt / NSEEG] * K \qquad (1)$$

More specifically, the parameter K is expected to take into account the populations' structural differences and the degree of children's integration between 6 and 11 years old in the elementary education. So it is equal to:

$$K = [DIEEAt / DIEEG]^{-1} * [PSAt / PSGr]^{-1} \qquad (2)$$

where the variables VEDEAt and VEDEE calculate the Degree of Integration of children from 6 to 11 years old in the Elementary Education for Attica and Greece. That is to say, the percentage of children that is found in the age of 6-11 years and goes to elementary school, to the total of what is found in the same age and should be included in the Elementary Education (in level of Attica and in national level). Therefore the equations are formulated as follows:

$$DIEEAt = NSEEAt / P(6-11)At \qquad (3)$$

$$DIEEGr = NSEEGr / P(6-11)Gr \qquad (4)$$

where P(6-11)At and P(6-11)Gr are the population of children from 6 until 11 years in Attica and in Greece respectively. At the same time, the variables PSAt and PSGr are indicators of the Population's Structure for Attica and for Greece respectively and they represent the percentage of children that are included in Elementary Education to the total population (in level of Attica and in national level). Therefore:

$$PSAt = P(6-11)At / PAt \qquad (5)$$

$$PSGr = P(6-11)Gr / PGr \qquad (6)$$

It becomes obvious that the result of combining equations (1) and (2) to (6) constitutes substantially an identity that is verified diachronically. So, after some simplifications, equation (7) is derived, and after some further simplifications we can derive equation (9), which gives the definition of the degree of Metropolitan Concentration:

$$MC = [NSEEAt / NSEEG] * [DIEEAt / DIEEGr]^{-1} * [PSAt / PSGr]^{-1} \qquad (7)$$

$$MC = [NSEEAt / NSEEG] * [NSEEAt / P(6-11)At / NSEEG / P(6-11)Gr]^{-1} * [P(6-11)At / PAt / P(6-11)Gr / PGr]^{-1} \qquad (8)$$

$$MC = [PAt/PGr] \qquad (9)$$

The data used to estimate the above relationship was taken from the Library of the National Statistical Agency of Greece (NSAGr) and the Department of Statistics of the Ministry of Education for the period 1961-2001. Having defined the variables AMDEAt, AMDEE, P (6-11) At (School Age Population in Attica), P (6-11) Gr (School Age Population in Greece), PGr and PAt, for the given years 1961,1971,1981,1991 and 2001, and using equation (8), it is possible to estimate the Degree of Metropolitan Concentration (DMC) for the period of 1961-2001 (Table 3). It is should be pointed out that the between prices of over time changes of the four indicators are calculated using the following equation:

$$Y_{t+10} = (1+r)^{10} * Y_t \qquad (10)$$

which gives us the possibility to calculate the annual rate of growth for each variable for the individual decades of the period 1961-2001. This particular method can be accepted since the periodic intervals are relatively very small.

Tab. 3: *Estimates of the Degree of Metropolitan Concentration (DMC) during the period of 1961-2001*

Year	*DMC*
1961	**0,2453**
1962	0,2491
1963	0,2538
1964	0,2637
1965	0,2652
1966	0,2755
1967	0.2855
1968	0.2911
1969	0.2967
1970	0.3086
1971	**0.3191**
1972	0.3362
1973	0.3449
1974	0.3488
1975	0.3501
1976	0.3522
1977	0.3522
1978	0.3510
1979	0.3498
1980	0.3497
1981	**0.3459**

1982	0.3459
1983	0.3488
1984	0.3474
1985	0.3514
1986	0.3517
1987	0.3530
1988	0.3515
1989	0.3474
1990	0.3507
1991	**0.3434**
1992	0,3436
1993	0,3438
1994	0,3439
1995	0,3441
1996	0,3443
1997	0,3444
1998	0,3446
1999	0,3448
2000	0,3449
2001	**0,3451**

Source: Authors' elaboration

Diagram 3: The evolution of the Degree of Metropolitan Concentration (DMC) in Greece over the period 1961-2001.

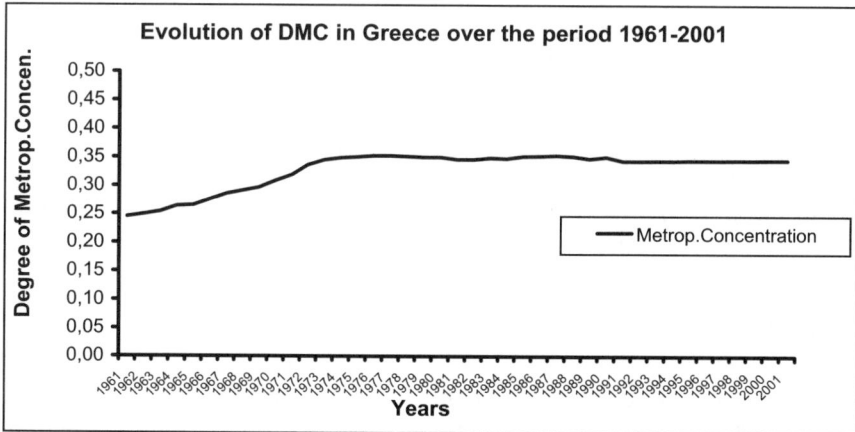

Source: Authors' elaboration

Observing Table 3 and Diagram 3, we can see that the degree of Metropolitan Concentration (DMC) increases continuously during the first 10 years (1961-1977), while during the four-year period 1978-1982 there exists a cease of growth to the point where can it be reverted. From 1982 and then, the values of DMC do not show a clear trend and they are tending to be around 34-35%. There is an explicit stabilization of DMC during the last decade at level little above of 34%.

Diagram 4: The Differentiation in the Degree of Metropolitan Concentration according to the Population of UCCC and the alternative method proposed.

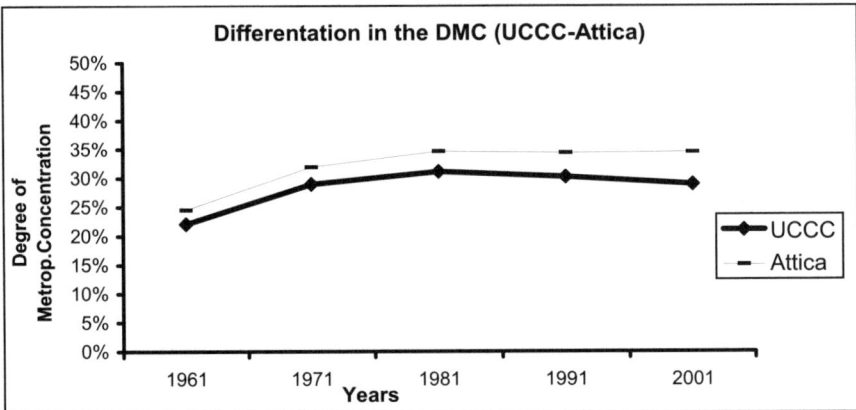

Source: Authors' elaboration

Finally, according to the data of the last census and the alternative method that was used earlier, we can conclude that the degree of Metropolitan Concentration in Greece tends to be stable, while in 2001 it is found to be around 34,51%. Comparing the estimates coming from Table 2 and our estimated values (Table 3), one can notice the diachronic differentiations (particularly for 2001) concerning the evolution of the Degree of Metropolitan Concentration. The estimates of Table 2 are clearly smaller, thus they should not be used in any kind of studies or as official data. These particular differentiations are portrayed evidently in Diagram 4 on the years of census 1961,1971,1981,1991 and 2001.

4. Conclusions

In the current study, we have examined whether the Greek urban system is still experiencing a trend of concentration or it is experiencing the first steps of deconcentration, and then we proposed an alternative method so as to estimate the degree of metropolitan concentration for the time period of 1961-2001. The estimated results indicated that especially during the last two decades, the small cities showed dynamics of demographic increase, which was intensified at the lower levels of the hierarchy. Given the fact that the rate of demographic increase of the Urban Complex of Athens, we can conclude that the system of Greek urban centers is led to stability.

However, taking our analysis further and investigating the geographic position of the cities that have the bigger positive demographic changes, it is observed that their spatial location is within the administrative boundaries of Prefectures of Thessalonica and mainly of Attica. These cities constitute important functional parts of the two big urban complexes and are not characterized by a stochastic distribution in the Greek space. More specifically, an important observation is that of the high rate of appearance of new small cities (over 5.000 residents) in these Prefectures (evident during the decade of 1981-1991), which has been slowed down and substituted the last decade, by a high rate of demographic increase in the already existing cities. Consequently, the idea of deconcentration of the Greek urban system cannot be proved in the current study; the superior trend, which is evident here, is that of the internal spatial restructuring and that of the enforcement of new urban concentrations (particularly in the Prefecture of Attica). As a result, the Prefecture of Attica can be considered as a wider multi-nodal metropolitan region, with the UCCC to be the sovereign urban core, which is connected with urban sub-centers in a framework of an urban network (picture 1). Nonetheless, Attica and the UCCC can be identified as a single ´urban formation´, in terms of the dynamics, the function and the metropolitan importance (Economou et al., 2001). According to the results obtained from our analysis, the degree of metropolitan concentration followed an increasing trend up to 1971, with consequent inclination to be stabilized at 34 -35% during the last two decades.

It is important, however, to make some remarks concerning the above results. First, it is known that the demographic data employed in our investigation does not expresses the absolute sizes of the reality, since a substantial number of residents of the cities is moving and registers at the places of origin. Secondly, the residents of big urban centers on the day of population census move to the places of origin or to the places of seasonal residence, and that is where they are registered. Finally, the foreigners from third countries are not counted. Thus, the population registration in any given census might not be the real one. Besides, taking into consideration the results of the research held by the company ´Attica Metro´, the population of Attica was appreciated to be in 1996 approximately 4.137.807 residents, while according to the population census of the NSAGr in 2001 the number of residents was 3.761.810. Consequently, the degree of Metropolitan Concentration in Greece is likely to be bigger. Furthermore, it becomes obvious that the examination of the parameter a (Pareto coefficient) alone is not sufficient for describing the trends of concentration or deconcentration in an urban system. As it appeared earlier, the analysis of the geographic dimension of the phenomenon is also essential, so that erroneous conclusions are avoided. Regarding the future development of metropolitan concentration in Greece, it is evident that the special role of capital, not only has not been decreased the last years, but also it is expected to increase itself in a national and international level. In the national level, the restructuring of the primary sector with the parallel reduction of the employment will possibly lead to mobility of additional rural population to the urban centers. If however, we take into consideration the fact that the smaller urban centers are not ready in terms of infrastructure to absorb the above population (Petrakos and Kotzamanis, 1994), then the bigger percentage of this internal immigration is likely to direct to Attica. This will contribute to the reinforcement of the Degree of Metropolitan Concentration. The opinion above is strengthened by the fact that already important infrastructure projects have been build, such as the new airport at Spata and the Subway, while several others are in the construction process for the preparation of the Olympic Games 2004. All these infrastructure projects will substantially improve the capital city and will increase its attractiveness. In an international level, the place of Athens is foreseen to strengthen, since in the new international reality, a progressive improvement of international intensities in the Balkans will emerge.

Regarding the future development of metropolitan concentration in Greece, it is evident that the special role of capital, not only has not been decreased the last years, but also it is expected to increase itself in a national and international level. In the national level, the restructuring of the primary sector with the parallel reduction of the employment will possibly lead to mobility of additional rural population to the urban centers. If however, we take into consideration the fact that the smaller urban centers are not ready in terms of infrastructure to absorb the above population (Petrakos and Kotzamanis, 1994), then the bigger percentage of this internal immigration is likely to direct to Attica. This will contribute to the reinforcement of the Degree of Metropolitan Con-centration. The opinion above is strengthened by the fact that already important infrastructure projects have been build, such as the new airport at Spata and the Subway, while several others are in the construction process for the preparation of the Olympic Games of 2004. All these infrastructure projects will substantially improve the capital city and will increase its attractiveness. In an international level, the place of Athens is foreseen to strengthen, since in the new international reality, a progressive improvement of international intensities in the Balkans will emerge.

Therefore, in the framework of the developing European integration, it is likely to have a more rapid economic growth, thus a higher demand for tertiary services and investments in Greece. Yet, because of the extended pressure of globalization, the need for improving the position of Athens in the existing European metropolitan hierarchy is increasing. An important factor that will contribute towards this direction is the exploitation of the fame that Athens is expected to receive organizing the coming Olympic Games.

In terms of policy, by examining the rank-size distribution of the Greek urban system and the Degree of Metropolitan Concentration (DMC), it is rendered to evaluate the prospects of a balanced growth of the Greek cities. This particular evaluation can possibly constitute the base for mapping out the strategy that will induce the balanced economic growth of the Greek cities. The new European and international role of Athens, allows us to follow a developmental path, one that offers more alternative opportunities of employment that can be similar to the productive models of European metropolitan regions. The last decade however, intense concerns are expressed for the growth level of the remainder regions of the country, since up to today it falls short comparing to that of Attica.

Accordingly, therefore, to the results of our investigation, it becomes obvious that the role of Athens has been strengthened and will be strengthened further, particularly in the framework of the European integration. Regarding the remaining cities, excluding the tourist destinations, that experience a recession due to deindustrialization, and because more generally, they do not have infrastructure so as to benefit from the European integration, are under the question of policy, since, this phenomenon is expected to continue. It is rendered necessary therefore, initially, the mapping out of a more general policy for establishing a balanced Greek urban system that will be based only on the exploitation of comparative advantages and local resources and on a series of selective policies. The latter are expected to solve the problems of each city individually aiming at the recovery of the urban centers that experience an extended delay of growth. This challenge of introducing such a policy will be an interesting field for future research. The degree of the policy's success will depend to a large extent on the level and the quality of the knowledge of basic characteristics of the Greek cities, such as their real population, their GDP, their productive structure and also the boundaries of their wider functional urban region. The characteristics above, even though that to know them is very important, have not been a matter of exploration in Greece yet.

References

Armstrong, H. and Taylor, J. (1985) Regional Economics and
Policy, Philip Allan.

Baldassare, M. (1986) Trouble in Paradise: the Suburban
transformation of America. New York: Columbia University Press.

Batten, D. (1995) Network Cities: Creative Urban Agglomerations for
the 21st Century. In: Urban Studies, vol.32, pp.313-327.

Beckmann, M. (1958) City hierarchy and the distribution of city size. In:
Economic Development and Cultural Change, vol.6, pp.243-248.

-,   and McPherson, J. (1970) City size distribution in a
central place hierarchy:an alternative approach. In: Journal of Regional
Science, vol.10,pp.25-33.

Berg, L. van den et al. (1982) Urban Europe: A Study of Growth and
Decline, Oxford, England: Pergamon.

Berry, J. and McGreal, S. (1995) European Cities, Planning
Systems and Property Markets. London: Spoon.

Cheshire, P (1987) Economic factors in urban change: European
prospects, Discussion Paper. In: Urban and Regional Economics, Series C,
vol.30, University of Reading.

-,   (1990) Explaining the Recent Performance of the
European Community's Major Urban Regions. In: Urban Studies, vol.27,
pp.311-333.

-,   (1995) A New Phase of Urban Development in Western
Europe? The Evidence for the 1980s. In: Urban Studies, vol.32, pp.1045-
1063.

-,   Carbonaro, G. and Hay, D. (1986) Problems of
Urban Decline and Growth in EEC Countries :Or measuring Degrees of
Elephantness. In: Urban Studies, vol.2, pp.131-149.

-,   and Hay, D. (1989) Urban Problems in Western Europe:
An Economic Analysis. London: Unwin Hyman.

-,   Carbonaro, G. (1996) Urban Economic Growth
in Europe: Testing Theory and Policy Prescriptions. In: Urban Studies, vol.33,
pp.1111-1128.

Ciccone, A. (2000) Agglomerations in Europe. In: European Economic
Review, vol.46, pp.213-227.

Ding, C. (2001) An Empirical Model of Spatial Development. In: The
Applied Regional Science Conference, vol.13, pp. 173-186.

Economou, D. et al. (2001) The International Role of Athens. University
of Thessaly Press, Volos.

EL-Shaks, S. (1972) Development Primacy and System of Cities. In:
Journal of Developing Areas, vol.7, pp.11-36.

Evans, A. (1972) The pure theory of city size in an industrial economy.
In: Urban Studies, vol.7, pp.49-77.

-,   (1990) The assumption of equilibrium in the analysis of
migration and interregional differences: a review of some recent research.
In: Journal of Regional Science, 30, pp.515-531.

Fielding, A. (1982) Counterurbanization in Western Europe. In: Progress
in Planning, no 17, pp.1-52.

Frey, W. (1988) The Re-emergence of Core Region Growth: A Return to the
Metropolis? In: International Regional Science Review, vol.11, pp.261-267.

Friedmann, J. (1969) A general theory of Polarized Development. Los Angeles, University of California.
-,   (1972) The Spatial Organization of power in the development of urban systems. In: Comparative Urban Research, vol.2, pp.5-42.
Fuchs, R.. et al. (1994) Mega-City Growth and Future. The United Nations University.
Gordon, I.R. (1985) The cyclical sensitivity of regional employment and unemployment differentials. In: Regional Studies, 19, pp.95-109.
Guerin-Pace, F. (1995) Rank-size Distribution and the Process of Urban Growth. In: Urban Studies, vol.32, 551-562.
Hall, P. and Hay,D. (1980) Growth Centers in the European Urban System. Berkeley: University of California Press.
-,   (1997) The Future of the Metropolis and its Form. In: Regional Studies, vol.31, pp.211-220.
-,   (1997) Modelling the Post-Industrial City. In: Futures, vol.29, pp.311-322.
Harris, N. (1997) Cities in a global Economy: Structural Change and Policy Reactions. In: Urban Studies, vol. 34, 10, pp. 1693-1703.
Henderson, V.J. (1986) Efficiency of resource usage and city size. In: Journal of Urban Economics, vol.19, pp.42-70.
Ingram, G. (1998) Patterns of Metropolitan Development: What Have We Learned? In: Urban Studies, vol.35, pp.1019-1035.
Isserman, A.M. and Brown, M.A. (1985) Suburbs in crisis, Totowa, NJ: Rowman and Alanheld.
Kotzamanis, B. (1988) The Reproduction of the Greeks, Myths and Reality. In: Review of Social Research, No.70.
-,   (1989). Le Mouvement Migratoire dans la Grèce de l' Apres-Guerre, Thèse, Paris.
Katachianou, D. and Theodore-Markogainnaki, E. (1989) The Greek Urban System. In: Scientific Studies, No 29.
-,   (1992) The Greek system of Cities. In: Ekistics, vol.59, no.352/353, pp.56-60.
Lichtenberge, E. (1976) The changing nature of European Urbanization. In: Berry B. (ed.) Urbanization and counterurbanization. Beverly Hills, California: Sage.
Leondidou, L. (1994) Mediterranean cities: divergent trends in a united Europe. In: Blacksell M., Williams A. (eds) The European Challenge: geography and development in the European Community. Oxford University Press.
McCann, P. (1995) Rethinking the Economies of Location and Agglomeration. In: Urban Studies, vol.32, pp.563-577.
McDonald, J.F. (1997) Fundamentals of Urban Economics. Prentice Hall, New Jersey.
McMillen, D. and Smith, S. (2003) The number of sub centers in large urban areas. In: Journal of Urban Economics, vol.53, pp.321-338.
Mills, E. and Hamilton, B. (1989) Urban Economics. Scott: Foresman and Company.
-,   (1992) Urban Efficiency, Productivity and Economic Development. In: The International Bank for Reconstruction and Development, The World Bank, pp.221-235.
-,   and Labuele, L.S. (1995) Projecting Growth of Metropolitan Areas. In: Journal of Urban Economics, vol.37, pp.344-360.

Moomaw, R.(1988) Agglomeration Economies: Localization or
        Urbanization? In: Urban Studies, vol.25, pp.150-161.
-,   and Shatter, A. (1996) Urbanization and Economic
        Development: A Bias towards Large Cities? In: Journal of Urban Economics,
        vol.40, pp.13-37.
-,   (1998) Agglomeration economies: Are they exaggerated
        by industrial aggregation? In: Regional Science and Urban Economics, vol.28,
        pp.199-211.
Moore, F. T. (1958) A note on city-size distribution. In: Economic
        Development and Cultural Change, 7(1) pp.465-466.
Myrdal, G. (1957) Economic Theory and Underdeveloped Regions. In:
        Duckworth, London.
Norton, R.D. (1979) City life-cycles and American urban policy. New
        York, Academic Press.
Parr, J. (1979) Regional economic change and regional spatial
        structure: some interrelationships. In: Environment and Planning A, vol.11,
        pp.825-837.
-,   and Jones, C. (1983) City size distribution and urban density
        functions: some interrelationships. In: Journal of Regional Science, vol.23,
        pp.283-307.
-,   (1985) A note on the size distribution of cities over time. In:
        Journal of Urban Economics, vol.18, pp.199-212.
Perroux, G. (1950) Economic Space: Theory and Applications. In:
        Quarterly Journal of Economics, 64, pp.89-104.
Peterson, P.E. (1985) The new Urban Reality. Washington:
        Brookings.
Peterakos, G. and Brada, J. (1989) Metropolitan concentration in
        Developing countries. In: Kyklos, vol.18, 4, pp.557-578
-,   and Kotzamanis, B . (1994) The level of metropolitan concentration
        in Greece: Estimating time series for the period 1961-1991. In: Kotzamanis B.,
        Maradou and Alibradi L. (eds.) The Demographic Evolution in Greece.
-,   and Mardakis, P. (1999) The Recent Changes in the
        Greek Urban System. In: Economou D. and Petrakos G. (eds.) The Growth of
        Greek Cities. University of Thessaly Press –Gutenberg.
-,   . and Tsoukalas, D. (1999) Metropolitan Concentration
        in Greece: An Empirical Exploration' System. In: Economou D. and Petrakos
        G. (eds.) The Growth of Greek Cities. University of Thessaly Press –
        Gutenberg.
Prevelakis, G. (2002) Metropolitan Planning in Greece: the case of
        Athens. In: Aeihoros, Issue 1, Department of Urban and Regional Planning,
        University of Thessaly, Volos.
Pumain, D. (1982) La Dynamique des Villes. Paris : Economica.
Rossen, K. and Resnick, M. (1980) The size distribution of cities: An
        examination of the Pareto Law and Primacy'. In: Journal of Urban Economics,
        vol.8, pp.165-186.
Schafer,R. (1978) Metropolitan Form and Demographic Change. In:
        Urban Studies, vol.15, pp.23-33.
Siebert, H. (1969) Regional Economic Growth: Theory and Policy.
        International Textbook Policy
Simon, C. (1998) Human Capital and Metropolitan Growth. In: Journal of
        Urban Economics, vol. 43, pp.223-243

Simon, H. (1968) On judging the plausibility of theories. In: Van Root –
    Seelar and Stall (eds.) Logic, Methodology and Philosophy of
    Science, 3, Amsterdam.
Smith, E.T. and Zenou Y. (2003) Spatial mismatch, search effort, and
    urban spatial structure. In: Journal of Urban Economics, no 54, pp.129-156.
Stastitical Yearbocj of Greece 1999 (2000) Athens: NSAG.
Suarez-Villa, L. (1988) Metropolitan Evolution, Sectoral Economic
    Change and City Size Distribution. In: Urban Studies, 25, pp. 1-20.
Vinnig, D. and Kontuly, T. (1978) Population dispersal from major
    metropolitan regions: an international comparison. In: International Regional
    Science Review, vol.3, pp.49-74
-,   and Pallone, R. (1982) Migration between core and
    peripheral regions: a description and tentative explanation of the patterns in 22
    countries. In: Geoforum, vol.13, pp.339-410.
Wheaton, W.C. and Shishido, H. (1981) Urban Concentration,
    Agglomeration economies and the level of Economic Development. In:
    Economic Development and Cultural Change, vol.30, pp.17-30
White, R.W. (1974) Sketches of a dynamic central place theory'. In:
    Economic Geography, vol.50, pp.219-227
Williamson, J. (1992) The Macroeconomic Dimensions of City Growth. In: Developing
    Countries: Past, Present and Future', The International Bank for
    Reconstruction and Development, The World Bank, pp.241-261

Towards a Peripheral Society?
Research Results on the Life Style in an East-German Region

Frank Eckardt

In recent debates on the relationship between societal constitution and spatial entities, new terms like "post-suburbia", "edge cities", "periphery" or "regional city" have been introduced. Although there is a wide range of meanings attached to the different uses, it can be said that these approaches intend to overcome the established dichotomy between city and suburbia which can be found in urban studies frequently (Beauregard 1993).

With regard to observations all over the world, the morphological changes in urban forms have not only been placed in relation to a physical process of urbanisation but have been seen as an expression of a society in a new phase of development. In other words, the emergence of a varied way of modernization leads to a different shape of spaces. At the same time, the "postmodern geographies" (Soja 1989) produce their own effects to ground a society that changes in a substantial or even radical way. The periphery is therefore seen as being a future form of urban life and a physical part of the "second modernity" or post-modernism (Prigge 1998). In this way, the analysis of the periphery has first been undertaken from a phenomenological point of departure and then linked to a broader dispute in social science about the general constitution of society. With the link to the debate on postmodernism, the interpretation of what is happening in the peripheral spaces refers to theories of disembedding, medialisation and globalization. It questions the relevance of space in the sense of traditional modernity where there is high congruency between personal life style, social position and spatial anchorage. With the acceleration of social and geographical mobility, it has been assumed that space has become no longer of any significance. In the most radical perspective, medialised and globalized communication generates life styles and the urban physis no longer plays a role as an important point of reference. In this way, the relationship between the individual and society becomes more direct and is lesser intermediated by a social field embedded in spatial milieus (Giddens 1990, Beck 2003). The contrary argument underlines the remaining significance of space and milieu and the new periphery is interpreted as a prolonged tradition of relationalist social space with all its practices of distinction (Bourdieu 2000).

Between Weimar and Erfurt

The research undertaken and presented here wants to contribute to the debate on societal analysis of the phenomenon of peripheral spaces; although there is no clear definition as to which places are to be seen as evident expressions of the introduced category of a post-urban and post-suburban "spatial fix" (Jessop 2002). However, since the theoretical reach of the hypothesis on a generally observed new spatial-postmodern space profoundly aims at being of relevance worldwide, it is legitimate and even necessary to look at micro-spaces like the one this study tries to highlight. In the following discussion, the results of a survey undertaken in those places between the two cities, Weimar and Erfurt, will be viewed in the light of the theoretical debates outlined above (Eckardt 2004).

Case studies, especially if they want to contribute to a wider theoretical debate, are always of a limited scope with regard to their generality of findings. With the selection of the area of research in this particular East-German region, it seems to be even more important to underline that it has to be taken into serious consideration whether the "globalization paradigm" is not competitively challenged by explanations derived from the other two theoretical frameworks about major changes in society. In the first place, one could argue that such a region is predominantly changed by those processes normally referred to as "transformation". It can be clearly shown that many relevant social phenomena are the product of changes in the political, social and cultural transition after the German re-unification. Secondly, there is a broader debate on pro-cesses, which are due to the "Politics of lifestyles" especially affecting the urban context (Hitzler 1994). In the run of both lines of argument, the visible changes in East German regions could be understood as not being linked to globalization. Obviously, this is true with regard to a more economically oriented definition of globalization. It remains, however, an open question whether the theories about transformation and social changes can exclude any reference to the accelerated global linkages if one assumes that "globalization (is) a social process in which the con-straints of geography on social and cultural arrangements recede and in which people become increasingly aware that they are receding" (Waters 1995, 3).

With this definition of globalization, two aspects are seemingly interesting to point out the degree of a globalization-indicated new form of urban life: a major linkage in a functional way to the outside world and a subjective way of awareness of those global interferences. With regard to the places between Weimar and Erfurt, it has been stated that the area shows morphological characteristics which underline the hypothesis of a new form of peripheral life style (Christ 1998). The area has been seen as symptomatic of the spatial transformation of many East German regions where "peripheral subcentrality" is observed as a general trend (Friedrichs 1995, 138).

The periphery between Weimar and Erfurt, when placed in a historical analysis, can be regarded as a traditional and nearly cliché form of agricultural area. It has surpassed the industrialization processes during the Prussian rule and even in the period of the GDR. Throughout centuries, the villages in this particular area have been host to a stable society with regard to their social, cultural and demographical homo-geneity. As a result of such a long duration of these stable relationships, a certain form of "particular narrow mindedness" has developed, which does not have much affection for the outside world (John 1995, 30). Nevertheless, the periphery played a major role in the constitution of Erfurt as an important place on the Via Regia, a central route of trade in Europe. With industrialization, the surrounding villages of Erfurt were used as a resource for labour forces. During the Socialist Republic, many of those functionally interlinked places were integrated into the administration of Erfurt and became an official part of the city. The pull effects of Erfurt on the surrounding periphery remained strong until the seventies which were merely caused by the comforts of modernized high-rise housing estates. Moreover, it became a common fact that the GDR-citizens sought to escape their homes by using garden houses ("datschas") during the year. In this way, suburbanization took place without the formal approval of property as is common in a market society. Therefore, especially in the case of Erfurt, we can consider the extensive reorganisation of certain rural places as a form of "internal suburbanization" (Ott 1997, 240).

After the German re-unification, both Erfurt and Weimar have lost inhabitants in a significant way. In general, the loss is caused by a three-fold of factors. First of all, there is an unstoppable trail to the West where work can be found more easily. Secondly, the general changes in the lives of the East German inhabitants have neared the demographic development in the West with a lower birth rate. And thirdly, in the later half of the nineties, those who could afford to realize their dream of living outside the city have contributed to a suburbanization of the periphery. Both cities have undertaken a set of measures to react upon the latter cause of depopulation. Especially the integration of some villages close to Weimar has helped to prevent the city from a further loss of inhabitants.

In the now established administrative form, the periphery is either a part of one of the cities or within the so-called "Land of Weimar" (Weimarer Land). In short, it is clear that today the periphery between the two Thuringian cities is highly integrated into their urban fabric. The space is used more as a living area than as an agricultural region, which it had been for so long. As the analysis of commuter activities shows, the new inhabitants of the periphery remain linked to the cities with regard to their economic and consumption needs. However, what confuses the simple observation of suburbanization is the fact that there are important developments in this ex-urban space which are mostly not common in the classical suburban space. Especially the lining up of shopping malls, logistic firms, hotels, and even entertainment facilities alongside the road between Weimar and Erfurt reminds the common observer of some US-style of regionalization, where it is no longer necessary to drive to the city centre, but where the most important features of daily life can be served in the periphery. This seems especially obvious in Bindersleben where the small village has become "Airfurt" because of its nearness to the newly established airport. The same can be observed in Salomonshorn or Schaderode which are officially part of Erfurt since 1994. These places have been typical villages since more than a thousand years and have received more than 1,200 new suburban inhabitants within a few years time. While confronted with this multiplication of their populations and the request for adequate public infrastructure, these villages have entered a new phase of their development with a "cultural attitude of the fifties" (Wenzel 1999, 44). Another prominent example is Nohra where 2,000 jobs have been shaped by localization of the "UNO economic zone" (Gewerbegebiet) and the middle age-style place became transformed into an area of superregional significance.

Not only does the offer of important aspects like work, leisure and housing disturb our understanding of a classical typology as "suburban", the same has to be said about the socio-cultural picture of the periphery. While the expected middle class households can be found to be over-represented in the Erfurt-Weimar periphery, these findings cannot be related to a higher degree in educational and occupational categories. In-habitants outside the cities are comparatively poorly educated and have to a lesser extent been holders of the highest degrees of the German school system (TLS 2001). While it is difficult to analyse this fact since a more detailed picture of the social data is not existent, the usual assumption that those better-off bear higher educational skills is in question. On first sight, this seems to support the theory on dis-embedded life styles as well.

Researching peripherization

Research in challenging concepts of urban theory requires a complex methodological concept that fulfils manifold expectations. It can be critically debated whether single case studies as such are able to give a satisfying clue to how globalization interferes in local processes of transformation. Weighing the influence of local particularities, a translocal research strategy should be preferred (Eckardt 2004).

Another limitation of case studies can often be found in the circumstance that they are mostly framed in an analysis of the objective transformation of the functional part of regionalization/globalization. While it is worthy to debate in extenso as to how the globalization of urban life is anchored in the functional aspects of city life and in which way the cultural side of globalization is linked to it, we can observe that the increasing aware-ness of the receding significance of space attracts little attention. At this point, research on globalization and urbanisation are placed in theoretic-cal frameworks mostly operating apart form each other. To overcome this scientific divide, a research strategy should reflect both "structuralist" and "subjective" worlds of space and globe (Eade 2004). The study undertaken here therefore emphasizes the micro-level of globalization and the perceptive side of the global flow so as to discuss some assump-tions on the subjectivity of peripherization often deriving from a more bot-tom-down approach within globalization research.

As a consequence, the main part of this case study is based on a telephone survey in the periphery of Weimar and Erfurt between the years 2000 and 2002. Until now, there are only a few scholars who have tried to define the criteria which should be regarded as fulfilled in order to ensure the representative character of such a study on regional pro-cesses (Bertram 2000). This is especially true when the limitation of administrative definitions of what are "urban", "suburban" and "rural" is left aside. As pointed out above, in the particular case considered here, the borders of the cities have been shifted to cope with the functional changes in the region. The peripheral society, if it has already emerged as a new type of societal life style organisation must also be looked after in areas already formally integrated into the urban boundaries. On the other hand, those areas not linked to the assumed autonomy of the peri-phery but still existent as clearly rural should not be included. Spatial nearness as such is no argument to assume a place as being host to the new type of societal space. As a result of this debate, the first challenge has been to develop a research map that answers the call for a legi-timated definition on the background of the defined research questions (Hoffmeyer-Zlotnik 2000, 322).

After this map was constructed in discussion with experts of different disciplines which tried to identify those places undergoing significant changes seeming to develop a new form of urban life, the survey had to answer what the indicators should be to identify a peripheral life style. This needs an operational definition about the "urban" and the "rural". While there are many works which could be cited reflecting this dif-ference, only in the work of Richter (1991) a reference has been made to current debates on the reshaping of society with the pluralism of different ways of urban and rural life. In other words, it seems to be adequate not to start by a simple dualism of the urban and the rural but to assume that we can find important differences in both spatial terminologies as well. Furthermore, Richter elaborated an approach which cross-refers to a work by Bourdieu, thereby allowing the case study to be closer to the overall discussion about the "disembedding" (Giddens) or "relativization" of the position of the subject in the social field (Bourdieu). To identify a new form of spatialised life style, beyond or besides the "urban" and "rural" way of life, the dual construction between the two has to be abolished and replaced by a variety of types.

Operationalizing peripheral research

Thus, the main question is whether in a newly constructed space, not only the morphological appearance is changed but a new form of spatialized life style is also generated. A research proposal with this objective faces several challenges, of which the first one is to define the research area and to limit it with regard to the existing spatial entities. In a series of interviews with local experts, architects, regional and urban planning offices, the area of the "peripheral society" between the two cities of Weimar and Erfurt was mapped. Most places were part of the administrative unit of the "Weimar Region" (Weimarer Kreis). As this Region surrounds Weimar in a circular fashion, the East, the North and a part of the Southern places in this "Region" were left out, as the interviewees denied their functional relation with the periphery. On the other hand, certain villages which have been integrated into the administrative borders of Weimar and Erfurt were also indicated to be part of the periphery. As the area has traditionally been agrarian land, the changes of these villages are visible in terms of new settlements and industrial activities. Introducing "some autonomy" as the main criteria to distinguish classical suburbs from the suggested periphery, the included places were researched with a variety of qualitative instruments. In a study group lasting half a year, led by the author and the architect Lars Bölling, these places were visited regularly and intensively. While some places were easy to identify as having a peripheral character, others remained unclear and needed to be observed for a longer period. In some cases, the inhabitant statistics gave already significant clues. In most places, the number of inhabitants remained stable which could have symbolized a variety of processes. As the afflux of people is rather high in East Germany, stability mostly means that there has been both an inward and an outward movement. Extensive participant observations at kindergarten, hair dressers, hotels, gas stations, schools, saunas and other places of social contact allowed us to gain an insight into these formerly rural areas, now subjected to heavy changes.As a result, a map for the further quantitative life style survey was produced which included all places where both traditional rural population and new dwellers could be found.

A second challenge to be addressed for peripheral research is caused by the overall research question itself. If, in these peripheral spaces a new life style is generated, the continuum between "rural" and "urban" has to be given up, allowing to conceptualise life styles in a non-dualist way. Furthermore, the suggested new life style has a particular quality which transcends the other two as it is more linked to non-space related pro-esses. The research attempted to take into its design this double de-and by progressing in two steps. First, a survey was realized that used an eight fold of combinations of life styles on a threefold continuum. By doing so, the possibility to combine characteristics of life styles which are usually bound to either a "rural" or an "urban" type of life was provided. In a second step, the results of the survey were analysed with regard to the strength of correlations between the life-styles and non-place bound activities and perceptions.

Defining a Peripheral Life-style

As the "urban" is often regarded as being active, mobile and extrovert and the "rural" as being passive, immobile and introvert, a predominance of these attitudes is assumed for both spatialised life-styles for the individual orientations regarding holidays , leisure time, working attitude, private life planning and other aspects. (Richter 1994 a, b) Nevertheless, in reality, the "rural" or the "urban" does not appear in the extreme or purified way but allows a variety of combinations and the three con-inuums between progressive-conservative, active-passive, and extrovert-introvert. Therefore, the duality between both can be broken up by defining a range of different combinatory clusters:

The Intellectual Urbanite: Work is an important feature in his life, but it does not fulfil as giving life the only sense. As an active participant in the urban life, he feels himself accepted in this society.

The Extrovert Urbanite: Work is the most central part of life here. The personal appearance in a manifold of activities within leisure time is important.

The Active Urbanite: Intellectual and extrovert as both the other groups, the active urbanite plays special attention to cultural and culinary ad-vantages of urban life. This becomes visible also with regard to his choice of neighbourhood.

The Passive Urbanite: The use of the city's infrastructure is an important factor in his life, but the significance of cultural offers is little. Instead, work gives life meaning. However, in contrast to the first two urbanites, there is no ambition for a career.

The Extrovert Villager: His acceptance of external orientation is a form of adaptation, while the activities in the "outside world" are frequently used to reassure one's personal identity.

The Active Villager: The dream of living in a village has been realised, mostly together with the family, which remains the most important source of recognition and orientation. There are high expectations regarding the future and openness to discuss general issues.

The Conventional Villager: Conservative, conventional and stabilizing points of references are common. Keeping up traditions and the established order of things is an important principle. Work and leisure are perceived differently: work is active, free time is passive.

The Introvert Villager: Close to the conventional style, the introvert villager would also refuse to move to the city. Fashion and recognition by the outside world (beyond the private sphere) is regarded to be of no importance. Being lazy is not accepted, even on holidays or during free time.

It is expected that these clusters have a strong link to their spatial framing. The villagers are predominately to be found in a morphologically rural area, while the urbanites inhabit urban settlements. A peripheral society, on the contrary, would not be characterized by a dominance of only one of them.

Research results

Based on this differentiation, a survey with 950 persons was realized, in which 65 questions regarding cultural preferences, opinions about work, life and other important features were asked in a ca. 25 minutes long interview. The questionnaire enabled responses on a scale of 1 to 6 (in accordance with the German grading system in schools). The questions were weighed and organised as indicators for the pre-formulated eight life styles.
As a first result, all clusters have been represented to a certain extent in the survey. Using the SPSS computerized analysis, the consistency of

pre-defined clusters has been controlled both with regard to its internal coherence and in difference to the neighbouring clusters.[1]

Life Style	Percentage of population
The Intellectual Urbanite	18,37
The Extrovert Urbanite	6,01
The Active Urbanite	15,26
The Passive Urbanite	6,66
Urban Life styles	**46,30**
The Extrovert Villager	16,72
The Active Villager	4,17
The Conventional Villager	15,01
The Introvert Villager	17,80
Rural Life styles	**53,70**

Tab. 1: Life styles in the periphery between Weimar and Erfurt. Own resource.

As table 1 show, the general expectation to find a mixture of life-styles in the periphery between Weimar and Erfurt has been proved by the outcomes of the survey. In attempting to understand more about the findings, the results have been re-grouped with regard to the three continuums. In this way, the predominance of extrovert and immobile/conservative life styles becomes visible (as in tab. 2).

	Life style in percent
Extrovert life styles	41,10
Conservative lifestyles	39,47
Active lifestyles	19,43

Tab. 2: Life styles in the periphery ranked according to the continuum active-passive, extrovert-introvert, and progressive-conservative. Own resource.

As it seems, this interpretation consists of a surprising element that the life style of the peripheral inhabitant is best characterized by a melange of attitudes which are regarded as being controversial and not integrated within one personal individuality. However, it seems that the majority of the interviewed persons have elements of both an extrovert and a conservative life-style integrated in their habits towards the world and their private life. This duality can be best illustrated by looking at the answers given to questions concerning the individual working attitude.

---

[1] The choice made here was not to let the analysis generate its own clusters according to the distances found in the sample. This would have led to other results where the link to the spatial categories would become invisible.

While work (with family life) has been given the highest priority as giving life a sense, this rather traditional opinion is counterbalanced by a high percentage of affirmation that work should be fun (see tab. 3).

	"I totally agree"
"One's own home is the most important thing in the world"	838
"One should try to make a career"	798
"Work should be fun in the first place"	760
"In general, only those performing well in their work should be supported"	749
"To go out once in a while is important"	749
"Without education, life is senseless"	710
"Every human being should live according to moral principles"	688
"At home, I want to relax".	665

Tab.3: Highest affirmation of single statements. Own resource.

While a conservative confirmation of wide spread agreements on the importance of "work" and "home" life is mixed up with rather post-modern values like "fun" and "going out", statements of a more introvert and passive life styles like "every human being should live according to moral principles" also do score high. It would therefore be appropriate to imagine the peripheral dweller as somebody who encaptures a variety of life style elements. This might indicate that the innovation of this new type of relationship between spatial morphology and personal habit is characterized by a mosaic of normative orientations.

A new type of society?

As outlined above, the wider theoretical debate about city regions, edge cities, peripheries etc. also puts forth the question of societal implications that this incoherent life style of the periphery generates. While the limited scope of the research undertaken does not allow drawing as far reaching conclusions which would contribute to this debate with an empirically underpinned statement, a small part of the survey has explicitly addressed this issue. Two major concerns are often put forth with regard to the emergence of a peripheral society where the cities are loosing their importance and where the inhabitants are creating a sphere of xenophobic NIMBYs. Both aspects have been integrated into the design of the survey with questions regarding the relationship to both cities, Weimar and Erfurt, and with a question about the interest concerning foreigners.

While the answers to the questions regarding the "external orientation" do not show extraordinary opinions about foreigners (More than 80 per cent agreed to the statement that foreigners enrich their personal life), the issue of the remaining importance of the city in a peripheral society appears more complex. The relationship with the cities has been tested by formulating questions with regard to both the scope of activities that link the peripherical inhabitants to the cities (work, leisure, shopping) and their general perception of Weimar and Erfurt (atmosphere). As the outcomes show, the autonomy of the periphery, which was the initial indication for including places into this research, is rather limited with regard to their functional interconnectedness with both cities (tab. 4).

"In the last years, I am visiting both cities…"	Percentage of answers
"more often"	41,02
"as much as ever"	35,28
"lesser"	21,40

Tab. 4: Visits to Weimar or Erfurt in the last years. Own resource.

A far reaching hypothesis about the irrelevance of cities in an age of peripherization cannot be supported by this finding. Thus, it then remains interesting whether we have to reconsider the whole area as simply being a suburban place and work commuting creates the increased visits to the city. Here, the answers reject this simplification of the socio-spatial processes as being a purely old style suburbanization (tab. 5).

Visits to work in Weimar or Erfurt	Answers as percentage
Never	59,61
Once a week	1,56
Several times a week	3,63
Nearly daily	31,67

Tab. 5: Work visits to Weimar or Erfurt per week. Own resource.

While it is apparent that a high percentage of the periphery people do commute to Weimar and Erfurt, there is no equivalence with the total working population (63 %) living in this area and which has been integrated into the survey in a representative way. Thus, it means that a relative share of the work is also located in the periphery and offers jobs to the peripheral population. In this sense, the criteria of a functionally divided city, wherein the spheres of work (city) and living (suburbia) are separated, cannot be upheld for characterizing the periphery in total. With regard to the other two reasons to visit the city (shopping, leisure), it becomes clearer how the increase of visits to both cities can be explained. The results show that Erfurt and Weimar are highly frequented for having a good time there or to go to the shops (tab. 6). As more detailed questions show, the attractiveness of the cities is due to the existing cultural and leisure time offers. However, it can no longer be said that cultural activities and shopping–only take place in the city centres. As also shown by qualitative studies, many periphery dwellers do spend their free time in their near surrounding and are not necessarily dependant on the opportunities in the cities.

	Positive answers in percent
Periphery	46,27
Weimar	54,38
Erfurt	70,87

Tab. 6: Attractiveness of different spaces. Own resource.

The city has not been abolished in its central role but is re-estimated as a place for temporary visits. The geographical orientation thereby represents the mosaic of attitudes found in the life style part of the survey.

Deterritorialization of the periphery

A second challenge faced by the research on the development refers to the fact that the new life style is due to cultural globalization or interferes with its disembedding mechanism installed in the due run of medialization and interconnectedness. As the survey was already blown up with sixty questions, only a little space was left to address this issue in a more comprehensive way. Questions about the use of media showed that the use of television is integrated into the patterns of spending free time. Seventy percent of all interviewed persons watch television for one to three hours every day. Nearly the same share of answers can be found regarding the number of readers of a local newspaper. In the Land of Thuringia, the "local" newspapers cover reports on Weimar, Erfurt, and the periphery alike. With regard to the non-local/regional newspaper (appearing nationally) nearly the same group can be found which states that it never or only seldom reads these newspapers. It is not clear whether television is used to be informed or entertained by broadcasting channels outside the region. As commonly observed in East Germany, the so called "Mitteldeutscher Rundfunk" (MDR) with particular attention to the East German regions is very popular, next to private entertainment channels like RTL and SAT1. It cannot be said, however, that the TV channels frequented block the peripheral observer from the outside world. Although there might be a certain navel gazing fostered by both the regional TV programmes and the "local" newspapers, it would go beyond reasonability to assume that there is no linkage to those dissemination processes of globalized cultural attitudes.

While a closer look at these phenomena could not be taken within the given organisational framework of this research, another way of analysis has been undertaken to give a first clue on the general interest for the relatedness/disembedding of the peripheral life-style outlined above. As an example, the analysis takes into account how strong the relationships are between generating factors like the "structural activities" (e.g. work) and more "disembedded activities" (e.g. leisure time visits) and the perception of the "urban" (Attractiveness of the cities) and the "periphery" (Attractiveness of the periphery). As it becomes obvious from the cor-relations represented in table 7, there is only a limited validity allowed to be formulated about the correlation between the different forms of space-related activities and the perception of the spaces.

	Perception of the city	Perception of the periphery
Structural activities	0,08	-0,03
Disembedded activities	0,14	-0,20

Tab. 7: Relationship between structural and disembedded activities and the perception of the urban and the periphery. Own resource.

It seems, on the basis of these weak correlations, that the influence of all kinds of activities is slightly higher with regard to the urban perception and vice versa. This means that the perception of the periphery is not so much linked to the real activities and both perception and activity are less bound to each other. A closer look-at correlations between the factors of the social field which determine the life-style and the factor "media" which is here seen as indicating the extent of deterritorialization shows the further significance of the embedding of the individual into the social context. The relationship between the peripheral life style and the level of education, household income and marital status has a higher impact on its development than any kind of spatial relatedness. In this way, the theoretical assumption in the run of Bourdieu's theory on the social field as predominating "spatial effects" can still be upheld. Nevertheless, this is not to say that the factor of dissembedding does not hold ground at all. In another step of analysis, the deterritorialization was measured with regard to the three categories of spatialised life styles. Here, it appears that rural attitudes seem to be lesser influenced by medialization than urban or peripheral ones which underlines the expected "nearness" of agrarian life to place.

Conclusion

The results of the illustrated research concerning the periphery between Weimar and Erfurt are of limited scope regarding their value for the overall debate on the emergence of new forms of spatialised life and society. The area integrated in the undertaken survey is rather small in comparison to other regions under suspicion of peripherization. This is especially true in an international perspective, but even if only Germany is concerned. Nevertheless, the number of interviewees integrated in the survey gives some clue to the tendencies of the newly developing peripheral life style. It might be critical to describe the peripheral society in a way which is based on a clear distinction between the "urban" and the "rural" way of life. Instead, a mixture of both worlds of life is more adequate to assume as sketching the newly generating life style. In the case of the Weimar-Erfurt periphery, this mix shows a colouring with rather contrasting elements of a conservative and extrovert attitude. This might be the consequence of a particular historical situation where the transformation of an agrarian region only started with the German reunification and was heavily influenced by a demand for suburban living unsatisfied so far. NIMBYism has not yet developed and the cities re-main important for the daily organization of life in the periphery. How-ever, the significance of the cities has been redirected towards a more cultural and leisure time oriented use and perception. Meanwhile, the economic, social and cultural autonomy of the periphery can be identified and is likely to increase.

The larger theoretical debate on the diminishing significance of space in times of globalization and medialisation of everyday life needs to be reconsidered. According to the findings of the represented survey, it cannot be said that space becomes irrelevant as such, indicated by the example of the newly viewed role of cities as cultural nodal points. Space seems to still have a lesser effect on the construction of individual attitudes as compared to the hard factors of the social field like education and income. Nevertheless, it seems that the peripheral life style, to some extent, is lesser influenced by the fact of its spatial situatedness. In conclusion, the process of disembedding seems to be most likely the one which reflects more the geographical than the social mobility of the individual.

References:

Beauregard, R. (1993) Descendants of Ascendant Cities and other Urban Dualities. In: Journal of Urban Affairs, No. 2, pp. 217-229.

Beck, U. (2003): Individualization: Institutionalized Individualism and its Social and Political Consequences. London: Sage.

Bertram, H. (2000) Einleitung. In: Bertram, H./Nauck, B../Klein, T. (eds.) Solidarität, Lebensformen und regionale Entwicklung. Opladen Leske+Budrich, pp. 7-16.

Bourdieu, P. (2000) Distinction: a Social Critique of the Judgement of Taste. London: Routledge.

Christ, W. (1998) Von Innen nach Außen. In: Kulturkreis der deutschen Wirtschaft im BDI (ed.) Von Innen nach Außen. Stadtentwicklung ohne Stadt? Weimar/Heidelberg: BDI, pp. 8-14.

Eade, J. /Mele C. (eds) (2002) Understanding the City: Contemporary and Future Perspectives. Oxford: Blackwell.

Eckardt, F. (2002) Eine periphere Gesellschaft. Regionalentwicklung zwischen Weimar und Erfurt. Marburg: Tectum.

-, (2004) Soziologie der Stadt. Bielefeld: transcript.

Friedrichs, J. (1995) Stadtsoziologie. Opladen: Leske + Burdrich.

Giddens, A. (1990): Consequences of Modernity. Cambridge University Press.

Hitzler, R. (1994) Radikalisierte Praktiken der Distinktion. Zur Politisierung des Lebens in der Stadt. In: Dangschat, J. /Blasius, J. (eds.) Lebensstile in den Städten. Opladen: Leske + Burdrich, pp. 47-58.

Hoffmeyer-Zlotnik, J. H. P. (2000) Methodische Aspekte der Anwendung regionaler Stichproben. In: : Bertram, H./Nauck, B./Klein, T. (eds.) Solidarität, Lebensformen und regionale Entwicklung. Opladen. Leske+Budrich, pp. 313-344.

Jessop, B. (2002) The Future of the Capitalist State. Cambride: Polity.

John, J. (1995) Erfurt als Zentralort, Residenz und Hauptstadt. In: Weiss, U. (ed.) Erfurt – Geschichte und Gegenwart. Weimar: Böhlau, pp. 25-44.

Prigge, W. (ed.) (1998): Peripherie ist überall. Frankfurt: Campus.

Ott, T. (1997) Erfurt im Transformationsprozeß der Städte in den neuen Ländern. Erfurt: Pädagogische Hochschule.

Richter, R. (1991) Der Orientierungsraum von Lebensstilen. In: Österreichische Zeitschrift für Soziologie, No. 16, pp. 72-81.

-, (1994a) Der Habitus von Lebensstilen in Stadt und Land. In: Dangschat, J./Blasius, J. (ed.) Lebensstile in den Städten. Opladen, S. 355-365.

-, (1994b) Stilwandel und Stilkonflikte. Zur Analyse von Lebensstilen und Mentalitäten im sozialen Raum am Beispiel kleinbürgerlicher Stilmerkmale. In: Mörth, I./Fröhlich, G. (ed.) Das symbolische Kapital der Lebenstile: zur Kultursoziologie der Moderne nach Pierre Bourdieu. Frankfurt/New York, S. 167-180.

Soja, E. (1989) Postmodern Geographies: The Reassertion of Space in Critical Social Theory. London: Verseo.

TLS – Thüringer Landesamt für Statistik (2001) Statistischer Bericht: Bevölkerung, Erwerbstätigkeit, Haushalt und Familie in Thüringen. Ergebnisse des Mikrozensus. Erfurt: TLS.

Waters, M. (1995) Globalization. London: Routledge.

Wenzel, H. (1999) Die ländlichen Siedlungen. In: Grundmann, L. (ed.) Weimar und seine Umgebung. Weimar: Böhlau, pp. 40-44.

The City and its Borders:
Some implications of the globalization of migration control for urban social space

Monika Krause

Up to the 19th century, legal and physical borders around cities were an accepted part of everyday reality. In most German states, cities had some measure of formal and actual control over who could enter when and who would be accorded which citizenship rights up to 1867. To some these border controls were a mere inconvenience. For others, these borders were a decisive barrier to the freedom and privileges that urban life afforded.

We know for example that Goethe's lover, Charlotte von Stein, resented the fact that she had to register with the city of Weimar's guards on her way to the poet's famed garden house, which was situated just outside the city's boundaries. The list of people who entered and left was shown to the Duke twice a year causing the married noblewoman considerable embarrassment. More was at stake for the impoverished peasants who for centuries were turned away from the city's borders and thus could not breathe the air that is praised to be liberating in the old German saying "Stadtluft macht frei" (Dohse 1985; Grawert 1973; Negt and Kluge 1993).

It was an integral part of state-building to abolish these borders around cities and others that had turned into "internal barriers" in the way of a supposedly unitary "national territory" (Dohse 1985). In this process, the privileges of urban residents were also abolished with the establishment of national citizenship. The national became the site of borders, which became guarded and fortified in the beginning of the 20th century (Torpey 2000).

The project of modern territoriality, marked by a unitary sovereignty over a clearly delineated territory has been fraught with its internal contradictions and the process of deterritorialisation and reterritorialisation has not ended with the establishment of the nation-state. After a period of comparatively aspatial analysis, researchers are now beginning to analyse territorial and other spatial changes (Agnew 1994; Agnew and Corbridge 1995; Brenner 2004). The recent globalisation of migration control forms part of a key shift in the political organization of space. In this paper I examine the implications of these developments for contemporary cities.

I will first sketch an analytical framework for comparing what I call "border regimes" across time or nations. Then I will examine recent changes in migration control in Western Europe. We do not see a simple return to borders around cities. The recent transnationalisation of migration control, the increasing complexity of regulation of non-nationals and the increase in migration, however, combine to a rise in internal borders in and around the city.

Elements of a Border Regime
A border regime is based on the legitimate power to regulate access to or exit from the territory. In analyzing a specific regime, we can ask at which institutional level such control is located: the national state, the local state, a supranational entity, or private actors. This dimension of a border regime is what Leitner calls the scale of control (Leitner 1997).

Secondly, we can ask around which entity the boundary is drawn ideologically and institutionally with regard to the primary institutional location of citizenship rights.

This border can be physically unestablished or established. In the latter half of the 19th century for example, the border was national in scale and scope but unestablished. If the border is established it can be selectively closed (such as in the late 1970s in Western Europe) or selectively open (such as prior to the 1970s in Western Europe).

Based on the regulate access and expel, the modern state has built a system of regulating the access of foreign citizens already on the territory to rights and resources (Dohse 1985). This leads to what Lockwood (1996) and following him Morris, call civic stratification: Civic stratification is a "system of inequality based on the relationship between different categories of individuals and the state and the rights thereby granted or denied" (Morris 2003). These regulations of the citizenry and resident population can in turn have spatial implications.

Fragmented Territoriality: the new transnational border regime
National borders were established and increasingly fortified in the decades since 1890. It followed a period of relative stability. Even though, in central Europe borders were redrawn in radical ways after both world wars, the framework of national border control was relatively unchallenged. Changes occurred mainly on the level of migration policy. Since the 1980s, we have seen a fundamental change through the internationalization of migration control (Sassen 1998b; Duevell 2002).

In the past decades, the institutional location of control ceased to be exclusively national. Since the mid-eighties, some control over migration policy in the European Union has shifted upward from the national level. Governments have established a variety of working groups, building on the early efforts of the Trevi group (1975) to address cross-border issues of terrorism through cooperation of law enforcement agencies. In 1985 the Trevi group's responsibilities were extended to matters of Immigration (Duevell 2002).

The original members of the Schengen group, Belgium, the Netherlands, France, Germany, and Luxembourg took a leading role in institutionalising cooperation. The Schengen conventions (1985, 1990) established the basis for a harmonization of asylum policies, a joint visa list, the reinforcement of external borders and a European information system (Cruz 1993; Meijers et al. 1991). The conventions have since been signed by all EU member states except the UK, Ireland, and Denmark.

EU members duplicated the Schengen agreement with regard to asylum in the Dublin Convention signed in 1990 by all member states meeting in the so-called Ad Hoc Immigration Group.

The Maastricht treaty of 1991 gave legal competence to the EU in the area of visa policy. It also lays ground for a formal institutional cooperation of member states in the realm of asylum policy, immigration policy and policies regarding non-EU nationals by incorporating it into the EU-treaty as the third pillar.

The Amsterdam treaty, ratified in 1999, has incorporated asylum and immigration in communal decision making, giving a significant role to the commission, and established a possibility for moving from the unanimity principle (Geddes 2001; Lavenex and Uocarer 2002; Leitner 1997).

Cooperation in migration policy in Europe has not only increased among EU member states. In a series of treaties with non-members, the EU has extended its migration policy beyond its territory. The 1990s have seen the imposition of a cordon sanitaire on Eastern Europe. All Eastern European states have entered into re-admission negotiations with the European Union and its member states. Poland, for example, undertook to re-admit any person who enters the EU-territory via Poland or any Polish national who does not fulfil conditions for entry or residence in the European Union. These agreements pressure states to in turn strengthen their external borders, thus extending the geographic scope of the migration framework (Lavenex 1999). In anticipation of the EU enlargement, German border police have been working with Ukrainian border police since 1997.

Re-acceptance clauses have also become an important part of aid negotiations with the south. A clause on migration control is part of every bilateral agreement with an ACP state since the summit in Seville in 2000 (EU 2000).

Migration policy has become an increasingly important part of the emergent EU foreign policy, thus turning immigration control into a matter of international co-operation in other policy areas, such as development aid, crisis management, the military (Lavenex 1999; van Selm 2002).

Transnational think tanks and agencies have also come to play an important role in migration policy, most prominently among them the International Organization for Migration (Duevell 2003). The IOM carries out governments work but also takes the initiative in providing research and formulating policy. It claims to have moved 450 000 people in the year 2000 alone. These movements were predominantly so called return migration into conflict zones.[1]

Some implementation and monitoring powers have been shifted downwards to a sub-national level of government. Local authorities have been given a significant role in policing migrants. In France, a 1982 decree requiring a housing certificate for being eligible to host a foreigner, has been used as a tool for migration control since 1993, when mayors were given the power to refuse to sign it. Some mayors refused to give out the form or systematically failed to deliver them. More than 50 % required papers not required by law (compare the study by CIMADE study, quoted in Guiraudon and Lahav 2000: 182).

The Dutch policy to link welfare allowances for newcomers with the attendance of Dutch language classes and other training is also one that requires monitoring by local authorities.
In France, the Netherlands and Germany, local authorities have also used the right to inspect the marriages between residents and foreigners for the control of migrants (Guiraudonand Lahav 2000).

Increasingly, actors within civil society are made responsible for the control of migrants. Governments have shifted responsibility by criminalizing citizen for supporting illegal migrants. Schengen's Article 27 calls for measures prohibiting aid to foreigners. In France, a measure in place since 1945, dating back to 1938, states that "any individual who either directly or indirectly, helps or tries to help the illegal entry, movement, or stay of a foreigner will be imprisoned for 2 months to 2 years and a fine of 2000 to 200000 francs" (quoted in Guiraudonand Lahav 2000). The Loi Debre of 1997, in addition, required hosts, who have guests on special visas, to inform the town hall, when their guests leave, allowing the French government to compile computer records on the movement of foreigners (Fassin and Moriceand Quiminal 1997).

---

[1] Critics contest the claim that these movements can be called voluntary return migration. Amnesty International and Human Rights Watch have accused the IOM of human rights violations by amnesty and human rights watch in detaining refugees in Papua New Guinea, Indonesia and Cambodia (Duevell 2003).

The border is drawn in the name of both the nation and the European Union. For EU-nationals, access is to EU territory as a whole. For third-country nationals, access at EU borders is thought to be to respective member states' territory only.

Physically, the border is established primarily on the European level. Among Schengen states, national borders have been defortified and replaced with a system of controls diffused surveillance throughout the territory.

On the level of migration policy, we have witnessed a move from selective openness to selective closure. Since the 1970s most states in Western Europe closed their borders towards economic migrants. In the UK successive governments limited the citizenship rights of former colonial subjects from 1962 onwards. Following the worldwide economic recession, Germany stopped recruiting guest workers in November 1973; France officially closed its borders in 1974. Parallel to the stop to economic migration, the harmonization of asylum policies on a European level since the late 1980s pushed by the signatory states of the Schengen agreement and the TREVI group meant a convergence towards the lowest common denominator. Especially after the fall of the Berlin wall, measures like the third country rule, the introduction of visa requirements for refugee producing countries, and the extension of the policing of borders have made it extremely difficult to claim or obtain political asylum in the European Union. The principal route of legal in-migration in the last two decades has been family re-unification.

In recent years, there has been a trend towards a more open migration policy, establishing opportunities for certain categories of migrants, such as the German green card scheme for IT specialists or the expansion of the UK's highly skilled migration programme.

Civic stratification has assumed a new significance given the rising number of non-citizen residents on European territory. The non-citizen population has risen in the UK, Italy, Spain and Germany throughout the eighties and nineties.[2]

The European Union has brought some leveling of status for EU citizens in other EU countries compared to nationals (Soysal 1994). The number and share of third country nationals, however, has also risen in almost all EU countries. While there is some evidence that international conventions and human rights have begun to play a larger role in national

---

[2] In Germany, the number of foreign residents has stagnated since 2001. In France it has declined during the nineties partly due to naturalization.

politics (Soysal 1994, Sassen 1996), there have not only been gains for non-citizen over the past decades. The trend towards a restrictive migration policy has made residents on the territory more depended on their present status. Most governments have sought to extend their powers to deport unemployed or offending foreign residents well before 9/11. The security laws enacted in many Western countries after that day have rendered foreign citizen even more vulnerable to the state's executive (IBA 2003).

The recent accession of ten new member states to the EU has added the Baltic's large Russian minorities to the number of Third Country Nationals. It has also created a further status: Citizen of Poland, the Baltics and other new members remain EU-citizen in waiting for the duration of the 7-year- transition period in Germany and Austria.

The growing population of illegal residents – some of whom have entered illegally, others have been illegalized while already on the territory – live the extreme end of the status hierarchy. In practice they are without rights and lack any legal protection.

New borders in the city
These developments of migration control have marked a departure from national territoriality, characterized by a clear demarcation of the inside and the outside. They underline the fact, that political space is perspectival, i.e. its form depends on one's position in complex social relationships. Borders are borders for some people but not others. We have also seen the rise of overlapping jurisdictions, outward projection of territoriality, internal borders, and extraterritoriality.

For cities, this new complexity of political space has not meant a return to a premodern autonomy or its own fortified borders. Recently, governments have put in place explicit spatial restrictions on a local level for some migrants. It has become common for asylum seekers to be assigned an obligatory place of residence while their application is being reviewed (Robinson 2003). In Germany, even recognised refugees remain confined to a given district (Landkreis) and have to apply for permission to leave it. Refugees caught outside their district without permission are brought to court and risk fines or imprisonment (see Figure 1).

Fig. 1: "Germany has many borders for refugees". Poster of the Advocacy Group Pro Asyl.

Against the metaphor of the rise of a "neo-medieval" spatial order, it is worth emphasizing that urban authorities in general have no control over access to city territory and the city or city region is usually not an entity to which access can be restricted to. Neither are spatial restrictions enforced in the name of the city. Yet urban spaces are affected by the larger process of restructuring of the political space by migration and the new migration regime.

The growth of budget airline travel has placed the most highly frequented national borders within large city-regions since the 1960s and 70s but especially during the 1980s and 1990s. The number of entries to the UK by airplane per year has increased almost threefold between 1982 and 2002, and has increased faster then entry overall (ONS 2002).

These borders are heavily fortified in almost all airports. While European integration has meant that for some intra-EU journeys passport controls have been lifted, the level of surveillance may actually have increased through the introduction of carrier liability. Carriers have long been obliged to transport ineligible passengers back to their country of departure at their own expense. Recently these measures have been extended to include heavy fines. In 1994, nine EU member states passed laws to extend the responsibility of carriers. "Thus, where the move toward free movement of persons has become critical to full European integration, the abolition of checks at internal borders has become essentially offset by the flurry of legislation and implementation of the carriers' liability to check passengers. Indeed, more stringent security checks at airports – of identity cards, tickets, boarding passes, baggage and so on – have made the absence of passport controls virtually irrelevant" (Guiraudon and Lahav 2000: 185).

For a number of city-regions within the European Union, the 1990s have also brought the phenomenon of extraterritoriality within their areas: In key airports within the European Union -such as Frankfurt am Main in Germany, Roissy Charles de Gaulle in France, Leonardo da Vinci in Rome- waiting zones have been created, wherein immigrants are detained. These immigrants are conceived to not be formally on the territory of the host country, which means that constitutional guarantees do not apply (Hughes 1998; UNHCR 1996; UNHCR 2000). Borders here are extended into zones of lawlessness (Agamben 1998; Noll 2003).

Schengen has spread border controls throughout the territory and has extended the power of border police on the territory and of police in general. Police is now authorised to execute controls "independent of suspicion or incident." The new role of private actors and civil society in monitoring immigration also geographically disperses controls. These new and dispersed powers to control become effective, however, only in concrete relationships, and become border controls especially for non-citizen, who throughout Western Europe are concentrated in large cities. Two types of controls can be distinguished. Some check for legality of stay and directly threaten the ability to stay on the territory. These are border controls in a classic sense and include controls by the border police but in some cases also regular police controls.

Others, which regulate access to resources that all citizen have automatic access to, such as work, or in some cases health care, can be called border controls of a second order. In this context, the British plan to introduce ID cards receives its real significance. The introduction of ID cards in Britain will extend border controls throughout the public health system and the school system.

The number and share of non-citizen in cities has risen dramatically in the past two decades. Let me discuss the cases of Germany, Italy, and the United Kingdom. In Western Germany's cities the percentage of foreign residents is consistently higher in cities than in the territory at large, where it lay at 7.3 percent in 2003. Offenbach in Hesse has the largest percentage of foreign residents in its population (25.8 percent). In Frankfurt, 22.4 percent of residents were not citizen of Germany in 2003, in Stuttgart 22.3, in Hamburg 15.3 percent in 2003 and in Berlin 12.3 percent. These shares have been rising strongly throughout the eighties and the mid-nineties with some stabilization in the new millennium.

In Italy, the share and the number of non-citizen has risen sharply in all major cities in the decade between 1991 and 2001. A fifth of non-citizen live in Italy's seven cities with over 500 000 inhabitants. Rome (3.9), Milan (7), Florence (5.3) and Verona (5.3), Torino (4.0) Bologna (3.9) have the highest shares of foreign residents (Istat 2004).

In the UK, London in particular has gained dramatically in net-inflow of international migration 1991-2001. At least 85 % of asylum seekers live in London. Other urban areas, such as Manchester, Bradford, Cambridge, Leicester, Loughborough Birmingham, Bedford, and Slough show a concentration of residents born abroad (ONS 2004).[10]

These numbers do not include the number of illegal residents, who are most strongly affected by the city's new internal borders.

Conclusion
The transnationalisation of migration control has contributed to establishing complex new forms of territoriality. Borders today cross-cut each other, borders are extended into zones, and borders are in the heart of the territory. Given the rising non-citizen population and the rising number of people on the move, we need to focus attention on the fact that

---

[3] The number of residents born overseas is not an ideal measurement of those civically disadvantaged. Some of those born overseas might be UK citizens born; on the other hand these numbers exclude people born in the UK without full citizenship rights.

borders always raise the question: borders for whom? Social scientists have yet to fully come to terms with the perspectival nature of political space.

Governments have over the past two decades institutionalised these new forms of control and new restrictions partly as a reaction to struggles by migrants and their supporters. They were designed to help circumvent some of the routes that resistance has traditionally taken, such as constitutional guarantees on a national level and national jurisprudence. Yet it is important to note that this new regime also creates its own new instabilities. In the 1990s, a novel form of transnational resistance a-gainst the control of migration and migrants has arisen, which questions these mechanisms of the control of movement.

The anti-border movement is new in that it directly targets the spatial dimension of migration control. Groups such as no one is illegal are also genuinely transnational and local at the same time. It should be clear from what has been said that cities will be a key site of this struggle.

References:

Agamben, G. (1998) Homo Sacer : Sovereign Power and Bare Life. Stanford.
Agnew, J. (1994) The territorial trap: the geographical assumptions of international relations theory. In: Review of International Political Economy, 1(1), 53-80.
Agnew, J. and Corbridge, S. (1995) Mastering Space. Hegemony, Territory and International Political Economy.(London.
Brenner, N. (2004) State Spaces. Oxford.
Cruz, A. (1993) Schengen, Ad-Hoc Immigration Group and other European Intergovernmental Bodies. Brussels.
-,   (1994) Carrier Liability in the member states of the European. Brussels.
Dohse, K. (1985) Auslaendische Arbeiter und buergerlicher Staat. Berlin.
Duevell, F. (2002) Die Globalisierung des Migrationsregimes. Zur neuen Einwanderunspolitik in Europa. Berlin.
Duevell, F. (2003) The globalisation of migration control. www.noborder.org.
EU (2000) http://europa.eu.int/comm/development/cotonou/agreement_de.htm.
Fassin, D.,Morice, A. and Quiminal. C. (1997) Les lois de L'inhospitabilité/ Paris.
Geddes, A. (1988) Breaching Fortress Europe? An institutionalist approach to analysis of migrant interest representation at EU level. Florence.
Geddes, A. (2001) International migration and state sovereignty in an integrating Europe. In: International Migration, 39(6), 21-42.
Grawert, R. (1973) Staat und Staatsangehoerigkeit. Verfassungsgeschichtliche Untersuchung zur Enstehung der Staatsangehoerigkeit. Berlin.
Guiraudon, V.and Lahav, G. (2000) A Reappraisal of the State Sovereignty Debate. The case of Migration Control. In: Comparative Political Studies, 33(2), 163-185.
Hughes, J.and Field, O. (1998) Recent Trends in the Detention of Asylum Seekers in Western Europe. In: Hughes, J.and Liebaut, F. (eds.): Detention of Asylum Seekers in Europe: Analysis and Perspectives.The Hague.
IBA (International Bar Association) (2003) Internacional Terrorism: Legal Challenges

and Responses. London.

Istat (2004) 14 censimento della popolazione. La popolazione straniera residente in Italia. www. istat.it.

Joppke, C. (1997) Asylum and state sovereignty - A comparison of the United States, Germany, and Britain. In: Comparative Political Studies, 30(3), 259-298.

Lavenex, S. (1999) Safe Third Countries. Extending the EU Asylum and Immigration Policies to Central and Eastern Europe. Budapest.

-,   and Uocarer, E. (2002) The Emergent Eu Migration Regime and its External Impact. In: Lavenex, S.and Uocarer, E. (eds.): Migration and the Externalities of European Integration. Lanham.

Leitner, H. (1997) Reconfiguring the spatiality of power: The construction of a supranational migration framework for the European Union. In: Political Geography, 16(2), 123-143.

Lockwood, D. (1996) Civic Integration and Class Formation. In: British Journal of Sociology, 47, 531-50.

Meijers, H. et al. (1991) Schengen: Internationalisation of Central chapters of the Law on Aliens, Refugees, Privacy, Security and the Police. Utrecht.

Miller, M. (1995) Employer sanctions in France: From the campaign against illegal alien employment to the campaign against illegal work. Washington, D.C.

Morris, L. (2000) Rights and control in the management of migration: the case of Germany. In: The Sociological Review, 48 (2).

-,   (2003) Managing Contradiction: Civic Stratification and migrants' rights. In: The International Migration Review, (37 (1).

Negt A.and Kluge, A. (1993) Vernunft und Eigensinn. Frankfurt.

Noll, G. (2003) Visions of the Exceptional: Legal and Theoretical Issues Raised by Transit Processing Centers and Protection Zones. In: European Journal of Migration and Law, 5(3).

ONS (Office for National Statistics) (2002) Travel Trends – A Report on the International Passenger Survey, www.statistics.gov.uk.

ONS (Office for National Statistics) (2004) Census 2001: Key statistics for urban areas in England and Wales, www.statistics.gov.uk.

Robinson, V. (2003) Spreading the "Burden"? Bristol.

Sassen, S. (1996) Losing Control? Sovereignty in an Age of Globalization. New York.

-,   (1998) The de-facto transnationalisation of immigration policy, in: C. Joppke (ed.) Challenge to the nation-state: Immigration in Western Europe and the United States. New York.

Soysal, Y. (2004) Limits of Citizenship. Migrants and postnational membership. Chicago.

Torpey, J. (2000) The Invention of the Passport. Surveillance, Citizenship and the State. Cambridge.

UNHCR (1996) Detention of Asylum-Seekers in Europe. Geneva.

UNHCR (2000) Reception standards for asylum seekers in the European Union. Geneva.

van Selm, J. (2002) Immigrants and Asylum or Foreign Policy: The EU's Approach to Migrants and Their Countries of Origin. In: Lavenex, S.and Uocarer, E. (eds.): Migration and the Externalities of European Integration. Lanham.

Urbanization of the Region or Regionalization of the City? Immigrants and urban development in Thessaloniki

Giorgos Kandylis

Introduction

As in other fields of social research, including among other things work relations, capital accumulation, housing provision and immigration flows, a 'critique from the South' (Gregson et al. 1999; also see Kourliouros 2003) has emerged in recent years concerning the spatial organization of cities in the era of so-called post-fordism and (in a way consequently) postmodernism. Socio-spatio-economic discourses about flexibility, restructuring, deregulation and so on, have enabled many scholars to search for their functional equivalents in the social systems of the Euro-pean South, where important 'postmodern' spatial arrangements do-minated, much before they be treated as requirements in advanced capitalist countries (Leontidou 1993). The peculiar pattern of urban development, composed by piecemeal, resisting to planning expansion, attaining to incorporate new massive populations without being based on industrialization, could be represented to some extent in the dialectics between urbanization (of regions) and regionalization (of cities). The Greek cities, exemplary cases of rapid, 'spontaneous' and unplanned urbanization of rural land which produced large urban areas of a semi-urban social as well as natural environment, are at the heart of this issue. In a context of low industrialization, other than fordist forms of work organization and exploitation (not only necessitating means of collective consumption, but also leaving enough space for self-development) have been crucial for urban development.

In that sense, one could attend the historical evolution of Greek cities through the transformations in labour integration into urban areas, namely through the ways immigrants of different periods became pro-ducers of urban space. I think that such an approach of 'labour geo-graphy' (Herod 1997 and 2003) could be very useful in the analysis of the contemporary urban transformations in Greece, considering its cities' new kind of participation in the 'age of (labour) migration' (Castles and Miller 1993). The emphasis of this study is given on the research of immigrants' everyday lives from a point of view that insists on their social role, as of carriers of labour power. Immigrants' labour (re)produces the urban environment, transforming spatial structures. It is through their participation in the production of social values that immigrants them-selves become subjects into their new social life. Farther, the dominantly unplanned pattern of urban development could be theorized as a pattern of urban-development-through-immigration. I propose a comparative study between different historical migratory movements towards Greek cities.

For decades, almost any attempt at studying the special features of urban development in Greece used to start from a central question: the factors that were responsible for what was considered as a differentiation or a divergence of the development pattern of the Greek cities, when compared with the urban development pattern in most (considered as "typically capitalist") European countries. Besides the evident disadvantage of such a comparative approach, that of the use of an unavoidably simplified and undifferentiated theory for urban development in advanced capitalism, another misleading hypothesis was often implied. The urban development conditions in Greece should be examined in terms of an underdeveloped – or not integrated – capitalist society that produced cities full of discontinuities, gaps and failures.

This kind of approach, part of a more general tendency to theorize the Greek social system through the 'norms' of the 'capitalist' center, was proved useful for the interpretation of the structure of the international capitalist chain and the position of Greece in it. However, emphasizing on divergent characteristics was hardly a convenient method for studying particularities in the field of spatial organization. Insisting in ascertainment concerning spatial disorder, limited spatial integration of certain areas, diffractions in market exploitation of land, discontinuities in the urban network etc, resulted to the disregard of the special development potential. The main consideration about Greek cities reflected a description of the abnormal, instead of a discussion about the actual development procedure – which was often very important and rapid. Moreover, such a discourse was not only the main direction of academic research. It also dominated the views about and the implementation of urban planning, producing for example provisions about heavy industry in cities where industrialization had never been the central precondition for development.

Low capital accumulation and restricted industrialization, the early expansion of the tertiary sector, the small size of land property, the comparative importance of middle social strata and the restricted development of the welfare state were some of the features that were at first taken to be "typically Greek" and then to explain the complicated land use pattern, the insufficiency of infrastructure, the irregular (and often illegal) construction, the degradation of the environment and the lack of spatial planning in Greek cities. I do not argue that this approach was false (on the contrary it contributed a lot to the comprehension of contemporary Greek society), but it was not apt to understand what was successful in the Greek cities, beside what went wrong. The rapid incorporation of refugee and immigrant populations, the resolution of housing issues, the important amelioration of living conditions, the income increase and a social division that was not straightly expressed in space are some of the 'good' and usually disregarded aspects of a peculiar urban development.

Vaiou and Chatzimichalis (1997) underlined the similarities between the development pattern of the Greek urban space and that of the semi-urban area of Italy, extending from Trentino-Altro Adige to Lazio and to Marche. In relevant literature, this area has been called 'Third Italy' (at first by Arnaldo Bagnasco in his homonymous work in 1977), in the sense of its intermediate character between the industrialized North and the agricultural South. Special emphasis has been given on the role of small enterprises and on subcontracting networks, resulted in diffused and horizontal organization of production.

The development pattern of "Third Italy" has been considered as a remarkable response to the declining fordist organization of production. Flexibility, specialization, horizontal networking are contemplated as requirements for the transition to post-fordism. However, at least two reservations have to be kept in mind from the beginning. First, that there is no sufficient evidence that what was successful in Italy or in the city of Thessaloniki would work anywhere else, in different socio-spatial contexts. Secondly, that flexible development was not free of collateral costs, such as the environmental one or the intensification of obscure (for not fordist) labour exploitation.

The dialectics of urban development in Thessaloniki
The city of Thessaloniki is the second largest urban agglomeration in Greece and a familiar field for urban planning innovation almost continually since its incorporation in the Greek state in the early 20th century (Yerolympos 1996). Already an important Mediterranean port in the era of late Ottoman Empire and a melting pot of different ethnic groups and cultures for centuries, Thessaloniki preserved its role as a major port and commuting center in Northern Greece. Its development rates were quite high during the post-war period, both in manufacturing and services, following the development potential of Athens (Pantazis 2000). The collapse of state capitalism regimes in Eastern Europe and the Balkans and the subsequent end of the dichotomy in its international neighborhood are deemed to have contributed to the restoration of the city's role as a central point of economic activity in the Balkans, the Caspian and the East Mediterranean basin. They definitely led, up to now, to the remarkable wave of immigration, which tends to restore the city's multiethnic character.

Exploring its historical preconditions from a labour perspective, one could sum up the terms of urban development in Thessaloniki after the World War II in the following selected (but multifold) points - although producing a rather simplifying diagram:

Remarkable immigration flows. Immigration flows resulted in a rapid urbanization of the city. The preceding refugees' settlement in the '20s was followed by the rural exodus after the War and by the new wave of international migration. Together these migrations constitute a more or less permanent influx of potentially urban population (see Sandis 1973 for a case study in Athens). The population size of the urban complex increased at impressive rates between 1951 and 1971 (more than 80% considering the expansion of the estimated as urban area) to be relatively stabilized after 1980 (Petrakos et al. 2000).

Diffused industrialization. The development of manufacturing of low capital accumulation not only meant a rather small average size of industrial productive units, but also an extended and operative sub-contracting network that connected different parts of the city into an aggregate economic structure (Vaiou and Hadjimichalis 1997). Employment in such units was proved very important as much to the economic integration of new populations, as to their positive social mobility.

Informal economy/labour. Informality was and continues to be a major component of the national economy, affecting all sectors of production. Some estimation raises the magnitude of informal activities to 1/3 or even 1/2 of the formal GNP (Delivani 1991; Kanelopoulos 1995). Informal labour was a substantial channel towards prosperity for urban populations, as it is today for new immigrants.

Multiple employment. Parallel employment in multiple positions, salaried as well as self-employed, formal as well as informal, 'enabled' significant parts of the population to avoid strict dependence on salaried work relations. From an additional point of view, multiple employment was a safety valve in a production system that did not produce massive jobs in the formal, salaried sector. This argument refers to the never-ending discussion about the class nature of the Greek social system (see Tsoukalas 1986 and Petmezidou-Tsoulouvi 1987 for two contradicting theses) but should not imply a general detachment from work.

Small land property. Small average land property, widespread over social strata is a historically formed condition that has not been seriously threatened up to now (Maloutas 1990). Small property was to some extent a political decision, targeted at an ordered assimilation of migrating populations, in the absence of positive welfare provisions.

Special conditions of housing production. The housing construction system, usually referred to as typically Greek, but actually being a part of a distinctive southern-European housing production system (Judith et al. 2004), was dominated by unplanned and even irregular/illegal housing construction. Land supply was also reinforced by institutional measures, such as the increase of building heights and antiparochi - a legal provision about the possibility of a land owner and a constructor to establish a joint corporation for the construction of a single building that permitted the continuous exploitation of urban land by enterprises of very small capital accumulation. Housing construction was also a significant lever for development in the whole economic circuit, with its 'forward' and 'backward' connections. Family practices also played a significant role (Maloutas 1990; Allen et al. 2004).

Typical spatial structure. As that of most other major Greek cities, Thessaloniki's spatial structure happens to be rather crowded and constricted, notwithstanding keeping the conditions of human-scale space. Almost chaotic urban segments, produced by rapid unplanned development based on equally rapid and unplanned labour integration, circumfuse ordered urban areas, produced by certain enterprises of city rationalization. Dividing lines between the urban tissue and the rural surroundings, as well as between private and public space are often vaporous.

The whole circuit provides an urban ensemble some parts of which are of a rather doubtful urban character, although participating into a less or more single economic structure. An effort of description should include, among many other things, neighborhoods that seem to be permanently under construction, of low-cost housing and poor infrastructure; traffic that exceeds what one would expect according to population size; a city center that preserves its importance in organizing the whole complex; urban segments facing functional and environmental degradation; the incapacity to determine the actual borders of different parts and of the whole city; the undefined pattern of land uses: all ingredients of an early regionalized city of a scale different from the Western European one. One might as well describe this urban phenomenon as an early urbanization of the region, since an important expansion took place in a quite short period, nearly without any welfare provisions and imposing a very low cost on the national budget. Producing new urban space, immigrants' labour urbanized the surrounding rural space. According to a certain approach, new urban populations achieved to put some parts of the urban space under their own control, having the ability to permanently resist state interventions (Leontidou 1989).
This development pattern was strongly linked to social reproduction procedures, as a multifaceted equivalent of underdeveloped welfare (Economou 1988; Maloutas 1988). Its linkage with the clientelist

structure of the political system has permitted the prolongation of its duration over several decades. However, it is now being challenged, having some of the system's stable terms changed. One of such crucial term is the appearance of a somehow 'unpredicted' wave of international immigration that (not surprisingly, if one takes into account the above historical circumstances) Thessaloniki and Greek cities in general were not prepared to receive. Moreover, major disadvantages had already become apparent before the massive arrival of international immigrants.

Immigrants in the city

More than a decade after the very first appearance of what was meant to be the large wave of new immigration to Greece, the discussion has necessarily gone further than the simple ascertainment of the reversal of the historical pattern of a country of emigration. Immigration to Greece, as many scholars have noticed, belongs to the broader context of immigration to Southern European countries (King 2000; Baldwin-Edwards 2001). It is a point of view that proved useful in turning the scientific attention once again to migration processes themselves (Anthias 2000).

While during the '80s a certain inflow of foreign immigrants, mainly from some African countries and the Middle East had already been established, not mentioning the beginning of 'repatriation' from the countries of the Soviet Union, massive immigration was a moment of the early '90s, just after the collapse of the state capitalism regimes in Eastern Europe. Immigrants from Albania were going to reign in the formation of the general phenomenon ever since then. A general estimation raised the total number of immigrants in Greece in 2000 to about 500,000 or one tenth of the economically active population – the highest proportion in the Southern European countries (Fakiolas 2000). In 2001 the general registration of population recorded more than 760,000 foreigners compared with about 167,000 foreigners in 1991). A rough estimation exclusively based on ethnicity (in order to exclude non-Greek citizens that would not be considered to participate in the 'from below' pattern of immigration to the South of Europe) gives a magnitude of more than 650,000 immigrants, still not including the non-documented ones that could not be recorded (Kandylis forthcoming). In the census data of 2001 a population of more than 50,000 non-European citizens were found to dwell in urban municipalities of Thessaloniki, representing a little less than 6% of the total usual resident population (National Census 2001). According to a registration that took place in 1998, in the context of the legalization procedure that the Greek state put in progress, about 26,500 non-documented immigrants lived in Thessaloniki and the surrounding rural area up to then (Cavounidis 2002/2003).

It is worth mentioning that available data tend to support the thesis of feminization of immigration. A significant part of the immigrants, especially of certain origins, are women and family immigration has already a very important presence. Family reunification seems to take place at a considerably more rapid rate than that in most countries of advanced capitalism, while 'reunification' itself becomes an inappropriate term when members of families practically immigrate together.

Apart from all other aspects of immigrants' social integration (the never ending catalog might include issues of employment, legalization procedures, language, education, management of cultural diversity, racist attitudes etc.), housing is a crucial point in the process of obtaining a position in the city.

Any effort to measure certain conditions of immigrants' life in Greece faces the obstacle of insufficient and ambiguous available data, due to the important presence of non-documentd immigrants in the total immigrant population and the slow correspondence of the Greek agencies. Even though there are quite reliable indications about demographic divisions by ethnicity, gender, age groups etc the picture becomes relatively unclear when one takes employment and work relations into consideration - and almost loose when considering settlement and housing conditions. Accordingly, it becomes necessary to utilize either previous surveys or new field research. Moreover, field research in the city's neighborhoods is needed in order to investigate what statistics could hardly describe, namely lived stories of immigration/urban integration that constitute a primary material for the representation of labour geography. For the purposes of this article, apart from previous literature (Lamprianidis and Lymperaki 2001; Nitsiakos 2001; Syrigou 2000; Cavounidis 2002; Hatziprokopiou 2003), some additional information was obtained through interviews mainly held in three "immigrant" neighborhoods in the periphery of Thessaloniki:[1]

Nikopolis, a spatially isolated part of the city on the borders of the municipalities of Stavroupoli and Polihni. A significant number of immigrants of Greek origin, coming from the countries of the former Soviet Union, live there. Many have selected this area, situated on the fringes of the city, to buy a small piece of land and build a house by themselves, in an insecure and risky (from a legal viewpoint) way.

Oreokastro, a quite remote suburb with many residents belonging to middle strata. A number of Albanian immigrants have settled here. An interesting pattern of employment is observed, as most immigrants work not far from their residence, men in construction and women in domestic works.

---

[1] Most interviews were held during the elaboration of my PhD thesis at the University of Thessaly (Kandylis forthcoming). Interviews in Phinikas were a part of the Local Governance project, supported by the European Union. University of Thessaly was one of the participants

Phinikas, situated on the opposite alter end of the city, is a neighborhood that occurred through a public housing project in the '60s, and nowadays attracts immigrant families. Its location in the middle of a rapidly developed urban area (right on the axis that leads to the city airport) happens to be another serious challenge in this case.

It proved necessary to reduce the field research to the two major immigration groups of the city, those of Albanian immigrants and immigrants coming from countries of the former Soviet Union. The two cases are not, of course, identical. The distinctive approach is evident in policy analysis, since the latter are supposed to be treated as people of Greek origin,[2] introducing further motivation for comparative analysis.

A detailed presentation of different housing careers exceeds the capacity of this article. Instead, we could stress some nodal points that many housing itineraries intersect. Thus, during their early steps in the city, immigrants' residence directly depends either on their employment or on existing informal networks that support their settlement. On the first occasion, they usually live near their place of work or even in the place itself, where a shelter is provided by the employer (as it is often the case in Oreokastro). The importance of informal but personalized work relations becomes very evident in this case, giving a cultural additional value to work. Personal relations between employers and employees are often considered as an indication of an immigrant's personal value and his/her success, a quite traditional method to soften devaluation of work. On the other hand, living with relatives, friends or other persons of the same origin, could be described as a method for initial protection out of the very field of work - or even as a first field of resistance, if one considers irregular activities of informal networks to facilitate 'illegal' arrival.

The reasonable next step of the housing careers concerns rented houses in different parts of the city, selected not only according to rent prices, but also (not rarely) through informal migratory networks. In the absence of welfare provisions, there is a reasonable correlation between tenure and employment of (some of) the members of households. A remarkable residential mobility among successive rented dwellings in same or different parts is often described in immigrants' testimonies, representing a continuous residential roaming around the city. Despite personal tragedies it could be supposed that the general level of housing conditions in rented dwellings has been improved during the last decade, usually through personal work that transforms old apartments or even dilapidated old cottages.

---

[2] Immigrants of Greek origin from the former Soviet Union are often referred to as 'repatriated'. It is not but an inaccurate term, carrying a certain national and emotional charge.

As soon as immigrant families have the possibility to obtain their own house, they tend to move to neighborhoods where land prices are affordable. Very interestingly, a specific part of immigrants are still able to possess a private dwelling not only through free housing market, but also through irregular construction, repeating traditional housing practices. This usually means a movement to the borders of the city and a simultaneous entrapment in the fragmented space.

Therefore descriptions related to the space of "repatriated" immigrants might differ from descriptions concerning Albanians. Albanians seem to face more difficulties in having access to private property, while "repatriated" immigrants enjoy some kind of welfare provisions (even the possibility to take a housing fees loan, or a certain degree of tolerance before irregular construction), thanks to their very origin (Papadopoulou-Symeonidou 1999). However, both groups experience some degree of spatial enclosure: new shelters for the latter, might indicate the beginning of a more normal urban life, but they reproduce some kind of spatial exclusion, not necessarily less important than that of the low-cost apartments in central city districts. In an urban context where social mobility is not necessarily connected to residential mobility (Maloutas 2004), one can now observe almost nomadic intra-urban movements that signify, at least in the short term, residential but no social mobility. Albanians' wandering around city's neighborhoods discourages explicit spatial expression of community relations, while some 'repatriated' immigrants have the opportunity to enjoy parts of the urban space, in a way that resembles to spatially concentrated, urbanized communities of the past. However, these new communities seem for the moment to lack the possibility to control their own space (as other ones did a few decades ago), due to more pressure from the state and more competition from the construction capital.

An adjacent field of research concerns the presence of immigrants in the public and semi-public spaces of the city. One could choose among umpteen moments of the respective spatio-temporal continuum. Public space is an organizing field for several activities, including work, free time, survival and well-being, as well as an expression of community solidarity. Streets and squares, parks and shops where one can meet members of different ethnicities and languages create a picture that rings a bell from the city's past. Deficiencies of private spaces might explain some part of the practices expressed in common spaces. However, the tendency to appropriate the commons goes much further than this point, to the right to reproduce everyday life in the city.

Seeking for a synopsis, we could notice some impressive similarities between the pattern of shelter (and therefore urban) development concerning internal migrants in previous decades and that of shelter development for new immigrants (in the cases that such a shelter begins to exist).

The massive arrival of population. Immigration meant an important increase of urban population and more especially of the population of Thessaloniki. Even though urban population increase was much larger in the case of rural exodus, it is worth mentioning the rapid rate of increase in both cases, as well as the fact that new migration becomes more important if one considers its proportion to the total active indigenous population.

The similar circumstances of absence of positive housing policy. Living in the era of the end of active urban planning in Greece (Economou 2000; Papamihos and Hastaoglou 2000), internal migrants were obliged to manage their housing needs almost by themselves. Despite housing provision, the circumstances were not at last very different for the refugees from Minor Asia. New immigrants are obliged to follow personal and family strategies, with very few or in the absence of policy provisions.

The similar expectances on 'housing itineraries'. In both cases, after a shorter or longer period of rental, owner occupation becomes a central point of family practices (although these practices are at present more rarely successful in the case of new immigrants). This effort requires an amount of personal and family savings accumulated through hard work. It also uses previous savings that had been accumulated in order to support migration.

The collateral appearance of almost *exclusively residential neighborhoods*, featuring a very low level of infrastructure and hardly any employment opportunities. Migrants living there have to work somewhere else in the city. As it will be argued below, community formation supported by that kind of spatial concentration, follows a rather rougher road than in the past.

The extended use of informal networks of families, relatives and friends, as an indispensable precondition not only during the first steps in the new urban environment, but also for long-term planning of housing solutions (Maloutas 1990). Testimonies about the first stages of house construction, when most residents of the neighborhood leave their work in order to help in heavy construction works, is not only typical, but also dia-chronic. People facing problems in mobilizing and profiting from an informal network, such as women and single-parent families, are likely to be in a more risky situation.

The significance of irregular/illegal construction of housing, obvious in the case of internal migrants and still present today (see Fatouros and Hadjimichalis 1974 for a case study), although concerning only a small part of new immigrants, as mentioned above.

Despite the presence of the above common characteristics, one should not simply suppose that an undifferentiated pattern continues to exist through four or five decades. A number of further clarifications seem to transform the general picture.

First of all, different immigrant groups do not follow identical patterns of housing. Albanians of non-Greek origin face more difficulties in their effort to move to a private house. No loans are provided to them and no attempts to enter into the irregular construction circle have been noticed. Non-documented immigrants should be supposed to be in a remarkably worse and more dangerous condition. On the other hand "repatriated" immigrants do sometimes have access to housing loans and more possibilities to take advantage of irregular housing. A discriminative approach, (unknown in the past, as the construction of national homogeneity averted national divisions) based on ethnic origin seems to be adopted by the Greek state.

New immigrant groups have to enter into a land market, which appears to be more liberated than the one that their precedents were familiar with. Institutional and implied regulations protecting small land property and its exploitation have not disappeared, but new residents find themselves competing with construction projects of more intense capital accumulation, even (but not only) in the field of housing production, These projects are sometimes parts of a more general effort to rationalize the urban complex through major and minor urban interventions (mainly urban renewals and transportation arrangements). This is remarkably evident in Nikopolis, where irregular self-production of housing by 'repatriated' migrants, is situated next to or inside cells of relatively large private housing construction and in Phinikas where large commercial units surround old public dwellings. Of course, what seems to be competition at the moment might produce new opportunities later, but rather not in the field of urban space appropriation.

New immigrants face some new obstacles such as the illegal status and more importantly a legalization procedure that tends to recycle illegal status or their stigmatization in the host society (see Pavlou 2001), both more crucial in the case of Albanians. Irregularity, usually cited in public discourses as 'illegality', is proved a serious barrier against the appropriation as well as the very presence in public spaces, especially in times of intense police controls and expulsions (known as 'broom-operations').

What has changed and what remains?
New immigrants in Thessaloniki have found themselves in an urban environment that already had a large 'experience' in integrating migrating populations. Sometimes, they even settle in neighborhoods that were at first formed by their precedents, neighborhoods that are consequently

characterized by nearly permanent migration. The procedure of obtaining some place in the competitive urban space still retains many 'conservative' elements of the traditional pattern. And from a specific point of view, the integration of their labour into the system of production and reproduction, involving informality, irregularity, multiplicity, ephemerality and uncertainty resembles to that of former migrants to the city. However, there is quite sufficient indication that things change. What is new seems to move simultaneously towards a more liberal approach on housing issues and towards a perspective of a more general rationalization of urban space. It seems to me that there are at least three emerging implications:

First, no facilitation for immigrants' settlement and no official regard for the amelioration of their housing conditions. Immigrants of both groups have to solve their housing and shelter issues in ways that do not differ much from the past and are mainly based on individual strategies. Notwithstanding, they do so in a more structured and more competitive urban environment. Complaints about unsafety and uncertainty caused by unsolved housing and shelter issues are added to those about unemployment and economic hardship.

Secondly, a tendency to ethnic discrimination on housing and shelter conditions, although not yet resulting in a radical redefinition of the dividing lines of spatial segregation, through some schema of ghettoization.

Thirdly, an urban space put under more surveillance and control. Fragmentation of immigrants' space is not a sufficient indication thereon – more research in other fields is required. However, social control on housing issues of recently arrived population could be proved a method as restrictive as simple police surveillance, border controls and expulsions and could additionally be useful in any further effort of rationalization of space. Some scholars argue that in certain cases one could even consider the production of periphractic spaces (Psimmenos 2000).

Further research is needed if it is to connect obstacles in housing careers and in appropriating public urban space to the actual transformation of work relations. However, there is already strong evidence that new immigrants, despite superficially congener employment terms are found in more vulnerable positions, due to regional and (therefore) global economic restructuring that puts cheap labour in the middle of economic priorities in different socio-economic contexts (Migione and Quassoli 2000; Psimmenos 2001; Iosifides 2001; Castells 1996/2000). Working in conditions of 'new labour' might differ from past vulnerabilities, since temporariness, low wages, absence of social insurance and uncertainty, seem to be a part of a major devaluation of labour. Devaluing labour might be devaluing immigrants (Sassen 1994).

A more general question emerges as well, having to do with the effects of such shifts on the local development pattern. If the traditional pattern was supported by decentralized and disordered spatial organization, more rationalized control on space might destabilize economic activities that were once and still are crucial for immigrants' incorporation, e-specially in an era of decline of some informal and diffused branches, such as façon cloth production. Could for example community formation occur in different pathways, overcoming the obstacle of occurring frag-mented spaces? Could immigrant families reproduce themselves and the city's space overcoming irregularity?

Consequently, several questions occur about policies that (should) treat the city as a regionalized (or under regionalization) spatial entity. Im-migrants' labour is still producing new urban space or renovating old one. However, if the space actually left for them restricts their possibilities – and if consequently they are not able to gain control on it – new political arrangements will then be required in order to exploit their potential. On the other hand, according to some analysis, such immigration policy con-tributes to the development of xenophobic reflects in the Greek society (Kourtovik 2001). The integration of immigrants' labour into the local economy could coexist with the appearance of minor racist attitudes to some extent, but more major racist events might destabilize once again the local social relations.

New immigrants did not meet a brand new city but a city in transition that, accordingly, has not yet shaped a transparent schema for their integration. Not few of them have improved their quality of life in a short period of residence, but socio-economic and spatial barriers darken the life courses of many others. Moreover, considering the above analysis accurate, a significant oxymoron seems to occur: provision about more deregulation and more flexibility in labour market along with a more regular and structured urban space. Rationalization might be a really ob-scure state of affairs.

References:

Allen, J et al. (2004) Housing and Welfare in Southern Europe. Oxford: Blackwell.

Anthias, F. (2000) Metaphors of home: gendering new migrations in Southern Europe In Anthias, F. and Lazaridis, G. (2000) Gender and Migration in Southern Europe: women in the move, Oxford: Berg.

Anthogalidou, T. et al. (1998) Pontian immigrants from Russia: life stories. [in Greek] In: Virtual School 1(3), www.auth.gr/virtualschool/1.3/Praxis/AnthogalidouImmigration.html.

Baldwin-Edwards, M. (2001) Southern European labour markets and immigration: a structural and functional analysis. In: The Greek Labour Yearbook, Athens: Panteion University.

Castells, M. (1996/2000) The Rise of Network Society. 2nd ed. Oxford: Blackwell

Castles, S and Miller, M. (1993) The Age of Migration: international population movements in the modern world. London: MacMillan.

Cavounidis, J. (2002) Migration in southern Europe and the case of Greece. In: International Migration 40(1), pp. 45-70.

-,   (2003), Gendered patterns of immigration to Greece. In: The Greek Review of Social Research, 110, pp. 221-38.

Delivani, M. (1991) The Economics of the Greek Informal Economy. [in Greek] Athens: Papazissis.

Economou, D. (1989) Land and residence system in Greece after the War. [in Greek] In: Maloutas, T. and Economou, D. (Eds.) (1988) Problems of the development of the Welfare State in Greece: spatial and sectoral approaches. Athens: Eksantas.

-,   (2000) Urban policy in the '50s. [in Greek] In: Urban Planning in Greece from 1949 to 1974. Proceedings of 2nd Conference of Urban History and Urban Planning Association. Volos.

Fakiolas, R. (2000) Migration and unregistered labour in the Greek economy. In: King, R. et al (Eds.) Eldorado or Fortress? Migration in Southern Europe, Hampshire: Palgrave Macmillan.

Fatouros, D. and Hadjimichalis, K. (1974) Self-generated settlement in the area of Thessaloniki. In: Dousmanis, O. and Oliver, P. (Eds.) Settlements in Greece .Athens.

Gregson, N. et al. (1999) The meaning of work: some arguments for the importance of culture within formulations of work in Europe. In: European Urban and Regional Studies, 6(3), pp. 197-214.

Hatziprokopiou, P. (2003) Albanian immigrants in Thessaloniki, Greece: processes of economic and social incorporation. In: Journal of Ethnic and Migration Studies, 29(6), pp. 1033-57.

Herod, A. (1997) From a geography of labor to a labor geography: labor's spatial fix and the geography of capitalism. In: Antipode, 29(1), pp. 1-31.

-,   (2003) Workers, space, and labor geography. In: International Labor and Working-Class History, 64, pp.112-38.

Iosifides, T. (2001) Working conditions of three migrant groups in Athens. In: Marvakis, A. et al. (Eds.) Immigrants in Greece, [in Greek] Athens: Ellinika Grammata.

Kandylis, G. (forthcoming) Immigration and Social Reproduction in Greece: the case of Thessaloniki urban complex. [in Greek] PhD thesis, University of Thessaly.

Kanelopoulos, K. et al. (1995) Informal Economy and Tax Evasion: measurement and economic impacts. [in Greek] Athens: Centre of Planning and Economic Research.

King, R. (2000) Southern Europe in the changing global map of migration. In King Russel et al. (Eds.), Eldorado or Fortress? Migration in Southern Europe .Houndmills-New York: Palgrave Macmillan.

Kourliouros, E. (2003) Reflections on the economic-noneconomic debate: a radical geographic perspective from the European South. In: Antipode, 35(4), pp. 781-99.

Kourtovik, I. (2001) Immigrants: between law and legitimacy. [in Greek] In: Marvakis, A. et al. (eds) Immigrants in Greece. Athens: Ellinika Grammata.

Lamprianidis, L. and Lymperaki, A. (2001) Albanian Immigrants in Thessaloniki. [in Greek] Thessaloniki: Paratiritis.
Leontidou, L. (1989), Cities of Silence: working-class settlement in Athens and Piraeus, 1909-1940. [in Greek] Athens.
Leontidou, L. (1993) Post-modernism and the city: mediterranean versions. In: Urban Studies, 30(6), pp. 949-65.
Maloutas, T. (1988) Spatial structure and social process in (under)development of the Greek welfare state. [in Greek] In: Maloutas, T. and Economou, D. (Eds.) (1988) Problems of the development of the Welfare State in Greece: spatial and sectoral approaches. Athens: Eksantas.
-, (1990) Athens, Residence, Family. [in Greek]. Athens: Eksadas.
-, (2004) Segregation and residential mobility: spatially entrapped social mobility and its impact on segregation in Athens. In: European Urban and Regional Studies, 11(2), pp. 171-87.
Mingione, E. and Quassoli, F. (2000) The participation of immigrants in the underground economy in Italy. In: King, R., et al (Eds.) Eldorado or Fortress? Migration in Southern Europe, Hampshire: Palgrave Macmillan.
National Statistical Agency (2001). Results of 2001 National Census www.statistics.gr.
Nitsiakos, V. Testimonies of Albanian Immigrants. [in Greek] Athens: Odysseas.
Pantazis, P. (2000) Urban tissue of Thessaloniki. [in Greek] In: Maloutas, T. Social and Economic Atlas of Greece. Athens: EKKE.
Papadopoulou-Symeonidou, P. (1999) Housing and Job Accession Project for Ethnic Greeks in Thessaloniki Urban Complex. [in Greek]. Thessaloniki.
Papamihos, N. and Hastaoglou, V. (2000). Urban and spatial planning in the '60s: the case of Thessaloniki. [in Greek] In: Urban Planning in Greece from 1949 to 1974. Proceedings of 2nd Conference of Urban History and Urban Planning Association. Volos.
Pavlou, M (2001) The 'smugglers of fear': racist discourse and immigrants in the press of a candidate metropolis. [in Greek] In: Marvakis, A. et al. (Eds.) Immigrants in Greece. Athens: Ellinika Grammata.
Petmezidou-Tsoulouvi, M. (1987) Social Classes and Social Reproduction Mechanisms. [in Greek] Athens: Eksantas.
Petrakos, G. et al (2000) Recent developments in the Greek system of urban centres. In: Environment and Planning B, 27(2), pp. 169-81.
Psimmenos, I. (2000), The making of periphractic spaces: the case of Albanian undocumented female migrants in the sex industry of Athens. In: Anthias, F. and Lazaridis, G. (Eds.) (2000) Gender and Migration in Southern Europe: Women in Move, Oxford: Berg.
-, (2001) New labour and informal immigrants in metropolitan Athens. [in Greek] In: Marvakis, A. et al. (eds) Immigrants in Greece, Athens: Ellinika Grammata.
Sandis, E. (1973) Refugees and Economic Migrants in Greater Athens. Athens: National Centre of Social Research.
Sassen, S. (1994) International migration and the post-industrial city. In: The Urban Age, 2(3), pp. 3-5.
Syrigou-Rigou, E. (2000) Talking with Linda. [in Greek] Athens.
Tsoukalas, K. (1986) State, Society, Labour in Post-war Greece. [in Greek] Athens: Themelio
Vaiou, D. and Hadjimichalis, C. (1997) With the Sewing Machine in the Kitchen and the Poles in the fields: cities, regions and informal work. [in Greek] Athens: Eksadas.

Yerolympos, A. (1996) Urban Transformations in the Balkans (1820-1920): aspects of Balkan town planning and the remaking of Thessaloniki. Thessaloniki: University Studio Press.

Melting Pot or Fragmented urban regions?
Social and Spatial implications of the 'two migrations' to Spanish city regions

Michael Janoschka

1. Introduction

Since mid-1990s, the former emigration country Spain is the European Union state which has suffered to most striking modifications of social and urban habits associated with the reorientation of international migration streams. From that time, more than 2.5 million immigrants arrived to this Mediterranean country, multiplying foreign population by six in only eight years. Foreigners mainly cluster in the two principal metropolitan regions i.e. Madrid and Barcelona, the Balearic and Canary Islands and parts of the Mediterranean coastal strip (Malaga and Alicante region, Figure 1). In these areas, about approximately one out of five citizens comes from abroad (EUROSTAT 2004, INE 2004a).

A more detailed look into the existing statistical data shows the necessity to distinguish between two totally different types of migration: On the one hand, a part of the rising number of foreigners is associated with 'amenity-seeking migration', mostly undertaken by retired and elderly citizens from western and northern Europe, chiefly from the UK and German speaking countries. The phenomenon of international retirement migration can be observed in the whole Mediterranean area from the western Algarve coast in Portugal to Turkey. However, the highest con-centration and most severe spatial impact can be observed throughout the coastal strips of the Spanish mainland and the islands (King et al. 2000, Casado-Díaz et al. 2004, Rodríguez et al. 1998; Huber and O'Reilly 2004, Friedrich and Warnes 2000). Regarding data sources, it is important to note that official statistics largely underestimate foreign population. Especially considering that retired people moving to the Mediterranean tend to keep registered in their home country to preserve fiscal and health service advantages. Despite this fact, in a dozen municipalities belonging to Alicante province registers count on more EU-foreigners than Spaniards.

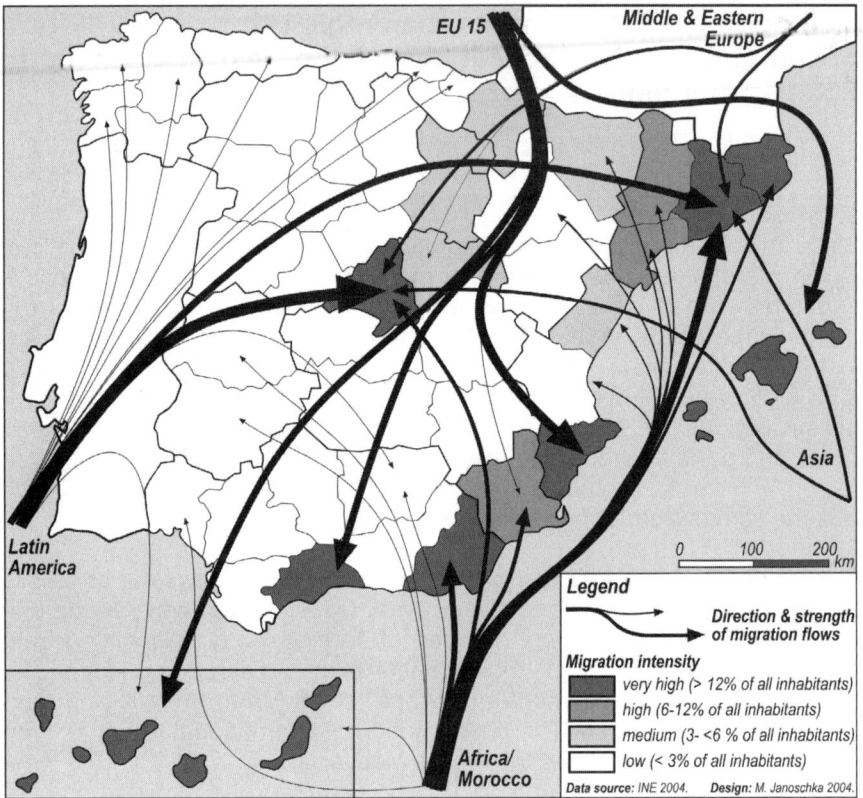

Fig. 1: The distribution of European (EU15) and Non-European immigrants in Spain

On the other hand, immigrants from outside the former 15-member European Union, mainly seek integration in (widely informal) urban labour markets of city regions such as Madrid or Barcelona. While Latin American and Eastern European immigration concentrates in the capital, Barcelona attracts a high number of residents from Sub-Saharan countries, China and some other Asian states (Riol and Janoschka 2004). In 2004, the number of immigrants only within the Metropolitan region of Madrid (about 5.8 million inhabitants) surpassed the million, i.e. ten times more than in 1998. Another concentration spot can be observed in regions where the highly specialized and competitive but labour-intensive agricultural production is found. Spain supplies most central and northern parts of the EU markets with fruits and vegetables grown in the *hinterland* of the Mediterranean coastline from Valencia to Almería. Agricultural expansion in this area would indeed have been difficult without the cheap labour force offered by Maghrebians and sub-Saharan immigrants. Further on, there is a rising need for employing migrants in leisure economy branches associated with tourism and residential tourism as shown in Figure 1 (Baldwin-Edwards and Arango 1999, Colectivo IOÉ 2003, Corkill 2001, Izcara 2002, Breuer 2004).

Within the target regions, the intensity of the mentioned two immigration flows is involving major social and spatial consequences. One important issue to consider is the multiplication of real estate market prices in the residential sector during the last decade. Several facts such as the progeny of the baby boom generation leaving the family household, an increasing suburbanization process and the acquisition of second or even third properties by wealthy Spaniards play a role on the exponential rise of housing prices (García-Montalvo 2003, Martínez and Matea 2003).
However, yearly growth rates of 15% in house prices, usual during the eight years of conservative government (i.e. 1996 to march 2004), can only be explained by the flow of immigrants towards Spain, which is occurring more intensively than anywhere in the European Union (EUROSTAT 2004, European Central Bank 2003, López 2001, INE 2004$_b$, *El Mundo* 2003).

Spanish coastal regions are especially developing towards a „laboratory of globalization" (Claret 2004), where the "new and poor" immigration from the southern and eastern hemisphere and the "rich residentialism" from northern Europe strongly clash. Potential conflicts for the physical and symbolic appropriation of urban spaces may proliferate within a situation of strong suburbanization led by an increasing Spanish middle class (Wehrhahn 2003). Since immigrants were a small group in Mediterranean countries until a decade ago, such states have limited experience in dealing with social and spatial problems with foreigners, which may exacerbate the occurrence of conflicts (De Lucas 2004, Carens 2004). Although the economic basis for integration in Spain is still intact (e.g. de-creasing unemployment rate, rising wages, improving social transfer system, high demand for less qualified and labour intensive work in lower income categories; Siebel 2004), the phenomenon is resolved as an "individual task". The concept of state-organized integration processes is barely restricted to the European legal frame and until recently, integration discourses were not a part of the social debate. In terms of immigration politics, Spain seems to repeat the same mistakes made by central European nations during the period of the *Gastarbeiter* (i.e. guest worker) regime (Kreienbrink 2004). The actual distribution of social and spatial re-sources and most negotiation mechanisms in Spain are bound to ethnic motivations and ruled by command and market laws.
Spain and especially the two city regions of Madrid and Alicante are excellent examples to discuss processes observable to a lower degree

throughout broader regions of southern Europe. Further discussion will concentrate on central topics related to the antonyms "integration" and "fragmentation". Especial attention will be paid to the analysis of spatial impacts and conflicts deriving from the massive migration process taking place during the last decade. On the other hand, the mentioned individual and "private" social integration mechanisms carried out by exogenous dwellers will be addressed and analysed. The paper will conclude with a discussion of some political consequences associated with the overwhelming migration process occurring in Spain.

2. Spatial Integration or Urban Fragmentation?
Effects of immigration on Spanish Urban Regions

The terms ‚fragmentation' and ‚fragmented city region' have been widely used to characterize transformations processes of urban societies in Western Europe and the US. However, only a few authors (e.g. Janoschka and Glasze 2003) clearly defined the analytical dimensions of the mentioned fragmentation processes. Within this discussion, processes of economic and territorial reorganization are somehow understood as 'diffuse' consequences of globalization, obviating any empirical evidence (Krätke 1995; Marcuse 1997). Many authors defend the existence of a direct correlation between economic polarization and urban segregation (Sassen 2004, Wehrhahn 2000, Prévot-Shapira 2000), a statement which is not verified in Western Europe. Within this scene, the *Leitbild* of the former modern époque, which was based on the principle of an integrative and open city, is replaced by mutual seclusion strategies. Results of such changes are observable in the urban structure with the appearance of functional islands of wealth, representative places for the international finance and real estate system, highly specialized consumption or urban night life (Marcuse 2004). In parallel, less favoured urban spaces transform towards "no-go-areas" where visitors and strangers feel physically threatened (Janoschka 2002). Such real or imagined fears can also be explained through globalized economic and social trends (Low 2003).

As noted by Wood (2003) and Siebel (2004), this argumentation is based on a pessimistic approach towards urban transformation processes. Change and evolution in the postmodern society is negatively interpreted as a resilience to the new reality, exclusively considering a fictitiously improved past situation. Subsequently, the term fragmentation is one of the basic elements to characterize this new and 'undesired' quality of spatial dynamics which are represented in many urban regions through the diffusion of new physical barriers such as access-restricted residential areas. According to this argumentation, a rising part of the population is overwhelmed with the prevailing individuality of life styles and the consequences of global interdependencies on a local and even individual sphere. With the raising degree of entropy and physical threats in many areas (beginning by the fear of getting unemployed up to the threat of terrorism), a retreat towards a homogeneous and organized private neighbourhood is understood as desirable by some society segments. As a consequence, possibilities of spontaneous and randomised inter-ction are highly reduced in contrast to the traditionally compact and his-orically developed city. The urban feeling and urbanity is limited to con-rolled consumption (Herlyn 2004, Selle 2004). These transformations have been studied with the example of the Californian metropolis Los Angeles, resulting in concepts such as *"postmodern Geographies"*, *"postmodern Urbanism"* and *"postmodern city"* (Davis 1990; Dear 1988, 1991, 2000; Ellin 1996; Scott and Soja 1996; Soja 1989). A common aspect of the different argumentations concerning postmodern urban development is the fragmentation of urban space in many independent and sharply separated parts. With special emphasis in the US, the widely homogeneous urban zones which were characteristic for the urban models of the Chicago school of social ecology, have been replaced by functional separations (Dear and Flusty 1998; Soja 2000). Despite urban development in Europe being clearly different from the US, trans-ormations of the global economic system also induced substantial changes in European city regions. On a local sphere, decentralization of urban structures and inside-oriented enclaves can be understood as products of the new, flexible economies and suburban life styles. From this point of view, the actual dynamics of urban development clearly differ from the industrial city of the mid 20th century (Borsdorf et al. 2002). Fragmentation processes in most European cities are limited by fundamental differences in the role of the state, the characteristics of welfare systems and the importance of public urban development and planning systems. But the occurrence of rapid transformations in Europe can be observed as clearly as in the US (Selle 2004). If as in the case of Spain, accelerated immigration processes are accompanied by strong suburbanization, the urban society may split, especially when state intervention is eroding. Such hypotheses will be discussed following the cases of Madrid and Alicante as shown below.

3. The laboratory of Globalization: Spatial and Social Integrationprocesses of the Immigrants

Aiming at giving a broad view of the processes of social integration and real estate market in Spain, the case of two completely different groups of migrants with absolutely different possibilities and goals will be analysed using the example of Madrid (i.e. massive migration in the search for a better life) and Alicante (i.e. retirement migration), re-spectively. Both migrant groups arrived with a reduced knowledge about how is life in the host country. However, the capacity to improve the knowledge status and to change own habits to accommodate to the new situation, clearly varies between both migrant groups.

Immigrants from third world countries aim at looking for occupational possibilities; their goal is to successfully integrate into the labour market. Very often immigrants got a bank loan to pay for the trip to Spain which must be paid back. Many of them commonly send remittances to the family on a regular basis. In such social conditions and due a relatively small ethnic business sector, the language competence is a corner stone for integration. Consequently and in contrast to for instance Germany, immigrants rapidly gain experience and familiarity with the Spanish language. People native from Latin America arrive at a pole position a due to a common language and religion with the host country. On the other hand, a series of charity, religious or ethnically-based organizations have been founded to help the newcomers improve the basic skills required for integration in the Spanish society and labour market. Such support organisations provide the only network to assist immigrants chiefly in terms of legal matters (e.g. Visa, legalization of residence status, real estate market and labour rights).

The situation for the residents and immigrants from EU 15-states is rather different. First of all, Germans, British and other Europeans usually move to Spain by retirement, hence counting on high retirement funds and savings. The achievement of a property and a life style change is the paramount target of these individuals. Retirement migrants do not usually have any economic restrictions. Integration in the host country implies making new friends and organizing leisure activities. As a result, they build a parallel society where the native language is the unifying aspect (e.g. Germans organize their daily life with other German speakers; British do the same). Social ties are made through common leisure interests. By this configuration, integration in the Spanish society is not only difficult as a consequence of substantial life style differences. But even excluding language and cultural barriers, interaction with the host is commonly not wanted. Interviews with residents in Costa Blanca region (Alicante) revealed that the *Spanish world* is regarded as an under-developed society, where local inhabitants do not share the same values. The aims and expectancies of the mentioned migrant types are crucial to understand the spatial implications and political consequences of migration as analysed below.

3.1. Immigrants in Madrid

Prior to discussing the spatial integration of immigrants in Madrid, it is useful to mention that the metropolitan region can be roughly divided between the wealthy north-western part and the poorer south-eastern zone. Differences in altitude of several hundred meters and the vicinity to attractive landscapes in the Sierra of Madrid were the base for the suburbanization process taking place in 1980s and 1990s. All efforts of local and regional planning institutions cannot neutralise this basic climatic difference, which is important for daily life organization. The proximity to private and public higher education institutions determines the direction of further residential expansion and also sets the guidelines for investment in human capital intensive economic branches (I+D activities). But within this scene, the massive investment required for the replacement of residential areas of lowest standards (i.e. the so-called *infraviviendas, chabolas*) by new apartments of a better quality, reduced the sharpest lines of urban segregation. The strong economic growth and European Union subsidies of the last two decades were employed on ameliorating urban infrastructures. The degree of segregation in Madrid is low as compared with other city regions in the Mediterranean area (Malheiros 2002).

The massive migration processes occurring since the last decade did neither induce an exacerbated concentration of immigrants nor led to the formation of ghettos. The concentration of immigrants in the historical city centre and in semi-peripheral quarters is lower than in other Spanish city regions (e.g. as compared to Barcelona according to Janoschka and Riol 2004), French cities as Paris, Marseille or Lyon or even Berlin, the capital of Germany. In Madrid, there is no neighbourhood in which the percentage of foreigner population doubles the mean of the city region.

The part of the real estate market in which immigrants are integrated has been recently established. Immigration is inducing a drop of the high vacancy of the residential real estate market. Only some years ago, more than 15 % of the whole stock was vacant and out of the market due to the low standards and a rising welfare of the Spanish society. The settlement of migrants stopped the loss of population of the central and semi-peripheral areas, reinventing and reinterpreting the dense city core of Madrid. Actually, immigration revitalizes the pubic sphere with new patterns of symbolic interaction in public spaces, counting on a dynamic ethnic economy sector. The area of "Lavapiés", once an urban niche for squatters, has turned into an important neighbourhood for low price textile wholesalers, mainly represented by Chinese people. In contrast to the cognitive image of the neighbourhood, statistical data show that the presence of Chinese residents in the area is low. Chinese immigrants concentrate in areas which are not bound to the commercial sector such as traditional working-class neighbourhoods (e.g. Usera, located in the South of the City). In case of economic success, Chinese have the same desire to publicly evidence the improved social status, among other mechanisms via moving to wealthy 19th century neighbourhoods such as e.g. *Barrio Salamanca* (Ayuntamiento de Madrid 2003). Regardless the nationality and in clear contrast to most immigration societies, all migrants in Spain try to acquire a home property. The prevalence of ownership versus property renting is a special trait of the Spanish society and local real estate market (i.e. more than 90 % of Spaniards own their house or apartment). Migrants adopt the same principle and engage on buying a property as soon as their legal or economic situation makes it possible. Since the normal mechanisms to acquire a property (e.g. getting a bank loan) are normally not accessible for migrants, an array of ethnically-bound business is flourishing for such purpose.

Regarding the location of migrants in Madrid, concentration processes are not only observed in the centre but also in suburban zones of the northern and western parts of the metropolitan region, the areas where the Spanish upper and middle classes live. These areas have two potentials for immigrants: On one hand, the proximity to personal services in wealthy households or work in construction is important fact. On the other hand and the same like in the city centre, immigrants move to vacant houses which were bought as second homes or with speculative interests. Migrants can be characterized as optimizers of the urban structure. The density in suburban spaces grows parallel to the rising intensity of use of the real estate stock.

As a summary, it can be said that the massive immigration from third world countries did not accelerate the segregation processes in the Madrid metropolitan region. In contrast to US city regions, it must be considered that immigrants have competences and possibilities to reduce exclusion through ethnic networks. Processes of ghettoisation and rising exclusion are not occurring with the same intensity as in Germany of France (Häußermann et al. 2004, Wacquant 2004). Thereby, increasing ethnic heterogeneity in Madrid cannot be correlated to a rising fragmentation of urban space.

3.2. Spatial Fragmentation by Immigrants and Foreigners in the Costa Blanca region: The case of Calpe

Spatial actions and insertion of residents from the European Union in the Spanish Mediterranean coastal strip absolutely differs from the integration of third world countries immigrants as shown for the case of Madrid. The real estate market can be differentiated in four sectors which cope with ethnic and social frontiers. First of all, there is a strongly segregated and separated segment of poor immigrants of African origin, in the case of the Alicante/Murcia region. Since this group works within the labour intensive agricultural sector, most housing is located in the proximity to production sites or even on the field (Martínez Veiga 1999). These peripheral, marginal and rural locations make the process of social integration more complicated as within metropolitan areas. But major local cities such like Alicante or Elche (i.e. with approximately quarter million inhabitants) also show high degrees of marginalization. Immigrants from third world countries have a clearly less favoured situation on the real estate market than in Madrid (CeiM 2003). If they want to live in tourist destinations, they have to cope with problems inherent to housing on the coastal strip. Rental possibilities are scarce and letting houses to tourists during the short vacation period is economically more attractive than offering longer term contracts to immigrants.

A second sector is constituted by the local population which has an increasing demand for flats. Actually, the last baby boom generation is searching for flats to leave parental houses. This group raises demand within the compact urban areas or in compact urban expansion areas. On the other hand, the increasing local middle class also looks for second homes on the coast. Many beaches near Alicante have been urbanized with skyscrapers and massive urban infrastructures. As a consequence, , a complete urban structure with leisure parks, restaurants and so forth, can be found on the beach strip in locations such as San Juan/Campello, (i.e. ten kilometres distance from Alicante city centre).
A desert of several ten thousands of flats has been constructed to reproduce urban life along the beach. The otherwise lonesome area, recovers the pulse of life on the week-ends, bank holidays or vacation periods chiefly in the summer. The local residential demand entered in competition with a rising group of wealthy people coming from Madrid. The Costa Blanca region around Alicante is one of the nearest beach destinations from Madrid and a historically preferred tourist and residential destination for the summer period. The scene is completed by presence of a space intensive real estate sector of investment for international residents, composed in many cases by retired migrants from Northern and Western Europe. Amenity-seeking migrants from the wealthy EU 15-region basically search for the most attractive sites on the coast and prefer single detached housing on extensive properties. To meet the wish to acquire the best spots, conflicts for the use of the coastal strips can be expected. Such configuration is a good example of fragmented urban development in postmodern leisure societies.
The processes of migration and population exchange strengthen the tendencies of fragmentation on different spheres. One basic problem in

these locations is the political fragmentation of the territory. Municipalities in areas such as around Alicante, rose from small historic villages and do not have the strategic and logistic capacity to cope with national and international investors. As a consequence, urban development is chiefly driven by the real estate market and not by state authorities. Uses in leisure oriented developments (e.g. commercial areas, leisure parks) are space intensive and exclusive. In the long run, social problems and environmental damage will also affect the residential sector: many residents do not like the intensive use of the coastal regions. Consequently, political problems between foreign residents and the existing local society are easily predictable.

In the next paragraphs the relationship between Spanish and EU-residents will be introduced via describing the case of Calpe, a coastal town of approximately 10,000 inhabitants. In Calpe, About 70 % of the population is not Spanish national and in particular, there is a highly representative German community. Products available in the supermarket are almost the same like in Germany, since international and German providers entered the market and many shops receive products from abroad. A whole array of personal services is available in German, as offered by native Germans or German speaking personnel. Satellite TV receivers and German newspapers delivered from Germany in time to be sold in stationeries from 9 a.m., make the unreal scene almost perfect. A wide range of German speaking leisure clubs and associations can be found anywhere throughout the coast. In autumn, a 15-days festival makes Bavarians enjoy the Oktoberfest, while in February the traditional Cologne carnival is held. Germans live in urbanizations without establishing excess contact with to the few Spaniards around. Their local linkage, public sphere and interpretation frame for the Spanish society is the vision given by the two existing regional German newspapers (i.e. Costa Blanca Nachrichten and Costa Blanca Zeitung, respectively).
Indeed, Germans from an urban and upper middle class background find themselves in a surrounding which was clearly rural until three decades ago and still cannot offer a rich cultural life in terms of what they may associate with "consume" and cultural activities (i.e. theatre, cinema, concerts, exhibitions or highly specialized shopping facilities). Consequently, German residents enjoy their own circuit of cultural activities, which are often organised by clubs.

Urban places are only a stage for European residents. The central symbol for the region is Alicante airport, which stands for mobility and social contact with the home country. The symbolic territorial appropriation by residents goes further than the real occupation of space. Concrete social or spatial problems provide the incentive necessary for the involvement of residents in local politics. They come to the conclusion that their engagement is necessary to help coping with raising problems associated with the environment and uncontrolled urban development. Approximately more than one third of the total number of EU-residents is registered in Spain and has active and passive voting right in local elections. This fact favoured a greater influence of residents in local politics than what immigrants are normally allowed to have in host societies. According to Giddens (1995), European residents appropriated a part of the authority resources and are able to use them for their particular interests. Consequently, there is a change of urban space and habits associated with the radical swing of urban politics, especially after 2003 municipal elections since which resident political parties assumed governmental responsibility. New infrastructures ranging from school programmes, to the plans for new yacht harbours or town squares are devised following the criteria of a central Europe society.

The design of these new spaces is successfully ruled by the values and opinions of the European resident group. An example to mention is the recent struggle between residents and the local population for the use of a central inner-town space in Dénia. In this case, residents influenced the design and – more importantly - the utility of the place to be constructed. The original idea of building a massive parking-building was modified until the development of an urban green area which was inaugurated in June 2004. The criteria for symbolic appropriation of this new space are clearly different from Spanish societal standards, since for instance, unusual gardening design elements were used.

Another example worth mentioning is a regional law draft leading to severe spatial and economic disadvantages for large property owners. EU-residents disconformities were publicized via numerous demonstrations and even with the support of the German and British embassies in Spain. Residents finally involved the European Parliament and appealed to the European Supreme Court, where the case was resolved against them and in favour of the regional authorities.

However and in order to respect the petition of residents, the government compromised to develop a new and modified version of this polemic law. These examples provide evidence of a phenomenon which contrasts with the usual mechanisms of urban governance in immigration societies i.e. the processes of political articulation of immigrants can no longer be blocked by the powerful local class. In the Costa Blanca region case, new trans-European characteristics of the postmodern international leisure society are appearing, since residents have sufficient intellectual, economic and authoritative resources to represent political power via the construction/building of symbols in public spaces. Such processes symbolically transform key spaces of villages and towns in the Mediterranean coast of Spain.

4. Conclusions

The examples analysed in this text clearly show two different patterns of social and spatial integration of immigrants in Spain. The case study of Madrid shows that immigration to the Spanish capital region has interesting characteristics under various points of view. The economic basis for integration of newcomers in Madrid can be assessed as highly positive and conducive to integration. Apart from this fact and in comparison with central Europe, the greater similarity with regard to cultural and social habits and also pre-existing linkages (e.g. due to colonization) between host and migrant societies, facilitate integration as shown to occur in Madrid. Following a sociological approach, the socio-ecologic and spatial pattern observed in Madrid reminds to the theoretical-abstract idea of a „Melting Pot" – despite the absence of any institutional and state-organized effort. Comparing the Spanish situation with the ongoing debate concerning social and spatial integration of immigrants in France, the Netherlands or Germany, the situation in Madrid appears to be less dramatic at all levels.

In the region of Alicante the case is basically different due to substantial variations in the social and economical conditions of immigrants. The coastal strip is a region of intense dynamics associated with divergent economic and social interests and the subsequent generation of conflicts between the actors involved. The tendency is towards the development of processes and politics which facilitate exclusive and excluding urbanization. Under the prevailing conditions in this postmodern leisure and recreational region, the occurrence of social and spatial fragmentation processes is not surprising. Interventions, actuations and settlement of the space intensive uses of EU-residents only complicate the situation. But on the other hand, the political and economic power situation and the resources of residents lead to a modernization of local political styles and structures. In international terms, the new mechanisms and political initiatives towards integration in an alien social environment can be evaluated as a first sign of a new spatial development strategy. In spite of the occurrence of fragmentation processes, the new local and regional political style in the Costa Blanca represent the efforts, the future and the soul of daily European integration.

References
Ayuntamiento de Madrid (2003) Población extranjera en el Padrón municipal de habitantes. Madrid.
Baldwin-Edwards, M. and J. Arango (eds.) (1999) Immigrants and the informal

economy in Southern Europe. London, Portland: Frank Cass.

Borsdorf, A.; J. Bähr and M. Janoschka (2002) Die Dynamik stadtstrukturellen Wandels im Modell der lateinamerikanischen Stadt. In: Geographca Helvetica 57, 4, 300 -310.

Breuer, T. (2004) Der geographische Raum und seine wechselnde Bewertung. In: Bernecker, W. and K. Dirscherl (eds.) Spanien heute, 11-50. Frankfurt: Vervuert (= Bibliotheca Ibero-americana 91)

Carens, J. (2004) La integración de los inmigrantes. In: Aubarell, G. and R. Zapata (eds.) Inmigración y procesos de cambio. Europa y el Mediterráneo en el contexto global, 393-420. Barcelona: Icaria (= Serie Icaria Antrazyt 199)

Casado-Díaz, M., C. Kaiser and T. Warnes (2004) Northern European retired residents in nine southern European areas: characteristics, motivations and adjustment. In: Ageing and Society 24, 353-381.

CeiM (Centro de Estudios para la integración social y formación de Inmigrantes, Fundación de la Comunidad Valenciana, ed.) (2003) Inmigrantes y vivienda en la Comunidad Valenciana. Valencia.

Claret, A. (2004) El Mediterráneo, laboratorio de globalización. In: Aubarell, G. and R. Zapata (eds.) Inmigración y procesos de cambio. Europa y el Mediterráneo en el contexto global, 15-20. Barcelona: Icaria (= Serie Icaria Antrazyt 199)

Colectivo IOÉ (2003) La Sociedad Española y la inmigración extranjera In: Fundación de las Cajas de Ahorro (eds.) Inmigración en España, 16-31. Madrid: Fundación de las Cajas de Ahorros. (= Papeles de Economía Española 98)

Corkill, D. (2001) Economic migrants and the labour market in Spain and Portugal. In: Ethnic and Racial Studies, 24, 828-844.

Davis, M. (1990) City of Quartz: Excavating the Future in Los Angeles. New York, London.

Dear, M. (1988) The postmodern challenge: reconstructing human geography. Transactions of the Institute of British Geographers 13, 262–274.

-, (1991) The Premature Demise of Postmodern Urbanism. Cultural Anthropology 6, 538–552.

-, (2000) The Postmodern Urban Condition. Oxford, Malden (MA).

-, and S. Flusty (1998) Postmodern urbanism. Annals of the Association of American Geographers 88/1, 50–72.

De Lucas, J. (2004) Ciudadanía: la jaula de hierro para la integración de los inmigrantes. In: Aubarell, G. and R. Zapata (eds.) Inmigración y procesos de cambio. Europa y el Mediterráneo en el contexto global, 215-236. Barcelona: Icaria (= Serie Icaria Antrazyt 199)

Ellin, N. (1996) Postmodern Urbanism. Cambridge (MA), Oxford.

El Mundo (Newspaper), June, 17th, 2003; October, 03rd, 2003.

European Central Bank (2003) Structural Factors in the EU Housing Markets. Frankfurt.

EUROSTAT (2004) Eurostat Yearbook 2004. Luxemburg: European Commission.

Friedrich, K. and T. Warnes (2000) Understanding Contrasts in Later Life Migration Patterns: Germany, Britain and the United States. In: Erdkunde 54, 108-120.

García-Montalvo, J. (2003) La vivienda en España: Desgravaciones, Burbujas y otras historias. In: Fundación de las Cajas de Ahorro (eds.) Financiación de la Vivienda, 1-44. Madrid: Fundación de las Cajas de Ahorro. (= Perspectivas del Sistema Financiero 78).

Häußermann, H.; M. Kronauer and W. Siebel (2004) Einleitung. In: Häußermann, H.; M. Kronauer and W. Siebel (Eds.) An den Rändern der Städte, 7-42. Frankfurt: Suhrkamp (edition suhrkamp 2252)

Herlyn, U. (2004) Zum Bedeutungswandel der öffentlichen Sphäre. Anmerkungen zur

Urbanitätstheorie von H. P. Bahrdt. In: Siebel, W. (ed.) Die Europäische Stadt, 121-130. Frankfurt: Suhrkamp (= edition suhrkamp 2323).

Huber, A. and K. O'Reilly (2004) The construction of Heimat under conditions of individualized modernity. In: Ageing and Society 24, 327-352.

INE (Instituto Nacional de Estadísticas) (2004a) Padrón Municipal Contínuo. www.ine.es

INE (2004b) Precio del metro cuadrado de vivienda según su antigüedad. In: Boletín Mensual de Estadística. www.ine.es

Janoschka, M. (2002) Wohlstand hinter Mauern. Viena: Austrian Academy of Sciences (= ISR Forschungsberichte 28).

-, and G. Glasze (2003) Urbanizaciones cerradas: un modelo analítico. In: Ciudades 59, 9-20.

Janoschka, M. and E. Riol (2004) La inmigración extranjera a Madrid y Barcelona. ¿Una nueva fase sociodemográfica y nuevas formas de segregación espacial? Paper presented at the IX. Congreso de Población Española; Granada, September 23-24th, 2004. Available online: http://www.ieg.csic.es/age/poblacion/granada2004.htm

Izcara, S. (2002) Infraclases rurales: Procesos emergentes de exclusion social en España. In: Revista Española de Investigaciones Sociológicas 97, 127-154.

King, R.; T. Warnes and A. Williams (2000) Sunset Lives. British Retirement to the Mediterranean. Oxford, New York: Berg.

Krätke, S. (1995) Stadt. Raum. Ökonomie. Basel, Boston, Berlin: Birkhäuser.

Kreienbrink, A. (2004) Einwanderungsland Spanien. Migrationspolitik zwischen Europäisierung und nationalen Interessen. Frankfurt: IKO-Verlag.

López, J. (2001) La coyuntura inmobiliaria de 2001. In: Ciudad y Territorio 33 (129), 559-572.

Low, S. (2003) Behind the Gates: Life, Security and the Pursuit of Happiness in Fortress America. New York: Routledge.

Malheiros, J. (2002) Ethni-cities: Residential Patterns in the Northern European and Mediterranean Metropolises – Implications for Policy Design. In: International Journal of Population Geography 8, 107-134.

Marcuse, P. (1997) The Ghetto of Exclusion and the Fortified Enclave: New Patterns in the United States. In: The American Behavorial Scientist 41, 311-326.

Marcuse, P. (2004) Verschwindet die europäische Stadt in einem allgemeinen Typus der globalisierten Stadt? In: Siebel, W. (ed.) Die europäische Stadt, 112-118 . Frankfurt: Suhrkamp (= edition suhrkamp 2323).

Martínez, J. and M. Matea (2003) Precios de la Vivienda en España y factores explicativos. In: Fundación de las Cajas de Ahorro (eds.) Financiación de la Vivienda, 77-100. Madrid: Fundación de las Cajas de Ahorro. (= Perspectivas del Sistema Financiero 78).

Martínez Veiga, U. (1999) Pobreza, segregación y exclusión social. La vivienda de los inmigrantes en España. Barcelona.

Prévot-Shapira, M.-F. (2000) Segregación, fragmentación, secesión. Hacia una nueva geografía social en la aglomeración de Buenos Aires. In: Economía, Sociedad y Territorio 2 (7), 405–431.

Rodríguez, V.; G. Fernández-Mayoralas and F. Rojo (1998) European Retirees on the Costa del Sol: a cross-national comparison. In: *International Journal of Population Geography, 4, 183-200.*

Sassen, S. (2004) Die Verflechtungen unter der Oberfläche der fragmentierten Stadt. In: Siebel, W. (ed.) Die europäische Stadt, 373-384. Frankfurt: Suhrkamp.

Scott, A. J. and E. Soja (eds.) (1996) The City. Los Angeles and urban theory at the end of the twentieth century. Los Angeles.

Selle, K. (2004) Öffentliche Räume in der europäischen Stadt. Verfall und Ende oder Wandellund Belebung? Reden und Gegenreden. In: Siebel, W. (Ed.) Die europäische Stadt, 131-145. Frankfurt: Suhrkamp (= edition suhrkamp 2323).

Siebel, W. (2004) Einleitung: Die europäische Stadt. In: Siebel, W. (ed.) Die europäische Stadt, 11-47. Frankfurt: Suhrkamp (= edition suhrkamp 2323).

Soja, E. (1989) Postmodern Geographies: The Reassertion of Space in Critical Social Theory. London.

-, (2000) Postmetropolis: Critical Studies of Cities and Regions. Oxford, Malden (MA).

Wacquant, L. (2004) Roter Gürtel, Schwarzer Gürtel: Rassentrennung, Klassenungleichheit und der Staat in der frazösischen städtischen Peripherie und im amerikanischen Ghetto. In: Häußermann, H.; M. Kronauer and W. Siebel (eds.) An den Rändern der Städte, 148-202. Frankfurt: Suhrkamp.

Warnes, T.; K. Friedrich, L. Kellaher and S. Torres (2004) The diversity and welfare of older migrants in Europe. In: Ageing and Society 24, 3, 307-326.

Wehrhahn, R. (2000) Zur Peripherie postmoderner Metropolen: Periurbanisierung, Fragmentierung und Polarisierung untersucht am Beispiel Madrid. In: Erdkunde 54, 221–237.

Wehrhahn, R. (2003) Postmetropolis in Spanien? Neue Entwicklungen in Madrid und Barcelona. In: Geographische Rundschau 55, 2, 22-28.

Wood, G. (2003) Die postmoderne Stadt: Neue Formen der Urbanität im Übergang vom zweiten ins dritte Jahrtausend. In: Gebhardt, H.; P. Reuber and G. Wolkersdorfer (Eds.) Kulturgeographie. Aktuelle Ansätze und Entwicklungen. Heidelberg, Berlin: Spektrum Akademischer Verlag.

Parallel Space Belsunce

Robert Grimm

The work discussed developed from a participant observation carried out over a period of two years in Belsunce, an inner city area of Marseilles. The paper was written in the context of a PhD that has the dynamics of Belsunce as object of study. The quarter has changed its social character several times during the last two centuries. Belsunce, it will be argued, became a central place of international passage for goods and people for the Algerian diaspora. Its central position within a network of the space of flows is sustained through Belsunce's particular geographic position within the city of Marseilles, an economic infrastructure, and distinctive social interactions. These are tailored to the specific needs of passage for the Algerian diaspora with a cultural and socio-economic sensibility that renders Belsunce different from or metaphorically parallel to Marseilles. My work is still in progress.

A short history

Belsunce has always been a space of transition and change. Planned after the visit of Louis XIV, the Sun King, in 1660, it was Marseilles first extension to the North of the old port. The oldest city of France was to be opened up to the kingdom it traditionally opposed[11]. It was to become the gateway of the rising colonial France to the new areas of influence on the other site of the Mediterranean and beyond. And indeed, Marseilles turned once more into a harbour of global importance[12], if only for a unified and absolutist France; a development that was to hold true until the end of the second world war and the beginning of the de-colonialisation period, the high point of which was the independence of Algeria in 1962. In fact, the increasing influx of migrants to the French metropolitan territory, including guest workers, former expatriates from overseas (the so called pieds-noirs), and also refugees from formerly French administrated regions, in short the implosions of the colonies on their 'mother county' have to be seen in this historic context. A context that closes the historic circle but not without pain and sparking new conflicts on all sides. Marseilles is its seismic centre.

The extension of Marseilles was a prestigious project. Part of an attempt to modernise the medieval city on the one hand and to glorify the powers

---

[11] A continuous moment in the history of Marseilles is its drive for partial or complete independency from any administration exterior to its city walls. See: Contrucci & Duchêne; (1998).

[12] Allied to Rome, Marseilles was one of the most important trading points in the known world until it was sacked by Caesar's troops during the civil war in 49BC.

of the autocrat on the other, the *nouvelle Cours*, a central boulevard with its bordering buildings and side streets was to become the *plus beau d'Europe* (Contrucci & Duchêne; 1998). It was inhabited by global traders from all over Europe. The architecture of the area reflected its purpose, its buildings were spacious and richly ornamented with renaissance and classical styles. Belsunce's street pattern was socio-scientifically ordered and geometrically outlined; a reflection on the Baroque functionalism that was seen as state of the art during Colbertism and prefigured the more ambitious reconstruction of the 19th century. Strikingly, the contradictions inherent in French absolutism, which preferred a bourgeois Colbert to an aristocrat like Fouquet as its finance minister, that needed increasingly educated administrators for its bureaucratised power structures, and that promoted national and international commerce to finance its war machine, nurtured the class that struggled for power. The *'battalion des Marseillaises'* departed on the second of July in 1792 from the Jacobin club in rue Thubaneau in Belsunce. It was the starting journey of the French national anthem. The bourgeois character of the area persisted until the last century and is still manifest in the built environment of Belsunce.

The socio-economic and political upheavals throughout Europe during the 19th century were strongly felt in Marseilles. Imperial France and the third Republic extended French influence in North and Central Africa. The Suez Canal opened trade to the Far East. Marseilles strengthened its position as lifeline for the new colonies and as an international trading point. At the same time, starting at the second half of the 19th century, the city became industrialised. Because of the lack of natural resources in the region, Marseilles specialised in the production of soaps and oils, which led to a high demand for cheap unskilled labour to be satisfied by the influx of in-migration or transit migration. But the Mediterranean port was also a gateway to the new worlds. One of the major resources of wealth became human trafficking from the Mediterranean basin to the Americas (Temime & Lopez; 1991). Marseilles became a place of passage.

Walter Benjamin (1985a; 1985b), during his short stay in Marseilles in 1927, catches the density of the inner city with its harbour. Marseilles is the 'maw' of a 'seal', a striking creature that lives on the ground and in the water, one that needs both habitats to survive but which, at the same time, is more specialised in diving and swimming. Benjamin's metaphor comes close to the popular saying: 'Marseilles is a city that turns her back on France and her face to the Mediterranean'. The seal gets nourishment from the sea and so does the city. Its 'gullet' swallows the 'black and brown proletariat' thrown to it from the ships. Surely, these are the workers on the boats or migrants using the increasingly industrialised sea transport system. 'Companies' timetables' are the temporal frames of harbour life. The arrival and departures of ships are the feeding times. But what is fed is not Marseilles but the promised land of consumption and labour to which it is a gateway. Marseilles's intake, crushed by the seals 'massive jaws' and sticking to it like 'tartar', 'exhales' a bad breath that 'stinks of oil, urine, and printer's ink'. The gateway creates its own dynamics and Benjamin encounters in the harbour a 'bacillus culture'; the 'harbour people', 'porters' and 'whores' already partially 'de-composed' who only 'resemble human beings'. Strolling around the harbour, the hashish eater Benjamin, empowered with 'immense di-mensions of inner experience' and 'illuminations', fixed his gaze on the faces of the true proletariat, 'Faces that [he] would normally have avoided for a twofold reason: [he] should neither have wished to attract their gaze nor endured their brutality'. Are they the products of the di-gestive system for which the *gullet* is the opening? Who or what could be infected by this transmittable disease?

In the areas around the harbour, every step is a new encounter with noises as loose 'as butterflies on a hot flowerbed'. Interestingly, sounds that belong to residential and industrial activities intermingle in the hybrid world of work and living in the harbour areas. Benjamin juxtaposes the 'bawling of a baby' with the 'rattling of boards'; the 'flapping' of freshly cleaned 'wet linen' with the 'clatter of buckets'. But the industrial character of the impressions, the working and living condition of the pro-letariat seems to be the major aspect of his observation. The 'grindstone impales' all other sounds 'from behind with its whizzing sting' and summons the experience into a truly modern phenomenon. In these quarters, the 'walls are politically mobilised' and proclaim with 'spacious red letters the red guards in front of the dockyards and arsenals'. There is a sense of hope in this reference to the revolution, and the ugliness of the faces who Benjamin encountered under the influence of hashish, transform into the 'true reservoir of beauty'; the 'inner gold' of the ex-ploited gleams from the 'wrinkles, glances, and features'.

Marseilles population was growing throughout the 19th century. Migrants were either attracted by the increasing demand for labour in industry and port activities or they were seeking a boat that would take them to new continents. Most of them came from South European countries. More than the UK or Germany, France is historically an in-migration country (Puzzo; 2003). High demand for labour during industrialisation and a notoriously low birth rate during the 19th century made international mi-gration a necessity (Viet; 1997).[13] Italians were by far the biggest group to pass through Marseilles but were not the only ones. Soon the city was

---

[13] 381,000 foreigners were represented in the 1851 census data and the share of the foreign population reached 6.58 % of the total population as early as 1931 (Le Moigne;1986), which is comparatively close to the present figure of 7.4% in 1999 (Boëldieu & Borrel; 2000).

segregated in communities with different origins, languages and costumes. Marseilles's city centre now thronged with a migrant under-class, and this increased fears of new outbreaks of diseases similar to the plague and the yellow fever of the 17th century and the beginning of the 19th century. The rich merchants who lived in Belsunce gradually left the inner city. At the same time, these gateways offered employment opportunities for the already deprived arrivals; the transit migrants were in need of cheap temporary accommodation close to the harbour and the railway station. Belsunce is situated between the harbour and the train station, both are at less than a 5-minute walking distance (Figure 1).

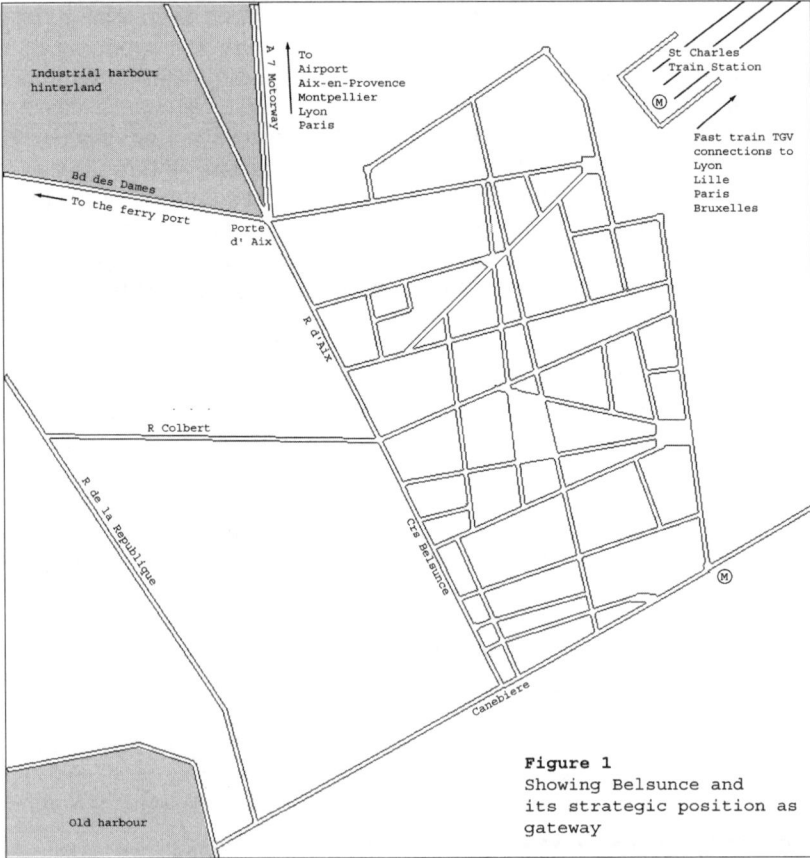

Industrial harbour hinterland

To
Airport
Aix-en-Provence
Montpellier
Lyon
Paris

St Charles
Train Station

Fast train TGV
connections to
Lyon
Lille
Paris
Bruxelles

Bd des Dames
To the ferry port

Porte
d' Aix

R d'Aix

R Colbert

R de la Republique

Crs Belsunce

Canebiere

Old harbour

Figure 1
Showing Belsunce and
its strategic position as
gateway

The strategic position of the area for the dynamics of passage comes out in a quote from Albert Londres (1999) who visited Marseilles the year before Benjamin: 'There are Marseilles settlers and then there is the flow of nomads who go from the train station to the port or from the port to the train station. If you are neither part of the settlers nor of the flows, you are nothing anymore. You are a daydreamer. You obstruct the traffic.' Belsunce, writes André Suarès in 1931(1998), becomes Marseilles's *'forum dans toute son odeur et sa force populaire'*. A market of crime, where everything is sold from women to drugs, the forum is dedicated to 'Mercury the money magician and Aphrodite', goddess of sexual pleasures.

Established as a centre of economic migration by the beginning of the 20th century, Marseilles and Belsunce become entailed in the political upheavals in the Near East and Russia throughout the Inter War period - Russian political refugees and Armenians, fleeing Turkish atrocities, arrive. Marseilles, as part of *'la France libre'* until 1943, was for many intellectuals, Jews, and anti-fascists the last hope to escape German Concentration camps. The German intellectual Anna Seghers, herself escaping Fascism via Marseilles to Mexico in '41, wrote a breathtaking account of her experience in the Mediterranean port. In 'Transit' (2001), she describes Marseilles as the sewer that channelled the flood of the lost European souls towards the sea. She too 'squatted' a Belsunce hotel which she described as 'a house of which one says: One holds out, because one leaves'. By that time, Belsunce had become a central point of in- and out-migration with a whole sub-economy dependent on it.

The 'Arab Quarter'
Marseilles always had a strong position between the Orient and Occident due to political alliances and trade. But the presence of a North African community remained marginal until the Great War. An 1874 *décret* allowed Algerian natives to leave French-Algeria only with special authorization. Exceptions were made for cattle exporters - the *convoyeurs Kabyles* - and traders who started to settle in Marseilles. Between 1906 and 1907, several hundred Algerians were invited to break Italian strikes in Marseilles's soap and oil production. They were later transferred to Paris and others were employed as complementary workers in the mines of the Pas-de-Calais or in the agricultural sector. By 1914, only 6000 Algerian workers were listed as resident in France. But as a response to the labour shortages in the war torn French economy, large scale migration started during the hostilities and the number of Algerian workers on French soil exploded to 240,000 in 1917 (Gillette A; Sayad A ; 1984). The 'perfume of the Orient' could soon be smelt in the migrant areas in the inner city of Marseilles, notably in Belsunce. 'Do you want to see Algeria, Morocco or Tunis?' asked Albert Londres (1999 / 1926) willing to take the curious reader away to the rue des Chapeliers. Butchered 'sheep are hanging from the doors' and goats run freely in the street. This is 'Arab territory'! But the Moslem community remains one among others and only concentrated in a few streets (Temime & Attard-

Maraninchi; 1991). The ethnic composition of the area was diverse, including migrants of different origins especially Italians and Armenian Turks; some elements of the bourgeoisie were still present (Temime; 1995). However, in comparing the area with the 'ghetto in Oran' and the 'Casbah', the poverty stricken old town in Algiers, Londres already stigmatises the quarter. Belsunce becomes an area where one needs to be careful and attentive: 'don't speak to the women, you might get into a fight'. The increasing number of cafés and hotels that attracted a doubtful clientele in search of work on the black market, faked identity cards, or for a room in one of the rather dark and cheap hotels, gave the area a dubious character. A tradition that holds true until the present day. 60.5% of the total population in the administrative quarter Belsunce were foreign nationals at the 1982 census, they represent still 40% at the 1999 census and 50% if one adds the foreigners who acquired the French nationality. 34% of Belsunce's total population come from the Maghreb (INSEE; 1999). The numbers are certainly underestimated as they don't include the many clandestine residents in the quarter. Ethnicity is not a variable in the French census, blurring the statistical image still further.

Physically, Belsunce is clearly defined by some of Marseilles's main roads. It thus appears as a closed space. Strolling through the streets of the quarter, one will be surprised by the dominance of the North-African community in public space. Groups of people hang around at corners or in the streets, others sit on cardboard that protects them from the cold stones on doorsteps. Many, the older generation in particular, wear traditional North-African hats, caftans, and turbans in the Saharan Touareg style. Cafés and the few open places found in the area are obvious meeting points. They are filled with people waiting or busily talking while enjoying a small cup of strong espresso or a tea sweetened with several pieces of sugar. Others are obstructing the traffic in the narrow streets, carrying full and heavy plastic bags between two people. It is not unusual to see men walk hand in hand. A striking sight is the large amount of cardboard boxes, left from the commercial activities during the day and that block the narrow streets in the evening.

There is a strong historic relationship between the immigration areas in Chicago, the great immigrant city, and Marseilles, the city through which many Italian and other migrants passed on their way to America. Early twentieth century migration flows formed 'twilight zones of deteriorating neighbourhoods and shifting populations' (Thrasher; 1966) in both cities. Belsunce can be understood as a transitional space similar to Zone II in Burgess's (1967) city growth chart with successive population displacements (from Italian and Armenian to North African) discussed in the human ecology approach (McKenzie; 1967). But there are also striking differences: Belsunce is more a space of 'sojourning' (Cohen; 1999) for the Algerian diaspora rather than a place of permanent settlement.

800,000 Algerians passed through Marseilles in 2002 (Aéroport Marseilles Provence; 2002; Port Autonome de Marseilles; 2002) only beaten by Paris Airports that transported 1,067,000 (Aéroports de Paris ; 2003) passengers between France and Algeria. But the port facilities give Marseilles a favorite position for small traders and merchants. The nonstop ferryboat connections between Marseilles and several Algerian ports allow traders to transport a wide range of goods from cars to heavy hand luggage. Sea transport is much more lucrative than air transport. Unlike international airports where border control has been tightened since the 9/11 attack, the control at Marseilles and the Algerian ports is based on informal networks, making it easy to smuggle stolen or un-declared goods. Belsunce is not only central for newly arriving migrants. The traveling Algerian diaspora, seasonal workers, and internationally operating Algerian traders pass through Belsunce before either joining the boat to Algeria or the train to the French and European hinterlands. Belsunce is an *'interstitial'* space, that is 'a space that intervenes be-tween one thing and another' (Thrasher; 1966) with a 'borderland culture' characterized through 'liminality, syncretism and ambiguity' (Cohen; 1999).

The economic organisation
The 'Chambre de Commerce de Marseilles' listed 718 officially registered businesses within the perimeters of Belsunce in April 2004. 305 of these businesses are owned by a landlord with a North African Muslim name; 147 businesses are owned by a identifiable Sephardic Jews community that settled in Marseilles in the wake of Arabic nation-alism in North Africa and the violence in Palestine (Temime & Sayad & Jordi; 1991). The cultural capital of the Sephardim – often first generation migrants still fluent in Arabic and Hebrew - clearly relates to their commercial activities amongst the North African diaspora. Only four categories – small retailer, wholesaler, hotels and travel agencies and catering services (including restaurants, fast food restaurants and café bars) – make up, with 632 listed businesses, the vast majority of the commercial establishments in the quarter.
65 of those businesses are hotels. The prices of their rooms are listed with heavy markers on cheap cardboard nailed to old wooden doors. They range from 6 to 12 Euros a night. Some hotels offer accom-modation on a monthly basis for around 250 to 350 euros for a single room.[14] Prices can be negotiated. Rooms are generally shared between two or more. Comfort cannot be expected in these establishments. A shower, if present at all, is generally communal. Sometimes the shower

---

[14] Some work has been done on the difficult living conditions in hotels and foyers by Ascaride & Condro (2001).

room only opens once a week. Rooms are generally without hot water. Plugs for basic electronic goods such as radios, shavers or mobile phone chargers are not installed. Some of the residents helped themselves and 'engineered' basic electrical installations. I saw dangerously un-insulated exposed electrical connections in some rooms. The toilets are in most of the cases 'Turkish'. At times there is one on each floor but generally there are even fewer. This 'hotel culture' is widely spread in Marseilles but concentrated in Belsunce. If one adds the 9 travel agents present in the area and the shops that sell bags and suitcases and metal boxes, one would arrive at up to 15% of travel related commerce in Belsunce. This is a clear indicator that Belsunce is a place of sojourning and passage.

Restaurants are a common sight – there are 73 catering businesses - in the area too. But 'restaurant' is a very relative term in this context. In fact, these places are sometimes called canteens among Belsunce population. The number of dishes available on these premises is restricted for a twofold reason: one is cultural – the food needs to be Hallal - and the other is the spending power of its clients. Couscous is on offer for only 3.50 Euros a plate. For around 5 Euros one can have with it a large piece of lamb, veal, chicken, a couple of Merguez, or mince-meatballs. The most common dishes include mashed potatoes, North African soups, basic rice dishes, chickpeas and green peas as well as lentils. The food is similar in nearly all restaurants. There is generally no menu apart from a list that might be found on the door. Alcohol cannot be purchased in any of these restaurants. I know of only one that attempts to appeal to the non-Moslem community. One can bring a bottle of wine and consume it with the meal there. Any symbolic values of the restaurants seem to be removed; functionality predominates. There is not much decoration in their interiors apart from a few mirrors and images that are either related to the homeland of the migrants, or have religious content such as phrases from the Koran. Separate tables for two or four are rare; they are often set up with places for 10 and more. A TV can often be found situated in a corner where it is widely visible to all. The programmes on show range from French to Algerian. It is normal to eat with ones hands (at least the meat) and indeed the men who come here (most of the clients are male and only a few of the restaurants offer a separated space for families) are visibly hungry. Up to 200 meals are served there at mainly peak times at noon and round 7 pm. The restaurants close at 10pm. Their service is sensitive to the cultural needs of the North African community. The fact that many hotels and apartments are without kitchens, and the overrepresentation of males without families explain the high numbers of restaurants. At the same time 'community centres', these establishments essential meeting places, crucial to the creation and re-creation of social networks, and informal business transactions.

While hotels and restaurants are situated in the centre and the surrounding main roads of Belsunce, the spatial distribution of the retail sector follows a north-south division, gradually declining in size and quality towards the north of the area. Belsunce comprises 176 officially listed wholesale businesses. Rue longue des Capucines, rue Tapis Vert, rue National and rue du petit Saint Jean have the highest concentration of wholesalers and form the *'quartier grossiste'* (Figure 2). The commerce is based on down market western fashion textiles, mainly coming from China but one can find goods from Algeria, Iran and Italy. Much of the merchandise is exported from Belsunce to Algeria and other North African countries. But smaller shops in the area itself and the local markets take their stocks from these traders too. National and International trade routes have their beginnings in these streets, delivering goods from Algeria, China and Iran to Paris, Germany, Holland and Belgium.

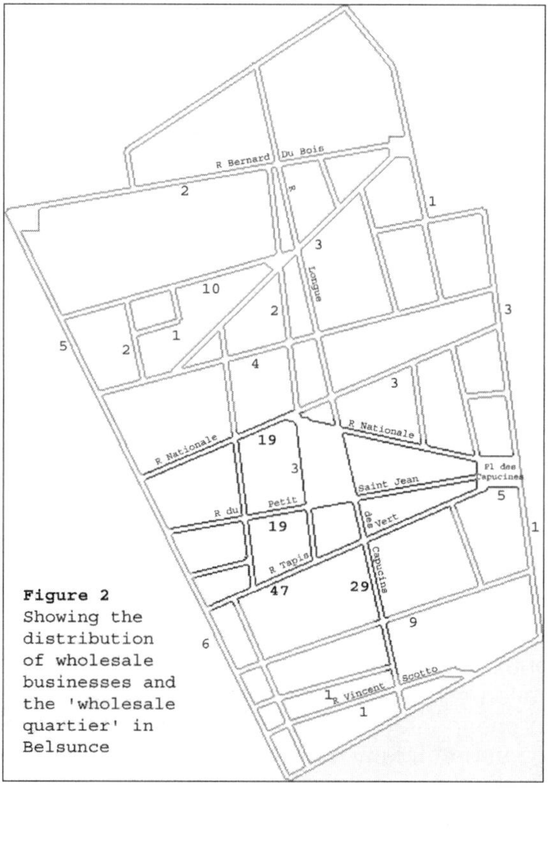

Figure 2
Showing the distribution of wholesale businesses and the 'wholesale quartier' in Belsunce

Small retailers account for 300 businesses in Belsunce. A bigger variety of goods is traded in the shops that are mainly concentrated in Belsunce centre and the rue d'Aix. Their status is sometimes ambi-guous as some goods are sold on a small scale and others can be bought in big quantities. Small retailers are much more culturally a-ware than wholesalers. Oriental tissues and dresses imported from Iran and China, oriental food stuff and kitchen utensils, jewellery but al-so popular culture such as Raï CDs and videos are on sale.

In the north of Belsunce at the port d'Aix, is the flea market, the centre of informal commerce. All imaginable items are sold here from clothes to shoes to electronic goods such as DVD players or tape recorders - but also cars and spare parts for cars, cigarettes, and gadgets are on sale from as little as 50 cents. Most of the goods on sale are used. Some have been found in the garbage and others might even have been stolen. Generally, it is uncertain whether the items actually function, but their low price make it often worth a try. The most deprived people work in this environment, offering their goods on improvised market stands built out of cardboard boxes. It is a 'wild' market frequently interrupted by police activity. Objects are used like currency, being exchanged several times a day for, hopefully, a little profit but sometimes with a little loss in value. The market is far from just serving the local community, some goods are destined for export. Mobile phones in particular among electronic goods and school text books will be bought by small scale merchants intending to sell them on in Algeria.

Belsunce provides other services crucial for commerce, passage, trans-port, and export and import. Black market taxis can be found at the port d'Aix, the gateway roundabout to the hinterland of the industrial harbour from which the ferryboats to North Africa depart. A motorway, connecting the city with the airports leads from the same roundabout. Banking is essential for the commerce between the two continents. Private persons coming from Algeria to France are only allowed to change a restricted amount of Dinars in Euros at a fairly high exchange rate. Furthermore sending money from France to Algeria or other countries is very costly in time and money and not reliable. There are some professional money exchangers and lenders in the area (changing 10,000 Euros and more is not unusual). Money can be paid in Marseilles one day and will be handed over in Algeria the following day. Merchants in need of money can borrow; others are given the possibility of exchange. Communication too is crucial. One ever-reoccurring sight in the inner city of Marseilles is the 'Taxi-phone'. In Belsunce, 15 were counted in April 2004. One could call it an alternative communications network. Taxi-phone shops specialised in cheap international tele-communication, including fax and, in-creasingly, Internet. Many of the migrants/traders are mobile and without a fixed address. Therefore they either can't subscribe for contracted mobile phones or fixed lines, or have Algerian numbers. Telephones are often absent in hotels. Taxi-phone shops therefore play a central role in the function of Belsunce as a site of communication. Car traders looking for cheap deals in Germany and the Benelux countries use the Internet increasingly as an information source. In case of a lucrative offer, the international phone line in the same shop will be used to fix a deal.

There are also black market medical treatments provided, often, through Syrian dentists; open air car services; job and housing agencies; legal advice through public notaries; public showers and baths.

One could include these commercial activities into the common framework of ethnic commerce and entrepreneurship in ethnic niche markets, or migration industries (Castles & Miller; 1998), the extent to which some services are over-represented in this small inner city area of Marseilles indicates a more global context for Belsunce than just a local ethnic community formation. With an estimated 500 million Euros turnover in 1994 (Tarrius; 1995b), Belsunce is a major commercial centre. Belsunce is a semi autonomous space that integrates a highly sophisticated and specialised infrastructure. Its economic importance extends from its physical boundaries to regional, national and international importance.

The walk
Belsunce has a peculiar relationship to time. Point of arrival and departure, the only constancy during the 20th century has been passage, a temporally restricted stay for some hours, days, weeks, months or even years. Until today, Benjamin's ships throw humans at the shores of Belsunce. The departure and arrival times of ferryboats from or to the North African coasts have a major impact on life in the quarter. Restaurants and hotels will fill and empty 'according to their timetables'. The passers have many faces and many reasons to come. Cars loaded with goods; men carrying heavy bags on heads and shoulders, ready to leave for good or to return immediately, are a common sight in the quarter. Some individuals staying around for months will suddenly disappear to other regions in search of work and papers in Europe, or be expelled and imprisoned; but equally they can reappear unexpectedly. Too many unknown variables determine the lives of the 'third world cosmopolites'. Delays at embassies; temporary visa restrictions; border and migration controls; expulsion; imprisonment; lack of economic resources; unexpected employment opportunities; sudden promises of regularisation; military conflicts; changes in political landscapes as well as threats of prosecution; all these can extend and shorten their stay in home or host countries. A defence against the hazards of hard necessity is the compactness of Belsunce, the density of the social interactions taking place – interactions that create their own dependencies (on Belsunce) and there-

fore need to be constantly reconstructed (in Belsunce). There is a necessity to pass via Belsunce as there is a need to pass (walk) in Belsunce itself, to make ones presence visible in places agreed to all, where the passer-by can be seen and met and thus take part in the *political economy of movement*:

A and I sit in a cafe. A is an Algerian asylum seeker. His social position is precarious: as an applicant for territorial asylum, he has neither the right to work nor the right to any financial aide from the French government. With us is K. He too is an Algerian asylum seeker. Both are friends and know each other from their little hometown. They discuss the prospect of a building site.

M. passes by in front of us. Recognising A, he joins us. They know each other from their home town too and had not seen each other for several weeks. M runs a building enterprise in Algeria that specialises in the construction of social housing. He travels to Europe via Marseilles on a regular basis. M buys machines such as cranes and bulldozers in France but preferably in Germany and the Netherlands. He has established business connections but always searches for new opportunities on the Internet. He sometimes stays in Belsunce hotels but occasionally lives with his uncle, where he leaves his Mercedes while he is away. Belsunce is vital for M. All of his business transactions are in cash. The local moneylenders offer him a preferable exchange rate. M's second interest is cars, especially Mercedes and BMWs with minor accident damage. These are cheaper. His connections in Belsunce will allow M to have them repaired at a low price, which increases his profit margins.

We leave the café and go to a local restaurant. M and A exchange information about home. Then the conversation switches to the German second hand car market. B the waiter arrives and tells us about rumours that there will be a wave of regularisation in Italy. Papers will only be given to the ones that have a work contracts. The contracts are on sale for around 3000 Euros. After a quick meal and a coffee, M goes to his room in the hotel to get his luggage. He will take the plane to Algiers in the evening. A and I decide to go for a tour in the quarter before heading home.

We take the rue X where T sits on a doorstep. He is teaching mathematics at a school in the hometown of A. Involved in the Muslim political opposition in Algeria during the 90s, T came with the local Emir to reestablish connections with the Islamic opposition forces that fled to Europe during the civil war. T and the Emir have been in Brussels and Antwerp previously. They are on their way are back to O. A exchanges some information about the political situation in his country.

D a Tunisian Jew has his shop some meters further down the street. A has been working for him several times. His present accommodation, a one bedroom apartment of 30 square meters where he lives with his wife and his two youngest children has been provided by D, as was the apartment he shared with four others before. A is in need of a bigger flat and inquires if there is anything available - at the same time he asks for work.

We hit upon M1. M1 has a 'commercial visa' allowing him to spend three months of the year on French soil. He has a little shop close to O, which he leaves with his older son to manage while he is away. M1 tries to earn additional money during his stays in Marseilles. He works on construction sites and does seasonal agricultural work. But he also exports and imports basic consumer goods for a little money. M1 has just come off the boat and A wants to know about his friends and family. There is some foodstuff M1 brought with him for A. He had left it in his hotel room and promises to pass it to A the next day.

A wants to buy some cigarettes and we turn into the rue Y where, at the crossroads with the rue Z, we know of some old and already retired 'guest workers' who sell Algerian tobacco. Purchasing a packet, we spot M2 who works in one of the shops in the rue Y. After two years in Marseilles during which he worked in a Belsunce shop for only 22.84 Euros a day, M2 will finally leave France and rejoin his family in the desert enclave around G. He promises to send a traditional hand made caml wool rug.

We head towards port d'Aix to have a look at the flea market. Looking at the goods on sale in the hope to find an interesting deal we stumble upon M3. M3 had just bought an Eriksson mobile phone for 15 euros and wants to sell it for 20 now. M3 has a commercial visa for France. He has a local small shop in Algeria and specialises in buying second-hand mobile phones in France in order to sell them for a little profit in Algeria or in Belsunce itself. He goes to the market early in the morning to find the most attractive offers and sells the items on in the afternoon. M3 buys also clothes and perfume from the wholesale traders among whom he has certain acquaintances. M3 knows people in N and G too where he can stay for some time to do a little business. He bought, for instance, 200 shirts for 2,5 Euros and sold them in N for 5 euros a-piece. M3 rents a room with three other men on a permanent basis in one of the Belsunce hotels.

On our way back, we meet N. A knows him from the town A where A has family. N works as the president of an organisation helping Algerian immigrants. He has some information about a possible 'regularisation of the 'sans papiers' in France.

We walk on only to meet K who is an old work colleague of A. Apparently there is a big building site coming up. A Jewish textile industrialist, who attaches fake trademarks to clothes coming from China, is looking for people that could help him to refurbish his factory in the hinterland of the industrial harbour. It sounds like promising long term work.

Finally, we arrive at the Canebiere, where one usually finds A1 in the late afternoon. A1 was a notorious criminal in Belsunce during his youth. He still survives on petty crime but his main asset is networking. A1 finds buyers and sellers for big amounts of smuggled marihuana and hashish. He talks secretively in kilos and about 'people' coming from the North of France for deals. A1 himself sells deals starting at 100g a piece for which he has a little 'work force'. But Leica photo equipment, stolen cigarettes, and postage stamp collections find a buyer too with A1. A has a little deal with A1 too. Regular on French soil and with a fixed address, A1 has the right to acquire an official invitation to France – an administrative paper - from his local town hall. Such an invitation is needed to obtain a visa to France in Algeria. The application is without any administrative fee but A1 will charge A 30 Euros for it.

This sort of stroll was not exceptional but a common occurrence. In fact, most of the time I spend in Belsunce, I spend sitting in cafes or walking. Walking generally took place during the great meeting times like lunch or dinner. Depending on the course of the stroll and the people en-countered, it took between thirty minutes and two hours. Walking is an important means of participation in the dynamics of Belsunce. Certainly, passing through Belsunce, strolling, is part of the creation of that place but it is at the same time a possibility to leave its narrow frontiers. If 'every body' passes through at certain times and places, it is most likely to be able to meet somebody eventually or exchange information via intermediaries. The area 'lives' through passage and makes passage possible through its social interactions and economic infrastructure. A knot of regional, national and international importance in the 'network of the space of flows' (Castelles; 1999) Belsunce becomes important as a place not in opposition to but precisely by facilitating interaction and mobility between itself and the global space of flows which pass through it.

Parallel space Belsunce

"Well, facing all this, I ask myself often, why a harbour is not used and developed like a harbour? It is like this that I saw the cultural revolution in Marseilles. The feet in the water first.' (Izzo; 1996)

Parallel, of course, is only meant to be metaphoric. In geometry, parallel lines never touch; they are continually at the same distance from each other. Marseilles and Belsunce however have a history in common. Marseilles has been the South for the North and the North for the south. Seghers saw a glimmer of Africa in its walls and Londres smelled the Orient. Marseilles had an intermediate position in the global structure of the colonial world with Europe at its centre and the Asian and African continents at its periphery. But the South, so Alain Medam (1995), re-treated from its North. With the rise of nationalism, France lost her colonies and Marseilles its key position in the logistic chain from and to the former regions of French influence. 'The city does not look at the Orient anymore' (ibid.) where throughout her history she had found her riches. Marseilles's new orientation is towards the north, the centre of the newly constituted Europe. At the same time, the economy shifted to-wards the service sector; Marseilles's industries, shipyards and re-fineries, broke down. The harbour, its activities cut back, relocated to the north, leaving abandoned docks behind. Marseilles, so Medam, finds itself in a double movement of retreat.

Belsunce is a remnant of the old Marseilles. Already physically se-parated, Marseilles and Belsunce seem to develop in different times and conflicting identities. While Marseilles attempts to catch up with the North - redefining itself as a city of tourism, attracting the crowds with her Mediterranean climate, fast TGV connections and luxury cruise-lines - the commercial and migration centre at its heart becomes an unwanted spot. Marseilles seems to be departing from her history as a city of exiles, of which Belsunce is the last survival, a reminder of an unwanted and troubled past, or to use Benjamin's metaphoric language once more: 'the tartar sticking to the teeth'.

Belsunce on the other hand has developed its own dynamics. The flavour of the orient has a homogeneous taste: life in its public spaces is dominated by the North African immigrant community that forms a cul-tural unit. While there might be national differences between the coun-tries of origin of this community, there are similarities in historic, lin-guistic, religious, and cultural terms that are shared between them. Belsunce is like the 'bled' (country in Arabic and generally relates to the country of origin) is a comparison I had heard often. You want to go to Oran? What for, you know it already! Londres ambiguity over which side of the Mediterranean Belsunce identity belongs at the beginning of the 20th century, remains valid at the beginning of the 21st century.

The presence of an international harbour is still hinted in Belsunce – an obvious trading-post for goods, a place of passage for people. The e-conomy of trust, its hidden passageways and trade routes, the face-to-fa-ce inter-business-actions and transactions with their lack of transparency to the outsider, are in strong opposition to generally accepted business practices. There is an absence of the regulating and controlling in-stitutions of a formal national economy. Belsunce is a problem of eco-nomic governance for the authorities.

As old port cities and former centres of production were excluded from economic growth during the last two decades, Marseilles lost her status as major trading centre and has now a merely peripheral position in the new hierarchy of cities (Sassen; 1994). However, if one were to leave the new geography of capital and investment flows and would conceive the world as comprising of several superposed and/or juxtaposed geographies with different centres, knots and hubs of varying importance depending on context and perspective, then Marseilles might be seen to have a different importance. Taylor, Walker and Beaverstock (1999) argue that metageographies are basic-scale spatial frames by which people order their world. Such a metageography is the now often dis-puted (Held McGrew & Goldblatt & Perraton;1999; Sholte; 2000) political geography of territorial sovereign nation states for instance. The authors (Taylor, Walker & Beaverstock; 1999) propose an 'alternative metageography' based on trans-national networks among global cities. One can similarly imagine metageographies for different diasporas, migration flows, and networks. These do not necessarily follow a pattern of the distribution of power among major global agglomerations. With 4,500,000 people travelling between Algeciras and the Moroccan coast in 2003 (Port Authority of Algeciras Bay; 2004), what is this town to Paris, London or Madrid for the Moroccan minority? A similar perspective can be taken on Belsunce in Marseilles and the Algerian minority.

Marseilles and Belsunce may have put some distance between each other. Marseilles moved away from its harbour and trans-nationality towards the European periphery. Belsunce on the contrary became a 'transborder' (Sholte J.A. 2000) space, an international trading centre for the Algerian diaspora, a place of passage. And it is in this sense that they became parallel and dislocated. But being part the one of the other, they are connected. It may well be that in the future, both will re-unite, leave their particular marginalisations and form a international centre of major importance that will connect both sides of the Mediterranean once more.

References :

Aéroports de Paris, trafic Maghreb par Pays, 2003.
Aéroport Marseille Provence, les trafics 2002.
Ascaride, G. and Condro, S. (2001) La ville Précaire. L'Harmattan, Paris.
Benjamin, W. (1985a) Marseills. In: One Way Street and other Writings.
    Verso, London.
-,   (1985b) Hashish in Marseilles. In: One Way Street and other
    Writings. Verso, London.
Boëldieu, J., Borrel, C. (2000) La proportion d'immigrés est stable depuis
    25 ans. Cellule Statistiques et études sur l'immigration. Insee, N° 748 Novembre
    2000.
Burgess, E.W. The Growth of the City. In: Park, R.E., Brugess, E.W.
    (1967) The City. The University of Chicago Press.
Castelles, M. (2000) The Rise of the Network Society. Blackwell, Oxford.
Castles, S. & Miller, M.J. (1998) The Age of Migration. International
    Population movements in the Modern World. Macmillan, London.

Chambre de Commerce de Marseille, Service des Renseignements,
Avril 2004.

Cohen, R. (1999) Global Diasporas. An Introduction. UCL Press:

Contrucci, J., Duchêne, R. (1998) Marseille. Fayard, Paris.

Gillette, A., Sayad, A . (1984) L'Immigration Algérienne en France,
Editions Entente, Paris.

Held, D., McGrew, A., Goldblatt, D., Perraton, J. (1999) Global
Transformations. Politics, Economics and Culture. Polity Press, Cambridge.

INSEE, Recensement de la Population, 1999.

Izzo, J. C. (1996) Chourmo. Gallimard, Paris.

Le Moigne, G. (1986) L'Immigration en France. Presses Universitaires
de France, Paris.

Londres, A. (1999) Marseille port du sud. Arlé, Paris.

McKenzie, R.D. The Ecological Approach to the Study of the Human
Community. In: Park, R.E., Brugess, E.W. (1967) The City. The University of
Chicago Press.

Medam, A. (1995) Blues Marseille. Eidtions Jeanne Laffitte, Paris.

Peraldi, M., (2001) Cabas et Containers. Maisonneuve & Larose, Paris.

Port Authority of Algeciras Bay, Customer attention service, 2004.

Port Autonome de Marseille, les Trafics 2002 / Bilan 2002 PAM.

Puzzo, C. (2003) Instruments of British and French Immigration Policy in the 70s: a
Comparative Analysis. Contemporary European History 12, 1, (2003).

Sassen, S. (1994) Cities in a World Economy. Pine Forge Press, London, New Delhi,
Thousand Oaks.

Sholte, J. A. 2000 18 Globalization a Critical Introduction Palgrave, New York.

Seghers, A. (2001) Transit. Aufbau Taschenbuch Verlag, Berlin.

Suarès, A. (1998) Marsiho. Editions Jeannes Laffitte, Marseille.

Tarrius, A., (1995a) Arabes de France dans l'économie mondial souterraine. L'Aube,
Paris.

Tarrius, A. (1995b) Economies Souterraines. L'aube, Paris.

Temime, E., (1995) Marseille Transit: les passagers de Belsunce. Éditions
Autrement, Paris.

-,   Attard-Maraninchi, M. F. (1991) Histoire des Migrations à Marseille. Le
cosmopolitisme de l'entre-deux-guerres. Edisud, Marseille.

-,   , Sayad, A., Jordi, J.J. (1991) Histoire des Migrations à Marseille. Le choc de
la Decolonisation. Edisud, Marseille.

-,   , Lopez, R. : (1991) Histoire des Migrations à Marseille. L'expansion
Marseillaise et « l'invasion Italienne ». Edisud, Marseille.

Thrasher, F.M. (1966) The Gang a Study of 1,313 Gangs in Chicago. The University
of Chicago Press.

Viet, V. (1997) Le cheminement des structures administratives et la politique
française de l'immigration 1914-1986. Migrations Etudes N°72-mai 1997.

Shaping Regional Governance in Metropolitan Regions – The Role of Spatial Planning

Markus Beier, Antje Matern

1 Metropolitan regions in a globalised world

A prevailing opinion in regional science is that under conditions of globalisation the influence of nation-state on economic processes is decreasing. This is seen as a result of the dissemination of information and communication technologies, which allow companies to reallocate their economic activities on a global scale. In a global economy with a differentiation of economic processes and globally diffused production sites, control centres are required where everything is linked. The control function, that is the headquarters of transnational companies (TNCs), is above all situated in 'global cities' (Sassen 1991, 1994) and metropolitan regions.

Metropolitan regions are on the one hand embedded in the global economic network; on the other hand they are part of the national economic system and often the country's growth poles. In other words: in metropolitan regions global economic networks are linked with local and regional economic activities (*'glocalisation'*, Swyngedouw 1992; Amin and Thrift 1994, 1995).

Therefore metropolitan regions play double role: following the logic of the growth pole theory (Perroux) spin over effects from metropolitan regions should set off economic development in more peripheral regions, and contribute to a reduction of geographical inequalities. Furthermore metropolitan regions should ensure a country's competitiveness in an international context. Because of their strategic role European and German spatial planning documents accentuate the importance of metropolitan regions for a balanced spatial development. But until now only a normative framework exists, however the empirical implementation lacks. This article deals with the implementation of regional governance structures in German metropolitan regions. It starts with the debate on metropolitan regions as a spatial planning concept. While this debate is to a great extend influenced by German spatial planning, the discussion on regional governance is more international. Regional governance is seen as a key concept relating to the challenges of metropolitan regions. The main ideas of the governance approach are presented in this article. Taking these theoretical discussions as a starting point, the article describes an empirical approach to implement regional governance in metropolitan regions. These descriptions refer to the results of a research project. The article ends with some concluding remarks on the role of spatial planning in implementing regional governance in metropolitan regions.

2   Metropolitan regions as a spatial planning concept

The overall aim of European spatial development policies is "a balanced and sustainable development of the territory of the European Union" (European Communities 1999). It is concretised by three fundamental goals that are

economic and social cohesion;

conservation and management of natural resources and the cultural heritage;

more balanced competitiveness of the European territory.

With regard to the economic and social cohesion and a more balanced competitiveness of the European territory, the development of a poly-centric and balanced urban system plays an important role (European Communities 1999: 19). The backbone of the urban system is a hier-archic structure of cities and city regions headed by metropolitan regions. Metropolitan regions can be defined as "agglomerations that are characterised by their extraordinary significance within the international network of city regions. They are distinguished by economic strength, strong infrastructure, political and economic decision-making levels, a small-meshed network of product-oriented service providers and a high demographic potential" (Network of German Metropolitan Regions 2003: 1).

Metropolitan regions as a spatial planning concept were introduced in 1997 by the German Ministerial Conference on Regional Planning (MKRO). As motors of economic, social and cultural development they should ensure Germany's competitive capacity and accelerate the Euro-pean integration process (BMBau 1997).

The MKRO defined seven German metropolitan regions, which are Ber-lin-Brandenburg, Hamburg, Munich, Rhine-Main, Rhine-Ruhr, Stuttgart, and the Dresden-Leipzig-Chemnitz region, the so called 'Saxon Triangle' (*Sachsendreieck*). Referring to Ritter (1997) and Blotevogel (1998) metropolitan regions can be mono- or polycentric, but decisive is the functional aspect. Their geographical delimitation may vary depending on the functions and they should be seen as a flexible and procedural con-cept (Scholich 1998: 77).

A central aim is to strengthen their competitiveness with regard to the international integration, environmental conditions, regional marketing in-itiatives, and geographic organisation and cooperation. A call for action can be detected concerning the self-organisation of metropolitan regions (BMBau 1997: 51).

The geographical localisation of special functions in metropolitan regions can be explained with reference to the theory of agglomeration ad-vantages. According to this theory the geographical localisation of economic activities may generate positive scale effects, documented in higher productivity of workforce and capital.

Therefore metropolitan regions have three main functions (Thierstein , Dümmler and Kruse 2003: 89), which are:

The *innovation-function* comprises two sectors: high-services and high -tech; whereas the first one stands for knowledge-intensive services, which rely on a skilled and often international workforce, the latter stressses rather the production aspect with innovative companies.

The *gateway function* emphasises the role of metropolitan regions as nodal points of national and international transportation networks.

The *regulation function* focuses on the political and economic head-quarter function of metropolitan regions.

The German discussion on metropolitan regions had great influence on European spatial development policies. Thus the European Spatial De-velopment Perspective (ESDP), adopted in 1999 by the Informal Council of Ministers responsible for Spatial Planning, emphasises the importance of metropolitan regions with regard to a balanced and coherent de-velopment of the European territory: "The creation of several dynamic zones of global economic integration, well distributed throughout the EU territory and comprising a network of internationally accessible me-tropolitan regions and their linked hinterland (towns, cities and rural a-reas of varying sizes), will play a key role in improving spatial balance in Europe" (European Communities 1999: 20).

Metropolitan regions first of all are a normative concept, which has to be substantiated by the regions itself. Therefore the seven German metro-politan regions started to build up a network ('*Initiativkreis Metro-polregionen in Deutschland*'). Their comprehensive goal is "to formulate the self-perception of German metropolitan regions and their demands on German and European spatial planning and development policies" (Network of German Metropolitan Regions 2003: 1).

To achieve this aim cooperation between metropolitan regions plays an important role, even if their relationship primarily is characterised by competition. Thus there are only some fields, where cooperation seems to be realistic, e.g. know-how transfer or articulation of common interests. In other fields like e.g. headquarter functions, travel hubs or large infrastructure facilities rivalry is dominating the relationship be-tween metropolitan regions.

Cooperation of municipalities within metropolitan regions however is an important step to foster their competitiveness. Thus a balance between competition and cooperation seems to be the best way in coping with the challenges of metropolitan regions (Göddecke-Stellmann, Müller and Strade 2000: 653). The metropolitan regions are called to intensify intra-regional cooperation to develop and implement concepts fostering their competitiveness. In this context the 'regional governance' concept seems to be adequate because it comprises competition, cooperation and co-ordination.

3 Collaboration through regional governance in metropolitan regions

Governance means "social coordination" (Mayntz 1993: 11) of collective action via control modes. Originally the term is derived from the new institutional economics (Williamson 1985; Richter 1990). In the meantime governance is used in a broader sense in economical, political and spatial spheres, despite of different connotations, e.g. corporate governance, good governance, sustainable governance, global governance, and urban or regional governance.

The debate on governance was significantly influenced by the international group of experts 'Commission on Global Governance' (CGG).[1] According to the CGG "governance is the sum of many ways individuals and institutions, public and private, manage their common affairs. It is a continuing process through which conflicting or diverse interests may be accommodated and cooperative action may be taken. It includes formal institutions and regimes empowered to enforce compliance, as well as informal arrangements that people and institutions either have agreed to or perceive to be in their interest" (Commission on Global Governance 1995: 4). A European Commission's White Paper describes governance as "rules, processes and behaviour that affect the way in which powers are exercised at European level, particularly as regards openness, participation, accountability and coherence" (European Commission 2001: 8).

In political science the term is used to make a distinction between 'governance' and 'government'. While the latter stands for the institutionalised state control system, governance is a mode for managing collective action: "[...] whereas government is vertical and firmly institutionalized, governance is horizontal and flexible. Whereas government is formal and directed from above, governance is informal and self-regulating. Whereas higher level government (e.g. states) connects to localities through demarcated procedures, lower level government (e.g. interlocal agreements) is looser and less confined by boundaries. Government emphasizes the centralizing features of regionalism, whereas governance stresses the decentralizing virtues of local co-operation" (Savitch and Vogel 2000: 161-162).

---

[1] The 'Commission on Global Governance' was established in 1992 in the belief that international developments had created favourable circumstances for strengthening global cooperation to create a more peaceful, just habitable world for its entire people

It has to be emphasised that governance is not a new organisational mo-del. In fact it is a regulation mode, which comprises hierarchical, com-petitive and cooperative elements. Governance is based on inter-dependency of private and public actors and stakeholders, maintained by formal and informal rules, norms, and conventions (Kooiman 1993; Le Galès 1997; Rhodes 1997).

The emergence of governance modes is the result of a paradigmatic shift from a relatively static "control of development" to a more dynamic "initialising and shaping of development" (IOEW 2001: 3). For some years, new forms of regional cooperation and regulation gain in im-portance, in particular in city regions. These 'bottom-up' approaches emerge in the context of agenda 21-processes, networks and new 'part-nerships' of public and private actors (public-private-partnership).

As there is no general textbook definition of regional governance, it only can be characterised by its attributes (Benz 2001; Fürst 2001; Healey 2000). Regional governance shows an inter-organisational character: actors from the public and private sector are collaborating on issues of regional interest. But regional governance shows a multi-level character as actors from national and to some extend supranational level are in-volved in the process. Actor networks, which are based on trust and communication, ensure a permanent cooperation.

The action framework is defined by formal rules and institutions as well as informal regulation modes. Actors are embedded in organisations which influence their action logics. Thus the institutional framework has impact on the interactions. Therefore regional governance is a com-bination of different action logics like hierarchy, network and market. Even if vertical control still plays an important role collaboration is characterised by negotiation.

Regional governance describes a regulated, nevertheless flexible form of collaboration, which requires a permanent adaptation and learning apti-tude. The 'success' of governance is based on a continual variation of structures and combinations of regulation mechanisms (Stoker 2000: 106). Therefore the concept is designed for situations of high complexity, dynamic and uncertainty. Nevertheless it should present answers to the challenges metropolitan regions are exposed to, as there are:

Metropolitan regions are more than other parts of a country affected by globalisation and global competition. Therefore spatial development of metropolitan regions shows more and more an external dependency, which leads to an uncertainty concerning future developments. Local and regional actors have to take this into account.

With reference to the debate on sustainable development economic, social, ecological and cultural concerns have to be reconciled. This is especially necessary in the context of land use patterns. Therefore the postulation of an integrated planning is up to date again, but using new modes of coordination.

By trends of regionalisation of politics like e.g. structural policy, labour market policy, local traffic the responsibility is transferred to the regional level. On the one hand this is a valorisation of regional politics. On the other hand this leads to the fact that the 'region' becomes the 'arena', where the different interests have to be negotiated. This means that in the context of regional governance the meaning of the term 'region' has changed. The region is no more seen as a geographical entity, but is constituted in the process of cooperation and communication.

On the one hand metropolitan regions are characterised by a high complexity. And in addition to this an increasing uncertainty concerning future developments exists. On the other hand existing administrative organisations do not correspond to these challenges and traditional planning and regulation modes are no longer suitable. Therefore the question arises how to coordinate the diverse and even conflicting interests on common grounds, e.g. land shortage. The answer is: by implementing regional governance structures in metropolitan regions.

Despite a multitude of studies on aspects of regional governance like networks, cooperation, and communication, the decisive step to an implementation of regional governance is still missing. Therefore the following chapter describes an approach to shape regional governance in metropolitan regions.

4 Implementing regional governance in Saxon metropolitan regions
Background and requirements

In the following an example will be given how structures of regional governance can be established in metropolitan regions. It is based on the results of a research project[2] which focused on new organisational models for planning and governance in city regions. The project aimed at improving the efficiency of planning processes in city regions by taking into account recent trends of urban development as well as environmental and social concerns of a sustainable development (Forschungsverbund 'Stadt und Region in Sachsen' 2003).

---

[2] The project was been initialised by the Saxon state planning authority and it was focused on an advancement of the 'central place theory' with special regards to city regions. It was accomplished by a research network (under direction of Prof. B. Müller) which comprised the Leibniz Institute of Ecological and Regional Development Dresden and the Leibniz Institute of Regional Geography Leipzig as well as chairs of regional development at the universities of Dresden, Leipzig and Chemnitz (so called Forschungsverbund 'Stadt und Region in Sachsen'). The following conception has been elaborated by B. Müller and R. Danielzyk in collaboration with the authors

The instrument should strengthen the inner-regional efficiency which includes advancing the competitiveness of these city regions as a part of the metropolitan region "Saxon Triangle"[3]. With regard to the requirements of sustainable development an instrument which combines planning, communication and management aspects is needed. Existing planning instruments are characterised by a lack of efficiency in respect of dynamic suburbanisation processes in the 1990s. These processes often resulted in undesired urban structures of fragmentation and specialisation within a city region. Besides these development patterns and their negative impacts a re-definition of planning competences is needed. The recent intergovernmental division of power between county, regional and state authorities in city regions leads to an inefficient fragmentation of political structures and responsibilities which often constrain problem-oriented development processes.

These aspects ask for more intensive coordination and intergovernmental cooperation within the city region as well as negotiation of conflicting interests between public and private stakeholders of the region. With regard to these needs important questions for the new concept had been:

What kind of issues and challenges can be addressed on the regional level?

What kind of instruments and planning methods can be utilised for addressing these challenges?

Who assumes duties and responsibilities for the urban development of metropolitan regions?

Concept idea
The main idea of the concept is to take regional stakeholders into charge for addressing main development challenges of planning and ongoing development processes instead of concentrating them on single municipalities or the central city in particular. Referring to the concept of regional governance common objectives, strategies and measures should be defined in a regional decision-making-process between public and private stakeholders instead of being given by legally binding guidelines and restrictions for an urban development of a higher hierarchy.

But in contrast to other regional cooperation processes the state planning authority initiates regional cooperation by defining basic conditions, using options for intervention or veto's and offering support for the cooperation process.

---

[3] The metropolitan region 'Saxon Triangle' comprises the city regions of Dresden, Leipzig-Halle and Chemnitz-Zwickau.

Concept design

To support regional cooperation processes '*Oberzentrale Kooperations-räume*' ('regions of cooperation') as a new spatial category for city regions will be defined which are functionally delimited. As cooperation is a crucial element of '*Oberzentrale Kooperationsräume*', they shall be understood as a platform for inner-regional negotiation be-tween stakeholders. The participating municipalities have a common re-sponsibility for the city region's development.

The negotiation processes shall cover all issues of city region's development: the development of urban structures as well as housing market, business development or social infrastructure facilities. The results of the negotiation processes should be fixed in financial, organisational or development concepts. Therefore the whole spectrum of existing, formal or informal planning and management instruments is adaptable which includes regional development or marketing concepts as well as legally binding land use plans.

Informal cooperation processes often exclude themes of conflicting interests, which can be seen as a weakness of these processes. To avoid such strategies issues of regional cooperation as well as the participating municipalities will be defined by the state planning authority.

Therefore the concept is based on an intergovernmental division of responsibilities between state and regional level. These levels interact during the cooperation process and have complementary responsibilities. The state planning authority defines the framework of the regional cooperation process. It provides the procedure, objectives and general aims of the cooperation and at the end of the procedure it approves plans and concepts of the city region.

Fig. 1: Players of 'Oberzentrale Kooperationsräume'
Source: Forschungsverbund 'Stadt und Region in Sachsen' (2003)

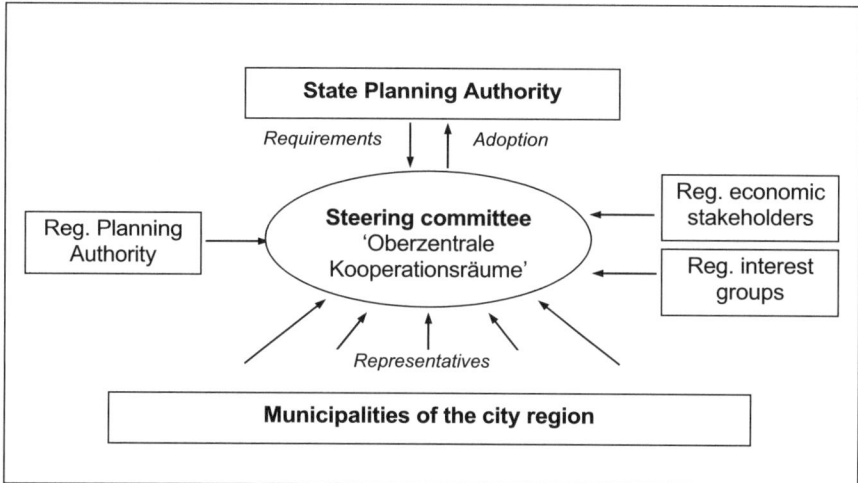

The main decision-makers of 'Oberzentrale Kooperationsräume' are the representatives of the participating municipalities. They negotiate conflicting interests, elaborate development strategies and concepts, plans and measures for recent and future challenges of the city region.
And furthermore it is in their responsibility to implement the adopted concepts (cf. Fig. 2). The representatives may invite further regional stakeholders like economic actors or other interest groups to join the cooperation process, if it is necessary.

Fig. 2: Procedure of *'Oberzentrale Kooperationsräume'*

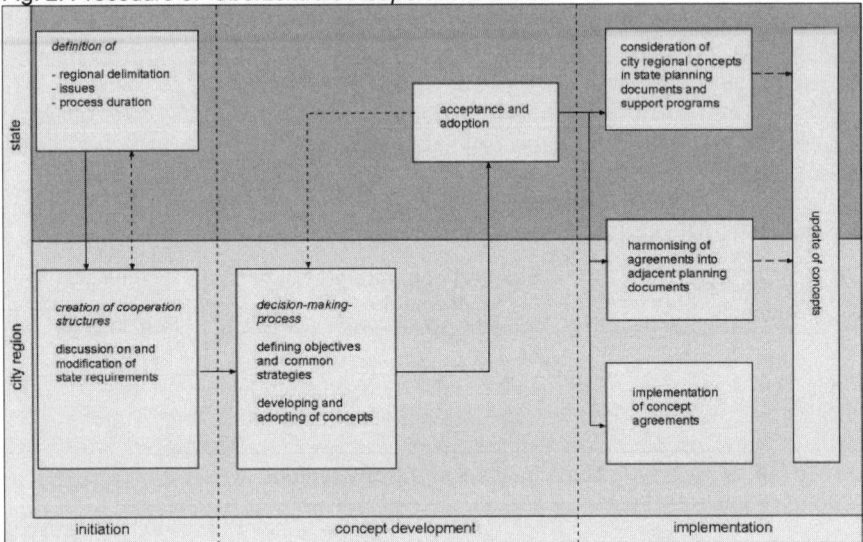

state	definition of - regional delimitation - issues - process duration	acceptance and adoption	consideration of city regional concepts in state planning documents and support programs
city region	creation of cooperation structures discussion on and modification of state requirements	decision-making-process defining objectives and common strategies developing and adopting of concepts	harmonising of agreements into adjacent planning documents implementation of concept agreements
	initiation	concept development	implementation

update of concepts

Source: Forschungsverbund 'Stadt und Region in Sachsen' (2003)

Innovations

Compared with existing planning procedures the new planning and governance concept of *'Oberzentrale Kooperationsräume'* offers some innovations and advantages, which are:

The concept of *'Oberzentrale Kooperationsräume'* can be understood as a process which combines existing, formal and informal planning instruments rather than providing absolutely new ones. Depending on regional demands the elaborated development concepts may include location-, financial-, and organisational concepts.

Regional stakeholders can utilise a bunch of existing planning and management instruments for elaborating the required concepts for their city region. Thereby the instruments can be harmonised by requirements of the issue as well as by preferences of the regional stakeholders. The developed concepts can become more problem-related than existing instruments.

By defining the framework for cooperation and negotiation existing functional structures and challenges of city regions can be considered. The efficiency of elaborated concepts is improved by the (intensive) involvement of regional stakeholders who are responsible for the outcome of their concepts as well as their implementation.

Following the concept of regional governance the importance of the regional level and its (public and private) stakeholders will be enhanced by assuming responsibilities for the city region. This can offer a decisive step for containing the fragmentation of (political) responsibilities in city regions. At the same time the state planning authority can keep its role as patron and observer of regional development and can enlarge its options of a more efficient use of state support to foster desirable regional developments and implement objectives for a sustainable development. Otherwise the adjustment of (financial) state-support on the instrument is necessary to foster the implementation of the instrument and the consistency of city regional cooperation processes.

Conclusions:
The role of spatial planning in regional governance
Referring to the outstanding role of metropolitan regions in global economy it is important to foster their competitiveness. The competitiveness of metropolitan regions otherwise depends to a great extend on appropriate governance structures. Starting from the previous interpretations the question arises, what the role of spatial planning and in particular regional planning in regional governance should be?

Besides its original responsibility the elaboration of documents and plans, spatial planning can assume the position of process management and facilitator. Regional planning is qualified for this function as it is embedded in the regional level and is not part of a local authority. It can be described as an expert on 'regional issues'; its focus exceeds the local authority area. Furthermore regional planning has a subordinating and integrating position as it is not part of the economic, social or environmental sphere.

The role as a promoter of regional governance requires a change in the main tasks of regional planning. Instead of elaborating zoning plans regional planning is more and more involved in development processes. This means e.g. supporting the self-regulation of networks and partnerships of public and private actors. Furthermore new modes and instruments of cooperative as well as competitive action have to be implemented. In this context regional planning plays a key role. One comprehensive objective of the changing role of regional planning is to foster implementation planning processes. The presented concept can be seen as an example how this could be performed.

References
Amin, A. and Thrift, N. (1994) Neo-Marshallian nodes in global networks. In: Krumbein, W. (ed.) Ökonomische und politische Netzwerke in der Region: Beiträge aus der internationalen Debatte. Münster, pp. 115-139.
Amin, A. and Thrift, N. (1995) Globalisation, institutional 'thickness' and the local economy. In: Healey, P. et al. (ed.) Managing cities. The new urban context. Chichester, pp. 92-108.

Benz, A. (2001) Vom Stadt-Umland-Verbund zu 'regional governance' in Stadtregionen. In: Deutsche Zeitschrift für Kommunalwissenschaft, 40, pp. 55-71.

Blotevogel, H.H. (1998) Europäische Metropolregion Rhein-Ruhr: Theoretische, empirische und politische Perspektiven eines neuen raumordnungspolitischen Konzepts. In: Schriften des Instituts für Landes- und Stadtentwicklungsforschung, 135. Dortmund.

BMBau Bundesministerium für Raumordnung, Bauwesen und Städtebau (1995) Raumordnungspolitischer Handlungsrahmen. Bonn.

-,   (1997) Entschließungen der Ministerkonferenz für Raumordnung 1993-1997. Bonn.

Commission on Global Governance (1995) Our Global Neighbourhood. New York.

European Commission (2001) European Governance. A White Paper. Brussels.

European Communities (1999) ESDP – European Spatial Development Perspective. Towards Balanced and Sustainable Development of the Territory of the European Union. Luxemburg.

Forschungsverbund 'Stadt und Region in Sachsen' (2003) Stadtregionen als Kooperationsräume. Zur Weiterentwicklung des Zentrale-Orte-Konzepts am Beispiel von Dresden, Leipzig und Chemnitz. Berlin.

Fürst, D. (2001) Stadt und Region – Schwierigkeiten, die regionale Selbststeuerung nachhaltig zu machen. In: Deutsche Zeitschrift für Kommunalwissenschaft, 40, pp. 84-96.

Göddecke-Stellmann,J./Müller, A. and Strade, A. (2000) Konkurrenz und Kooperation
    – Europas Metropolregionen vor neuen Herausforderungen. In: Informationen
    – zur Raumentwicklung, 11/12, pp. 645-656.

IOEW Institut für nachhaltige Wirtschaftsforschung (2001) Local und Regional Governance für eine nachhaltige Entwicklung (unpublished paper). Wuppertal, Berlin.

Healey, P. (2000) New Partnerships in Planning and Implementing Future-oriented Development in European Metropolitan Regions. In: Informationen zur Raumentwicklung, 11/12, pp. 745-750.

Kooiman, J. (1993) Social-Political Governance: Introduction. In: Kooiman, J. (ed.) Modern Governance: The Government System in England. Birmingham.

Le Galès, P. (1998) Regulations and Governance in European Cities. In: International Journal of Urban and Regional Research, 22, pp. 482-506.

Mayntz, R. (1998) New Challenges to Governance Theory. Jean Monnet Chair Paper 50. Florence.

Network of German Metropolitan Regions (2003) Strategy statement (draft). Berlin.

Ritter, E.-H. (1997) Europäische Metropolregion Rhein-Ruhr oder: Kann aus einer Städte-Agglomeration eine Metropolregion werden? In: Akademie für Raumforschung und Landesplanung (ARL): Räumliche Disparitäten und Bevölkerungswanderungen in Europa. Regionale Antworten auf Herausforderungen der europäischen Raumentwicklung: Forschungs- und Sitzungsberichte, 202. Hannover, pp. 156-171.

Rhodes, R.W.A. (1997) Understanding Governance. Policy Networks, Governance, Reflexivity and Accountability. Buckingham, Phil.

Richter, R. (1990) Sichtweise und Fragestellung der Neuen Institutionenökonomik. In: Zeitschrift für Wirtschafts- und Sozialwissenschaften, 110, pp. 571-591.

Sassen, S. (1991) The Global City. Princeton / NJ.

-,   (1994) Cities in a World Economy. Thousands Oaks / Ca.

Savitch, H.V. and Vogel, R.K. (2000) Paths to New Regionalism. In: State and Local Government Review, 32(3), pp. 158-168.

Stoker, G. (2000) Urban Political Science and the Challenge of Urban Governance. In: Pierre, J. (ed.) Debating Governance. Authority, Steering, and Democracy. Oxford, pp. 91-109.

Scholich, D. (1998) Diskussionsbericht. In: Akademie für Raumforschung und Landesplanung (ARL): Deutschland in der Welt von morgen. Die Chancen unserer Lebens- und Wirtschaftsräume. Wissenschaftliche Plenarsitzung 1997: Forschungs- und Sitzungsberichte, 203. Hannover, pp. 77-78.

Swyngedouw, E. (1992) The Mammon quest. 'Glocalisation', interspatial competition and the monetary order: The construction of new scales. In: Dunford, M. and Kafalkas, G. (eds.) Cities and Regions in the New Europe. London.

Thierstein, A. and Dümmler, P. and Kruse, Chr. (2003) Zu gross, um wahr zu sein? Die Europäische Metropolregion Zürich. In: DISP, 152, pp. 87-94.

Williamson, O.E. (1985) The Economic Institutions of Capitalism. New York.

„City of Regions" – Improving Territorial governance in the Zurich „Glatttal-Stadt"[1]

Alain Thierstein, Thomas Held, Simone Gabi

1. Introduction

Globalisation "hits the ground" in Glatttal-Stadt in the form of a growing working and living population, building activities triggered by the demand of international corporations, activities of real estate developers and the overwhelming influence of the international airport on the quality of future urban development and environmental conditions. The challenges that accompany economic growth and social change in metropolitan regions have mobilised politicians and actors towards activities and innovative approaches for improving existing institutions and problem solving capacity in Glatttal-Stadt. However, there is a lack of genuine political projects. The shaping of future development requires careful attention and action. New forms of metropolitan governance are necessary.

The central questions guiding our research are: who controls the development of this area, increasingly perceived as an urban conglomeration, but which has neither a city president nor a parliament? How succesful are existing governance bodies in solving spatial problems? In what way does the mismatch between spatial and sectoral scope of government bodies and the objectives and functional areas of private sector action networks complicate the political control of problems? Our research on Glatttal-Stadt is a contribution to current Metropolitan Governance discourse, laying out perspectives for metropolitan regions in Switzerland.

In the following, we outline the challenges for spatial development in Glatttal Stadt, pointing out the need for new forms of metropolitan governance. Building on this background and the findings from the case study in Glatttal-Stadt, we elaborate the „City of Regions" action-oriented model, consisting of the three elements „structures, behaviour and activities" of governance. We will close the chapter with a perspective on further research that builds on the action-oriented model, combining it with a „regional park concept" for better control and management of open space.

---

[1] This article draws from research at the chair for territorial and spatial development at the Swiss Federal Institute of Technology, Zurich. The article is based in large parts on a contribution by the same authors to a publication by«Avenir Suisse. The think tank for economic and social issues»: «Urbanscape Switzerland», published by Birkhäuser, Basel (2003); see references.

2. Glatttal-Stadt as a „City of Regions"

2.1 Challenges for spatial development in Glatttal-Stadt

Glatttal-Stadt, the area between Zurich and the Unique Zurich Airport can be perceived in various ways: as a collection of towns and communities in the central Glatttal, as part of the inner agglomeration belt around Zurich, as a shopping and leisure paradise, as a hotel and conference city or as the „gateway" to the biggest metropolitan region in Switzerland. Statistically, Glatttal-Stadt with its 170'000 inhabitants (Canton of Zurich 2002; City of Zurich 2001) is defined by eight political municipalities, which are located between the international airport and the city of Zurich, plus the two northernmost districts of Zurich.

The shape of Glatttal-Stadt is not the result of grandly structured urban designs or regional planning visions. It's emergence can be best described through the driving force of economic development in the context of „glocal transformation processes".

"Glocalisation" (Swyngedouw 1992) denotes the synthesis of global market orientation ("globalisation") and local (or regional) embeddedness ("localisation"). Glocalisation thus describes two sides of the same coin: international competitiveness and the centripetal needs of the local quality of life. The way globalisation „hits the ground" (Sassen 2001: 345) in Glatttal-Stadt, and attempts on local and regional levels to shape urban realities and life quality may be best described through three complex, intertwined spatial problems.

First, the overwhelming influence of Zurich's international airport along with the land use demands of international corporations has triggered growth of the living and working population and tremendous building development throughout Glatttal-Stadt. While in the hearts of its towns and communities small-town and village structures continue to exist, built-up areas have spread to the edges of their respective municipal boundaries, and open spaces have disappeared or shrunk.

Second, accessing prospective and existing development areas, including land access to the airport, can no longer be achieved in Glatttal-Stadt without an overall concept involving a considerable role for public transport. In order to tackle the urgent problem of increasingly overloaded roads, the project of an urban light railway for Glatttal-Stadt has been launched.

Third, the airport as a motor for the economic development of Glatttal-Stadt is at the same time the cause of serious problems. The air and noise pollution that air traffic produces has massive consequences for the quality of life in the residential, working and local recreational areas of the surrounding towns and municipalities. This can be seen in the extreme case in the concentration of socially disadvantaged population groups in particularly noise-polluted areas (Stieger 2001).

A closer look at the problem complexes aims to shed light on the question of who controls the development of this area, increasingly perceived as an urban conglomeration, but which has neither a city president nor a parliament.

Deficits in the control of development of built-up areas
As a result of their planning autonomy, towns and municipalities in Glatttal-Stadt play a dominant role in administrating building development. In this their goals are community-oriented and competetive despite the need for intercommunity coordination of planning issues. Eight municipalities in Glatttal-Stadt have joined together into the "glow. das Glatttal" organisation. The organisation's aim is to work on joint projects in the areas of economics, traffic, sports, culture, location marketing and design of living space. However, the development of built-up areas continues to be seen by the actors in "glow.das Glatttal" as the responsibility of the individual towns and municipalities; municipal autonomy is not to be encroached on.
With the instrument of the cantonal structure plan (Richtplan), the cantonal planning authority has laid down core development areas as focal points for future building activities in Glatttal-Stadt. This is intended to ensure development areas in appropriate locations at the same time as achieving the goal of an economical use of space. Sceptics, however, maintain that the core development areas do not have any strong administrative effect, but merely represent planning approval of development which will take place in any case. Also, the Zurich planning group Glatttal (ZPG) as regional planning institution between the municipalities and cantonal planning has been criticised as being a committee without any decision-making authority (Neue Zürcher Zeitung 17.4.02: 47).

Inter-municipal cooperation for an urban traffic system
In order to tackle the urgent problem of the increasingly overloaded roads, at the beginning of the 1990s the eight municipalities of Glatttal-Stadt formed an "Interest Group for the Future of the Glatttal" (Interessengemeinschaft Zukunft Glatttal), the precursor of the "glow. das Glatttal" organisation, in order to push forward the idea of an urban light railway for Glatttal-Stadt. The interest group was successful in obtaining a hearing at cantonal level for its inter-municipally developed proposal. The government of the Zurich canton assigned the project management to the Glatttal Transport Authority (Verkehrsbetriebe Glatttal, VBG). The project management from the start involved administrators and politicians at all levels in the working and decision-making process. In spite of various hurdles, the cantonal parliament approved the financing of the project in September 2002. The first stage is to be brought into service in 2006. However, cantonal structure planning played a subdued role, there was hardly any opportunity for decision making in sounding out alter-

natives to the urban light railway. Neither a simplified option nor more complex solutions for a transport system with a larger perimeter were brought up for consideration.

Deficits in control of airport - and building development
The negative influence of the airport on live quality and development perspectives in Glatttal-Stadt was by no means inevitable, but is the result of political, economic and planning decisions over decades.
As the highest authority, the Federation in its Sachplan Infrastruktur Luftverkehr (SIL) (UVEK 2000) has for years neglected to make binding stipulations for the downstream levels and actors. Thus, there is a lack of usage restrictions for the airport's noise impact zone. At the municipal level, construction continues in the airport's pollution zone for the period of the missing operating rules. Utilisations with detrimental cones-quences for quality of life and investments continue to be created in pol-lution zones.The protracted negotiations on a new international treaty with the German government on the number of arriving flights and the ban on night flights over southern Germany are a cause of further un-certainty for future development.
Not only because of the lack of guidelines from the Federation, but also due to its own misjudgement and lack of political drive, the canton of Zurich as the level between the Federation, municipalities and the operator Flughafen Zürich AG has for a long time neglected to regulate the correlation between settlement and airport development.
In spite of the current state of problems, neither the "glow. das Glatttal" organisation as supra-municipal committee, the regional planning of the Zurich planning group Glatttal (ZPG) nor the umbrella organisation Zu-rich and district regional planning (RZU) have incorporated the question of aircraft noise pollution in their problem portfolio. Also, the Greater Zurich Area (GZA) marketing cooperative has largely excluded the ne-gative aspects of airport development in spite of the fact that the peri-meter of the GZA and its location quality is closely linked to the problems created by the effects of the airport.
Prudent solutions geared to the overall situation can only be obtained with difficulty out of this initial situation characterised by vested interests and "material constraints". The debating of solutions to problems with representatives from municipalities, cantons, the Federation, neigh-bouring Germany and with organisations and affected citizens at open forums has taken place decades too late.

Deficiencies in governance capacity to handle spatial problems
The governance bodies from municipal to federal levels show de-ficiencies in governance capacity for inter community or even inter-cantonal problems of spatial development. The problem complexes pre-

sented here illustrate first, that they cannot be treated separately from each other. Secondly, that there are deficiencies in vertically and horizontally coordinating cooperation of institutions towards a sustainable spatial development.

The current deficit in building adequate institutions with problem solving capacity is outlined in the following quotation: "Technically speaking this policy deficiency does not exist, since there is no institution responsible for it. None of the various political levels has been given the job or the competence to create new, innovative structures" (Behrendt and Kruse 2001: 202).

From the examination of the three problem fields it can be concluded that Glatttal-Stadt as an area of complex governance levels needs institutional reforms.

2.2 Regarding Glatttal-Stadt as a „City of Regions"

A look at the functions of institutions and actors of the three problem complexes of building development, Glatttal urban light railway and airport development shows that Glatttal-Stadt is not a homogeneously distinguishable "region". The problem fields are, in fact, part of diverse institutional spheres of operation. The institutions cover operational areas of varying perimeters with different, partly overlapping responsibilities and functions. Experts refer to the overlap of operational levels and functions as "multilevel governance". In order to explain Glatttal-Stadt as an area consisting of overlapping "regions" or "operational spheres", we refer to it as a "City of Regions".

Based on the description of the "City of Regions" we are developing an action-oriented model in order to approach the complex issues of capacity and deficiencies of governance bodies.

The development of Zurich airport and its function as an international hub is an example for functional relations exceeding community, cantonal and even national borders. Evidently, problems of urban areas like Zurich are not confined to the core-city and its environs or an area statistically defined as the agglomeration of Zurich. Behrendt and Kruse (2001) propose a "polycentric metropolitan region of Zurich" as a spatial dimension defined by functional interrelations which includes the cities of Basel, Lucerne and St. Gallen as well as the southern German border. The European Metropolitan Region of Zurich (EMRZ) is proposed as a potential operational level capable to meet the challenge for an efficient metropolitan governance spanning more adequate spatial dimensions. Thus, with the EMRZ we define a metropolitan level for the development of the "City of Regions" action-oriented model. The polycentric European metropolitan region of Zurich and its functional interconnections includes des and corridors of development, municipalities within 60 minutes by car from Zurich and arrows symbolising the large user area of the Zurich International Airport (Behrendt and Kruse 2001: 210, adapted).

3. Improving Metropolitan governance

3.1 Metropolitan governance discourse
The problems and deficiencies pointed out for Glatttal-Stadt need to be reflected in front of an international discourse on new forms of „metropolitan governance".

The term „governance" was originally exclusive to the classical sense of government. Today governance describes the organisation and administration of regional authorities and institutions on different levels as well as processes of decision-making, cooperation, and exertion of influence (OECD 2001). The governance discourse debates innovative forms of governance based on new spatial alliances and partnerships between central government, territorial public authorities, the private sector and civil society.

In Switzerland, a debate on the conditions of future governance of urban regions has evolved in the past decade. A lack of genuine political projects for metropolitan societies has been stated, however, there are several initiatives and programs for improving metropolitan governance (Bassand and Kübler 2001). The principle of vertical and horizontal function fulfilment and competence distribution also characterises the efforts towards spatially-related administration which have been under way since the mid-1990s (Schenkel 2001). The Federal Council founded the Tripartite Agglomerationskonferenz (TAK) in 2001 as a political platform for the promotion of vertical cooperation between the Federation, cantons, towns and municpalities. The Federation's 2001 agglomeration policy complements these steps. Its aim is to support the cantons and municipalities in their activities and improve horizontal cooperation within agglomerations. In an initial phase the Federation supports and encourages innovative model projects. It promotes projects for cooperation within the agglomerations or between towns and agglomerations (Federal Council 2001, ARE 2002).

3.2 Institutional change needs „awareness, products and processes"
An inevitable change in the political system to deal with the problem solving deficit of existing government bodies will involve a change in our understanding of democracy and the will to rethink the essence of existing federal democratic political structures (Michalski 2001). The OECD (2001) maintains that improved metropolitan governance would not result solely from the reform of institutions and finances. It was rather a question of changing behaviour and governance culture as well. As a guidance for the member countries, the OECD elaborated eleven „Principles for Metro-

politan governance" in order to define adequate systems of governance in the 21st century. With reference to the OECD principles and the requirements arising from glocalisation, metropolitan governance aims to achieve mutual improvement of international competitiveness and local quality of life, creating „more livable and competetive cities for citizens".

Change of government institutions needs to be based on an evolutive and not a deterministic understanding of spatial development. In order to describe and develop this circumstance, we use the terms of "awareness, products and processes" as a "key to insight". Static "products" such as too rigidly determined operational areas and transport infrastructures or inflexible developmental and procedural organisations will not attain their objectives; indeed they are inconsistent with the open goal horizon of sustainable development. In the same way, one-sided focusing on quickly attainable results will not be far-reaching enough. People "still think and plan far too often in terms of products instead of processes" (Thierstein 1999: 27). In order to implement new forms of governance, there has to be a process rather than formal measures to create new government forms. "Products" often become future-viable only when they are "produced in a socially robust way" (Nowotny 2000:1).

In policy and planning practice, the importance of creating awareness in change processes has often been underestimated (Minsch et al. 1998). Insufficient awareness of problems and by actors often leads to inappropriate or tardy action. The reform of federalist institutions requires corresponding learning processes between the democratically legitimised decision-makers (the electors), the users and those who pay. "The future development of urban regions needs policy learning. It is a process of collective learning geared to a strategy of regional development with those actors participating who contribute to regional development" (Benz and Fürst 2002: 22).

Governance of urban regions according to the key to insight "awareness, products and processes" involves learning, both by actors and institutions. At the same time it is essential that awareness-raising for efficient co-operation, between the levels of state politics and between spatially relevant fields of activity, be linked with new administrative forms and economic equalisation instruments.

3.3 „City of Regions" action-oriented model

As we transfer the three-part key to insight "awareness, products and processes" to tasks of spatial development and control, applying elements of the St. Gallen management concept (Schwaninger 1997), we create the "City of Regions" action-oriented model.

The model views institutional change in a comprehensive way, dividing it into three interconnected areas:

The "structures" denote relatively stable arrangements in time and space. This means both information and management systems in the sense of sets of rules which support the fulfillment of functions, and also developmental and procedural organisation. We speak of the governance structure of the action-oriented model.

The "activities" describe the tasks, which arise from a region's conception of itself, including the functions, which the region fulfills in its wider spatial and functional context. Here we speak of the governance activities of the action-oriented model.

The "behaviour" means behaviour patterns, especially cultural attitudes, values, principles and norms, the recurring routines and trusted forms. We speak of the governance behaviour of the action-oriented model.

Our "City of Regions" action-oriented model can be understood as an evolutive system that is open in its development: multilevel governance adapts itself to the times and the changing problem areas as a process of discovery. Improvement of metropolitan governance means a simultaneous and mutually coordinated development of structures, activities and behaviour.

The framework for future governance needs to consider the premises of the"City of Regions " action-oriented model and be oriented towards the OECD's "Principles of Metropolitan Governance" (OECD 2001: 18). On this foundation "action principles" can be derived with varying degrees of relevance for the three governance aspects structures, activities and behaviour (Table 1).

Action Principles	Structures	Activities	Behaviour
Socially robust searching, learning and creative process	•	•	•
Evolutive governance	•	•	•
Transformation of urban areas from the viewpoint of glocalisation	•	•	•
Complex "City of Regions"	•		
Reference size of a functional metropolitan region	•		
Subsidiarity	•	•	•
Horizontal and vertical coordination	•	•	•
Coherence in policy		•	•
Endogenous development		•	
Efficient financial management		•	
Flexibility		•	•
Participation		•	•
Particularity		•	•
Social cohesion		•	•

Table 1: The Action Principles for Metropolitan Governance and their Importance for the Three Governance Aspects of the "City of Regions" action-oriented model.

4. Metropolitan governance in Glatttal-Stadt and the European Metropolitan Region of Zurich

4.1 Precondition: institutional learning within a coherent framework

The "drama" of Zurich airport development and insufficiently controlled growth of built-up areas is an expression of too much fragmentation and a principle of subsidiarity applied too linearly. Although the operating competencies of the actors involved are defined, their individual activity fails to result in an integrated whole. The incentives for orientation towards a superordinate spatial development advantageous to most of those involved are insufficient. Also the existing framework is not coherent or binding enough. In complex problem situations, solutions can neither be achieved by a single politically/administratively defined regional institution.

In planning practice, the conviction is slowly growing that overall responsibility can only be exercised through concerted action of various institutions. This orientation can be observed in new cantonal structure planning in the canton of Zurich. With improved metropolitan governance, regional development administrators and planners, such as "glow.das Glatttal", the Zurich planning group (ZPG) and the Glatttal Zurich and district regional planning (RZU), would accomplish more than handling issues of spatial development "remaining" from cantonal planning. Rather, for problem complexes in Glatttal-Stadt like building development, an urban transport system or the development of the Airport City, the various levels of actors would work on the same subject matter according to a negotiated subsidiarity scheme.This observation is not a rejection of subsidiary function fulfilment in the Swiss federal system. However, subsidiary function fulfilment can only lead to the development goal of "more competitive and liveable cities" when governance in Glatttal-Stadt and the Zurich Metropolitan area is a coherent institutional framework, which comprehensively covers the multi layered political sphere. Improved governance in Glatttal-Stadt and in the Zurich metropolitan region requires municipal autonomy to advance and take into account the widely spreading spatial linkages in the context of glocalisation.

A coherent interplay covering several spatial levels, in addition to awareness and the will for multilevel cooperation, requires new forms of relationships between the levels as well as a robust mutual accountability (Sabel 2001). We call this form of institutional innovation "mutual participation and accountability ". This mutual accountability is a part of regional knowledge management and helps in early identification both of innovative ideas and areas where coordination is needed, in supplying the results of an independent evaluation and promoting them more vigorously by publishing "best practices". This again gives a firm base for a multilevel institutional learning process improved over a series of stages.

One example of the application of "working with mutual participation and accountability" is provided by the model projects of Swiss agglomeration policy. The Federation and cantons are obliged to change their structure, activities and behaviour. The multi-faceted agenda of the model projects (ARE 2002) could be the beginning of a lasting experimental and exchange phase with gradually growing content, leading to improved horizontal and vertical coordination in urban areas. Beyond any project the "competition for good ideas" would promote the discovery of promising governance structures, activities and behaviour patterns.

4.2 Permanent Institutions and Ad-Hoc Institutions

The "City of Regions" action-oriented model is based on the present institutional complexity of Swiss spatial organisation (Federation, cantons, municipalities; regions, partially state-run or private institutions). There is no actual local government reorganisation at the forefront of the governance reforms, where formerly independent regional authorities would be compelled by law to merge. As described, our governance model is based on a multilevel system of permanent institutions. These would be complemented by problem-oriented ad-hoc institutions.

The situation of the "City of Regions" shows the complex issues of multilevel governance and deficiencies of governance bodies in handling complex problems. It becomes clear, that a congruence of operational levels of institutions on the one hand and functional areas of ever changing spatial problems complexes will not be achieved.

Thus, complex problems like the airport development or a solution for an urban traffic system need situation-oriented project organisation of a limited time-span. Ad-hoc institutions form a framework in which otherwise vertically linked organisations, from the Federation down to private actors, are organised horizontally and work together on the common issue. It is of central importance that the results achieved are transferred to the democratically legitimised developmental and procedural organisation of the state system.

4.3 Area-wide metropolitan structure

Which institution might be a candidate for metropolitan knowledge management and long-term spatial development strategy? As mentioned before, the European Metropolitan Region of Zurich (EMRZ) qualifies as a suitable spatial unit to tackle even complex and cross-border questions, such as airport development, properly. Schamp (2001: 177) defines European metropolitan regions as node regions important Europe-wide and sees them "in the current globalisation debate as decision-making, control and coordination centres of international importance". Behrendt and Kruse (2001: 202), however, point out the "emergence of a sub-political sphere" and "politics without policies". The trend towards a loss of democratic legitimisation in multilevel governance must be taken very seriously. It is precisely because of de facto existing "sub-political spheres" extending beyond political borders, that efficient governance structures and activities and corresponding governance behaviour should be developed at the metropolitan region level. As one example the EMRZ could take on the function of a coordinating hub, together with the cantons for the above mentioned model projects of Swiss agglomeration policy.

This joint exploration could be described as "experimental democracy" (Sabel 2001). Structural innovations such as this area-wide metropolitan structure are part of institutional reforms in favour of a future-viable development of urban areas. In concrete terms this objective can only be achieved if there is a close linking between the political planning of a metropolitan area (long-term analyses, legislative goals and programmes), metropolitan spatial development planning and financial planning (inter and intra-cantonal fiscal equalisation; settlement of social-economic benefits).

Only an optimal linking of financial policy and governance will achieve this objective. An initial, although not sufficient instrument exists in Switzerland with the upcoming "intergovernmental equalisation" (Neuer Finanzausgleich).

The implementation of the proposed changes come up against obstacles which in Glatttal-Stadt stem from municipal autonomy and in the Zurich metropolitan region from the "canton centered spirit". How can one persuade the Glatttal municipalities or the "glow.das Glatttal" organisation to be accountable to the Zurich and district regional planning (RZU) or to the canton, and vice versa? The precondition for this must be a composite of intellectual, financial and normative incentives, which will lead to function-oriented performance and settlement agreements and mutually implemented controlling.

5. Perspectives for research on „Metropolitan Governance" in Switzerland

Consideration of Glatttal-Stadt and the Zurich metropolitan area has brought forth proposals for concrete action in the urbanised landscape of Switzerland by working out a description of the "City of Regions" situation. "City of Regions" is a metaphor for an urban area made up of unequally wide-ranging, overlapping regional operational areas with different responsibilities and functions. The"City of Regions" action-oriented model, based on the three elements "structures, behaviour, activities" has been drawn up. It may be generalised and thus offer opportunities for specific solutions for an individual urban area.

There is no such thing as the ideal spatial boundary or the ideal regional institution. Thus, "governance" is becoming a complex continuous function, although not as a disquieting improvisation, but as strategic consideration of institutional answers tailored to needs. The "City of Regions" action-oriented model is a part of this answer. It includes the local, regional and metropolitan spatial dimension; it is evolutive, process-oriented and promotes experimental policy; and it regards governance as a mutual development of structures, activities and behaviour patterns.

Internationally, governance has become an important field of research (OECD 2002). At Swiss Federal Institute of Technology, this will be reflected by one project within the research programme „The future of urbanised landscape", at the „Urban studies and landscape planning and design network" (NSL), submitted to the research comission for grants. The interdisciplinary research programme, aside from socio-economic aspects, will cover ecological, engineering, architectural and landscape development and planning issues of urbanised landscapes such as Zurich's Glatttal-Stadt. We will take a closer look at the research project within above mentioned programme, which is going to combine the "City of Regions" action-oriented model and a "regional park concept": The concept draws from the example of "Regionalpark Rhein-Main", initiated in the Frankfurt metropolitan region in Germany (Rautenstrauch 2001). The relevant idea is to create an interlinked system of open spaces connected by paths within the urbanised landscape, extending beyond existing communal borders. The regional park includes elements such as designed parks for recreation, former industrial sites, historic monuments as well as natural elements as rivers and forests and protected habitat areas. The research project will investigate the hypotheses that a „regional park concept" is an effective policy, design, and planning instrument for control and revaluation of open space in the densely urbanised region of Glatttal-Stadt. Also, the regional park project is stated to be able to serve as a mobilising concept to support a collective learning process towards new forms of governance. According to the hypotheses, the "City of Regions" action-oriented model will be the suitable basis for a strategy to implement the regional park project in planning and policy practice. „Structures" are represented by the physical shape and design of the regional park as well as planning instruments and regulations and the organisational body put in place for the management and planning of the project. Activities" are to be described as the interactions of actors, actor groups and institutions who are shaping the process to design and implement the regional park project. „Behaviour" describes the climate, routines and will in local and regional policies, administration, private and semi-private actor groups and population to support and put forward the vision.

The strategy for a regional park system throughout Glatttal-Stadt will be a step towards a regional initiative capable to improve the quality of urban life according to the principles of sustainable urban development.

References:

Behrendt, H. and Kruse, C. (2001) Die europäische Metropolregion Zürich - die Entstehung des subpolitischen Raumes. In: Geographica Helvetica (56) 3: 202–213.

Bassand, M. and Kübler, D. (2001) Conditions and Prospects for Metropolitan Governance in Switzerland. In: Swiss Political Science Review 7 (4) 146-150.

Benz, A. and Fürst, D. F (2002) Policy Learning in regional networks. In: European Urban and Regional Studies 9 (1) 21-35.

Bundsamt für Raumplanung (ARE) (2002)Agglomerationspolitik: Modellvorhaben: URL: http://www.are.admin.ch/are/de/raum/politiquedesagglomerations_5/index.html

Bundesrat (2001) Agglomerationspolitik des Bundes; Bern.

Campi, M.; Bucher, F. amd Zardini, M. (2001) Annähernd perfekte Peripherie: Glatttalstadt/Greater Zurich Area; Basel.

Eidgenössisches Departement für Umwelt, Verkeher, Energie und Kommunikation (UVEK) (2000) Sachplan Infrastruktur Luftfahrt (SIL) Teile I-III B; Bern.

Kanton Zürich (2002) Statistisches Jahrbuch des Kantons Zürich 2002; Zürich.

Mlichalski, W.; Miller, R. and Stevens, B. S. (2001) Governance im 21. Jahrhundert: Machtverteilung in der globalen wissensbasierten Wirtschaft und Gesellschaft. In: OECD (ed.) Governance im 21. Jahrhundert, Paris: 9–36.

Minsch, J., F et al. (1998) Institutionelle Formen für eine Politik der Nachhaltigkeit. Berlin.

Nowotny, H. (2000) Sozial robustes Wissen. In: GAJA (9)1: 1.

Neue Zürcher Zeitung 17.04.02: Kanton will die Planungsgruppen aufwerten: 47.

OECD (2001) Cities for Citizens: Improving Metropolitan Governance; Paris.

-,   (2002) Territorial Reviews: Switzerland; Paris.

Rautenstrauch, , L. (2002) „Regionalpark Rhein-Main", in: Longo, A. et al. (eds.) Spazi aperti – offene Räume: Dortmunder Beiträge zur Raumplanung (103).

Saberl, C. F. (2001) Eine stille Revolution demokratischer Gouvernanz: auf dem Weg zu einem demokratischen Experimentalismus. In: OECD (ed.) Governance im 21. Jahrhundert, Paris: 145-178.

Sassen, S. (2001) The impact of the New Technologies and Globalization in Cities. In: Graafland, Arie (ed.) Cities in Transition, Rotterdam.

Schamp, E. W. (2001) Der Aufstieg von Frankfurt Rhein-Main zur europäischen Metropolregion: In: Geographica Helvetica (56) 3: 169–178.

Schenkel, W. (2001) Die Agglomeration im schweizerischen Föderalismus. In: Schweizer Zeitschrift für Politikwissenschaft (7) 4: 141–146.

Schwanninger, M. (1997) Reflexion über Veränderungsprozesse aus der Managementperspektive, in: THIERSTEIN, A. et al. (eds.) Tatort Region – Veränderungsmanagement in der Regional- und Gemeindeentwicklung; Baden-Baden.

Stadt Zürich (2001) Statistisches Jahrbuch der Stadt Zürich 2001; Zürich.

Stieger, U. (2001) Räumliche Entwicklung der Flughafenregion Zürich, Fragen und Aufgaben. In: Scholl, B. (Hg.) Flughafen und Raumentwicklung, Karlsruhe.

Swyngedouw, E. A. (1992) The Mammon Quest. ‹Glocalisation›, interspatial competition and the monetary order: the construction of new scales. In: Dunford, M. und Kafkalas (eds.) Cities and Regions in the New Europe, London

Thierstein, A., Hled, T. and Gabi, S.(2003) City of Regions. Glattal-Stadt as an Area of Complex Institutional Levels needs reforms. In: Eisinger, A. and Schneider,

M. (eds.) Urbanscape Switzerland, Basel. (im Erscheinen)

-,   (2001) Der Flughafen Zürich als Produktions- und Innovationssystem, in: Die Volkswirtschaft 8: 46.

-,   (1999) Mythen in einzelnen Politikbereichen: Regionalpolitik – Regionale Entwicklung im Umbruch. In: Walker, D., Thierstein, A. and Betz, P. (Hg.) Mythen und Märchen in der Politik; Chur, Zürich.

New Forms of Urban Governance in European Cities: Focusing on Cultural Policies

Jussi Kulonpalo

In this paper I will discuss the transformations in the mode of urban governance by examining urban cultural policies in European cities. The paper is part of my Ph.D. research project in which I am examining these questions more in detail by conducting comparative case studies of selected European cities. As most of the research work is yet to be done at the moment, I will concentrate mostly on exploring some background for these themes.

Urban Governance and Cultural Policies

By focusing on urban cultural policies, my objective is to investigate and analyze recent changes in forms of urban, or local, governance. Central questions will be about the implications of these developments for urban politics, economy and the social sphere in European cities. The simultaneous competition and networking between cities on different levels and the use of cultural policies and culture instrumentally as a tool in this competition are particular points of interest.

I have chosen cultural policies as focus of my research partially because of practical reasons. I have worked as a researcher in Urban Cultural Profiles Exchange Project EuroCult21, which is a thematic network financed by the European Commission under the 5th Framework Program for European Research, coordinated by Eurocities -organization. There are 31 partners of which 22 are mid-sized cities and eight are universities and academic networks. Project's aims include, among other things, increasing its members networking and the knowledge of the issues concerning urban cultural policies. Besides professionals working in cultural administrations of the cities and municipalities, the scientific branch the network includes researchers from universities and research institutes from the field of inter-disciplinary studies connected with urban cultural policies and local governance. This paper and research work is not, however, directly linked to Eurocult12 –project.

Urban Governance Framework

Urban governance has been vigorously discussed, debated and studied during the recent years. However, amidst all the different theoretical stances and rhetoric statements there does not seem to exist clear common acceptance of how urban governance should be defined let alone approached through research, besides some general lines but those are hardly useful as tools in strict scientific analysis. This ambivalence of the concept, on the other hand, is also one of the reasons contributing to the discussion. In this discussion most common hypothesis is that government as a way of governing nation states, regions and cities has given way, or is giving way, to new forms of governing, the governance. Emergence of these new forms of governing has been particularly evident in the case of cities, city governments and metropolitan governing bodies. Many authors have suggested that transition from government to governance has already taken place as during the last two decades or so, as Europe has gone through many structural transformations in the social, political and economic spheres of societies and in the global networks.

In the subsequent discussions within the social sciences these changes have been recognized as a series of transformations in which the traditional institutions of representative democracy weaken and other actors, namely private sector, are becoming increasingly involved in public decision-makingand policy-making processes.
These developments are not, however, usually interpreted so that the traditional government, political decision-making and participatory representative democracy are losing their meaning or functionality. Rather, new possibilities have opened up to meet the new demands posed by rapidly changing environment. We have not only been witnessing a dramatic growth of city governments', municipal administrations' and local governing organizations autonomy and authority as political, economic and social actors but also the emerging of new forms of urban governance (Harvey 1989; Goldsmith 1995; Kooiman 1993; 2003; Le Galès 1998; 2002; Lefèvre 1998; John 2001).

In the most common governance discourse, the transformation from traditional local government to urban governance is often interpreted at least partially as a consequence of global economic developments. This has been linked to structural socioeconomic changes associated with the transformation of new global economy and economic globalization created by the liberation of international financial systems and rapid development and rise of information technology (Sassen 1994; 2001; Castells and Hall 1994; Castells 1994; 2000). In order to be competitive and to attract international investments and capital in this context, the institutions of representative democracy on all levels in each country, region and city are under strong pressure to build new partnerships, especially with private sector economic actors, to ensure the efficacy of their policy making. Public-private partnerships have become the most common tool in this and according to many authors they are key-elements of governance as vehicles for resource sharing, resolving conflicts and discovering mutual interests. Stoker (1995) goes as far as claiming that besides public-public partnerships, public-private partner-ships are key elements of governance as vehicles for resource sharing, resolving conflicts and discovering mutual interests. Public-private partnerships are, however, often considered as inherently problematic con-cept because of the threats they pose towards democratic com-munal decision-making and transparency of governance systems. To add to this, Harvey (1989) has argued that public-private partnership could very easily be a source of urban instability and potential causes for social problems because these projects are inherently speculative by na-ture and managed by business logic demanding always profit. Besides that, the execution and design of public-private partnerships projects is very often such that the risk is to a large extent carried by the public side of the partnership. According to distinctly Marxist view supported by Harvey, these projects contribute to the problem of over-investment and over-accumulation, which will cause in larger scale periodic crisis characterizing capitalistic economy system. On local urban scale, these kinds of projects also act as barriers to rational planning and democratic coordinated development. It has also argued that projects based on pub-lic-private partnerships, for example urban regeneration projects, are al-so often more concerned with construction of place, or enhancement of the image of a specific place and the of property values, rather than im-proving the local living conditions (housing, health and educational ser-vices, special segregation and polarization etc.) of the city or region where the place is located (Harvey 1989). The significance of global competition is further heightened because it takes increasingly place between regions instead besides the obvious level of nation states. The abundant and broad lines of discussion about long term structural changes in economy associated with the neo-liberal politics of many national and local governments and the suggested shift from Fordist to post-Fordist phase of production and economy in western societies provides some background for these theories (Bell 1973; Aglietta 1979; Piore and Sabel 1984; Harvey 1989; Jessop 1994). For more historical background of defining urban governance and changes in governance, Harvey (1989) has argued that governance has been moving from 'ma-nagerialism' more towards 'entrepreneurialism' already since the 1973 Oil Crisis. According to Harvey, after the mid-70s the urban governance has become more and more preoccupied with trying to find new ways to foster and encourage local development and employment growth. This trend towards 'entrepreneurialism' in governance can be seen in many ways as being in strikingly strong contrast to the era of the strong welfare states of earlier decades since the second World War. During that era many urban governments, especially in many European countries, were preoccupied with their redistributive roles, meaning the local provision of services and facilities to whole urban population. It should also be noted that some authors such as Lefèvre (1998), make a negative distinction between the current developments in urban governance since late 1980s and 'the other boom period of urban governments' in the 1960s and 1970s claiming that a different approach is needed in examining these two periods.

There seems to exist more of an agreement on what Harvey (1989) presented early on about how the fundamental shift in the philosophy and practices of urban governance has been related to changes in macro-economic relations between nations, regions and cities in the global level. The process of globalization brought along with it increasing instability, which manifested in the de-industrialization of areas of the former western and northern industrial core countries. The declining power of the nation-states to control multinational capital flows almost forced urban governments to take a more proactive stance as these developments have been advancing (Castells 2000). This has been clearly evident in Europe throughout the whole nineties and continues to be even more so now in the 21st century.

As a consequence of this and in this climate of changes many European cities are have rebuilt, or have been building, their roles in relation to the power vacuum that has appeared as national states have been gradually losing their authority and political power, as a consequence of globalization of economy, European Union integration and accelerating competition between nation-states, regions and cities (Bagnasco and Le Galès 2000; Le Galès 2002). In this sense we are not only witnessing a dramatic growth of city governments', municipal administrations' and local governing organizations' autonomy and authority as political and economic actors but also the emerging of new forms of urban governance. This is not to claim that city administrations are not substituting national states or challenging their legitimacy but instead they aim at using their resources and newly found political power in much more effective way. Within the current attempts to reconnect formal politics to economics and social spheres of society, there are struggles over whose discourse will dominate the recasting of governance forms and whose strategies and interests are promoted by emerging new modes of governance (Coaffee and Healey 2003).

European Cities and Urban Governance

"European cities, more particularly those that together make
up the urban structure of Europe – a fabric of older cities over
100 000 inhabitants, regional capitals or smaller state capitals
as well as perhaps the huge conurbations such as London
*or Paris." (*Bagnasco and Le Galès 2000*)*

One of the key concepts of my research project is the European city as defined above and the theoretical framework of this paper is based on the argument that European metropolitan areas, or in administrative sense of the term cities, have become international and transnational actors by building multiple networks and actively developing foreign policies thus challenging nation-states which previously had a monopoly over the relations at the international level (Bagnasco and Le Galès 2000). Seen this way, European city becomes a major political, econ-omic and social actor for which governance is the most important tool in running the city in all the spheres of the society. Historically this is by no means a new phenomenon as networks of cities, national or regional ca-pitals or local centers have formed the fabric of urban Europe since the medieval times. On one side these recent development can be seen leading to returning to the classic role of the European cities as autonomous political actors as defined and historically identified by Max Weber in his classic work, "The City" (1958). Haila and Häusserman (2003) discuss this theme and argumentation further in their article about of the neo-Weberian framework in current governance research in the European context.

Culture, Urban Cultural Policies and Local Economies
At the same time with these developments European cities are emerging as new identity-forging powers, or depending on how one interprets the-se changes, regaining once more their true role. Culture, no matter how it is defined, is a major part of any city's identity and particularly when speaking of older European cities. The connection between cities and culture is strong and the identification between culture and cities has been constant throughout the history of mankind. In this sense it is not an exaggeration to say that in some sense culture and city is the same thing.

In historical perspective in many European countries the issue of culture and cultural policies became increasingly significant through the 1960s and 1970s, as consequence of general socio-economic developments and improvements in the quality of life, which most importantly brought more leisure time for a growing part of the population as well as an increase in the proportion of the disposable income to spent on leisure activities (Schwab 2002). It has also been argued that the 1968 students' protest movement and its critique of high-culture caused the cultural policy to be pushed more to the centre of the public agenda in Europe. In this context the domain of culture in a democratic western society, and particularly as a service or a set of services, provided by the all-encompassing welfare state in direct connection with increasing simultaneous commodification and popularization of art and culture and development of consumer society also eventually led to democratization of cultural policies on a certain level. Besides the open critique of and even revolt against what was considered to be elitist high culture before late 1960s, this caused a new and much wider demand for the governments to provide cultural services and to develop their cultural policies further. Providing subsidies for museums, classic performing arts institutions and schools, and other established cultural organizations was not enough anymore as governments were expected to provide more and much more varied selection of cultural services and policies. Urban politics were at the same time going through more or less the same set changes when in many western European countries socialists and other politically left-leaning young officials were bringing along progressive, if often strongly contested, ideas and ideals. The emerging new pressure to develop cultural policy was also in this sense two-fold, as it was coming both from the outside and inside. As an example, Vivion and Le Galès (1998) argued in their French case-study, and on a general level in France as a whole, that the multiplication of cultural organizations and different socio-cultural programs and projects during the 1970s, 1980s and the 1990s can be examined in the light of successive ideologies of cultural democratization and development. The growth of city governments', municipal administrations' and local governing organizations autonomy and authority as political, economic and social actors from the 1970s and through the 1980s, which brought along new forms of urban governance also included and was clearly reflected in cities cultural administrations. From the viewpoint of this paper, one particularly interesting part of this is the fact that role and importance of culture in the governance of cities increased strongly during this period and been growing ever since. Almost without an exception, city governments and administrations all over Europe have had a strong renewed interest in developing culture in its many forms to their benefit. In the eyes of many city governments and regimes, the vehicle for achieving at least some of these goals is often the cultural policy.

I am arguing that as a consequence of these developments today in Europe, more than ever before, cities' development strategies are often embedded in urban cultural policies as an integral element. The reasoning behind these visions can be found in the arguments by many authors (Scott 1997; Florida 2002; Markusen and King 2003) claiming that culture, art and cultural values also bring competitiveness to urban regions by attracting companies, capital and innovative people, allowing them to compete in global economy. In direct connection to this, new cultural industries are often considered highly important creator of jobs and economical prosperity. This view is reflected in many nations', cities' and regions' future visions as well as strategic and operational plans. City administrations and governing elites throughout the world appear to be increasingly interested in the idea of marketing cities (Martinotti 1999). Strong renewed interest in the city's past, history or heritage and the cultivation of physical settings and cultural milieu that distinguishes city from others, or other competitors have been very common phenomena lately (Evans 2003).

Post-Fordist Economy as the Basis of New Cultural Economy

"By the early 1990s, the city-branding campaigns devised by place marketers during the era emphasized the promise of a re-born city that had left behind a polluted and blue-collar past for a future in which it was becoming vibrant, stylish, confident, cosmopolitan and innovative (Hannigan 2003)."

In past twenty years, the relationship between cultural expression and the city has been turned on its head as cultural expression in thought of less as a socio-economic practice that follows in the wake of urban life, but it is regarded instead as the motor of the urban economy (Bianchini and Parkinson 1993). On the level of urban policy, politics and governance, the move of the focus from technology to culture in the economy of the cities also implicitly suggests a transformation cities' economic base from industrial production to services, or at least towards a much more service-oriented economy base. These developments match what has been suggested in the discussion about of the post-Fordist mode of production and post-Fordist society. As a result of the division between culture and economy becomes blurred with the necessity of dealing in both (Barnes 2003). Effects of the shift from Fordist to a post-Fordist society are reflected in the sector of economy linked with culture and cultural production, often altogether labeled as new cultural economy. In the beginning of the twenty-first century, the contemporary city has become a stage and a prime site for consumption-related activities related to tourism, sports, culture and entertainment (Hannigan 2003). Amin and Thrift (2002; Amin and Graham 1997; Thrift 2000) argue that in our times the urban economy increasingly operates as a discursive construction blending economy and culture. Effects of this shift are also reflected in the sector of economy linked with culture and cultural production, often roughly put together without much consideration on their actual contents and labeled as the new cultural economy. Scott (1997; 2000) sees the location of cultural industries within cities as vitally important to the competitiveness of urban economies on global scale. Whereas globalizing processes allow cultural products to gain access to wider ranges of markets, the cultural economy has been re-localized at nodes of global transaction flows (Zukin 1995; Castells 2000; Sassen 2001).

Scott (1997) sees the location of cultural industries within cities as vitally important to the competitiveness of urban economies on global scale. The idea of cultural city and the use of arts and entertainment as tools in urban regeneration can now be considered almost universal phenomenon, which has accelerated in the era of the 'city of renewal' (Evans 2003). The projected image of a particular contemporary city may very well play a greater role than the actual reality in shaping the views of visitors, investors, and, even residents. High-pressure marketing and sales techniques are frequently used to help troubled cities in their transition to post-industrial centers of tourism, culture and reinvestment. Tourism, which can also be seen as the cultural component of globalization, and especially cultural tourism in its various forms – heritage, arts, convention – is an increasingly an urban phenomenon MacCannell (1999). In the context of cultural production and new cultural economies in cities, many academic critics seem to believe that small-scale cultural producers tend to be excluded from the new entertainment economy and they may even be actively forced to move because they can no longer afford the rents (Zukin, 1995; Hannigan 2003). The counter-criticism to that argument goes that conversely, that for example tourism offers increased opportunities for local people who are involved in the production of culture and providing culture-related consumption opportunities (Hannigan 2003). Harvey (1989) has noted that rapidly growing inter-city competition exerts an external coercive power over individual cities to conform to the rules and logic of capitalist economy and accumulation. And although the consequence of this can be a forced uniformity of cities, all in the provision of a good business climate, the orchestrated production of urban image for a city can also help to create a sense of social solidarity, civic pride and loyalty to place (Harvey 1989). However, Harvey has also argued that the concentration on spectacle and image rather than on the substance of economic and social problems can also prove to be harmful in the long run. Zukin (1995) has voiced her concern by noting that greater attention should be paid to the material inequalities that are at stake in cultural strategies of economic growth and community revitalization. Different generations of cities and especially different groups of city users as defined by Martinotti (1999) also have an important role to play. The question of 'who the city is for' and 'who is it (effectively) marketed to' by using culture and cultural aspects has its implications for cities. This brings about the central question of the consequences of these developments for the societies and particularly for the social sphere of societies. These developments contain linkages to many much debated urban issues and problems, some of these more obvious than the others. One such issue is gentrification, namely people with middle-class –backgrounds finding housing opportunities, investing is and moving in working- or lower-class neighborhoods for various reasons. Besides upgrading the physical environment of the neighborhood, this is often seen leading to displacement of original residents and the break-up of the local communities, which in turn is seen to leading eventually to growing social polarization and segregation of cities, the 'dual-city'-phenomena being one of these issues (Mollenkopf and Castells 1992).

Research Design
Based on the discussion and notions laid out above, my basic argument and hypothesis is that on the city level cultural policies are used more and more as marketing tools and as urban regeneration schemes and less as officially and explicitly intended in the policies where the emphasis tends to be on issues concerning arts, educational aspects and community cohesion. The problem associated with this is the assumption that when urban cultural policies are submitted to capitalist market logic according to the governance theories, these ideals are turned into mere marketing tools. Problematic consequences of this are already felt in many cities in the form of cultural administrations' troubles caused by cuts in financing and budgets. The neo-liberalist politics of many city governments are manifested as demands for the cultural sector to show financially profitable and above all measurable results of their actions.
In many cultural administrations it is felt that the new strategic visions based on the promises of culture and cultural sector as the provider of new economic growth are steering the cultural policy away from itself and towards something completely else than what is its traditional core focus areas.

In order to examine the hypothesis and to operationalize the plan into a concrete research work, research questions of the project have been formulated as follows:

> How do urban cultural policies reflect changes in local governance and the changing role of the contemporary European cities?

What are the elements, functions, practices and goals of urban cultural policies in European cities' social, cultural, economic and political development strategies?

If urban cultural policies are used more and more as marketing tools in the competition between cities to attract capital, investments, enterprises, highly educated professional workforce and tourism, what will be the implications for European societies?

The empirical part of the research work will consist of separate case studies of selected cities' governance systems, cultural administrations and cultural policies, which will then be analyzed by comparative methods. Different types of data will be used in the research. The data will consist of cumulative material that is already available and of data collected specially for this purpose. This will include research done previously on the subject, official policy documents, issued statements and reports. Different types statistical data collected and provided by different organizations as well as the cities in question will also be used as well as interviews conducted with key-people. Qualitative material will be collected from the case-study cities within the Eurocult21 project's framework. I will rely on inductive empirical theory in explaining and prescribing the cases, based on empirical observation and accumulation of evidence from testing the hypotheses set in the theoretical framework the research. By investigating, analyzing and explaining policy decisions and strategies produced by urban governments and administrations of the case study cities, I will look at these as functions of these organizations' decision-making structures and their mode of governance. I have adopted the case study approach in my research even when I have acknowledged the problem of finding common measurability and comparability between different cities. The idea is to use this approach in order to be able both to investigate these cities cultural policies and governance strategies individually but also to analyze them comparatively despite the limitations of this approach.

Urban Cultural Policy Models
On very general level, cultural policies tend to cover and affect a wide ranging array of different activities including classic high-art and museum institutions, cultural heritage and tourism, regeneration of cities, public space and architecture, media and advertising. The definitions of culture used in cultural policies are often wide-ranging but they can also be very tightly defined to consist only of the so-called "high culture". Culture is often seen as a potential source of economic prosperity as well as an important contributor to social cohesion through development of common social values and recreational expectations.

During the course of my research work so far, I have constructed a pre-liminary typology based on very simple ideal types describing four different types of urban cultural policies and cultural administrations in the cities participating in Eurocult21-project. Models were built using empirical data gathered through the project and include only cities within the project. It must be stressed that at this point the models are still rather rudimentary, they do not allow for wider generalizations and important exceptions do exist.

Nordic Model:
Culture and contents of cultural policy are defined broadly to include a wide variety of activities, from classic performing arts to integration of different ethnic and other minority groups and activation of long-term unemployed. Besides classic high-art, community cohesion, and educational and civilizing aspects, main focus on special groups forms the central theme. Heritage or tourism does not have a strong role on policy level but is stressed more in cities strategies'.

Central European Model:
Policy focus is on organizing cultural events with strong high-art preference but attracting cultural tourism is also often high on the agenda. Preservation of cultural heritage and increasing the youth involvement and participation in cultural activities as a means of improving social cohesion are also important aspects.

British Model:
British cities have no specific cultural administrations, the main reason for this being the fact that British law does not require cities to have cultural services except for public libraries. Cultural services are usually under the control of The Department of Leisure and Culture/Community Services/Learning. They consist of individual cultural services such as Libraries, Sport and Recreation, Parks, Museums and Galleries, Arts, Events and Tourism. There are also often other public services, which could be considered non-cultural, included as for example Youth, Education, Jobs and Childcare Services. On the policy level there is strong emphasis is on community cohesion and integration, prevention of exclusion, educational and civilizing aspects of culture.

Southern European Model:
The cultural issues are an integral part of the municipal administration. The model stresses very strongly importance of tourism for the cities' economies. Cultural events and cultural heri-

tage and their marketing for tourists are main themes in cultural policies and strategies. Of the cultural activities organizing events and festivals are usually the most important. The central element of this model is the marketing of the cities, creating awareness of the cities cultural heritage and attracting visitors.

The typology above is also partially structured on national differences because cultural policies in most European countries are still strongly linked to national policies on state level as well as the cities' and municipalities' policies and strategic visions. The differences in cultural policies are also strongly linked with the differences between forms or organization models of cultural administrations of individual nations. In the other hand there are obvious general common features such as the fact that, at least on the outset, in all cases cultural policies and strategies are planned and decided by elected political city government officials and so on. Even through such superficial analysis as presented here, it becomes quite clear that national differences and traits still remain, even if there are also many obvious common themes. The pressure of globalization or European integration has not been able to transform all national differences, at least not yet. However, according to my view this does not contradict the idea of cities becoming more and more independent and active political actors. Quite the contrary, it will rather make these developments more complex, potentially more prone to tensions and most importantly, from the viewpoint of scientific research, more interesting.

Conclusion
The most important preliminary finding so far in my research has been that cultural policies, urban governance in connection with them and the context of competition between cities has not been very much researched before. However, some interesting research linked to the theme has been recently published on place-marketing (Philo and Kearns 1993; Ward 1998), different groups of city-users (Martinotti 1999), branding of cities (Evans 2003), marketing urban culture and cultural diversity as an tourist attraction (MacCannell 1996; Hoffman 2003), arts and artists contributions to regional development (Florida 2002, Markusen and King 2003). My argument, however, which I will try to find proof for in my PhD research project, is that culture plays currently an increasingly important role in the governance of contemporary European cities. I also strongly believe that these developments will be even more evident in the future.

References

Aglietta, M. (1979): A Theory of Capitalist Regulation. Verso, London.

Amin, A. and Thrift N. J. (2002): Cities: Re-Imagining the Urban. Polity, Cambridge.

Amin, A. and Graham, S. (1997): The Ordinary City. Transactions of the Institute of British Geographers, Vol. 22, pp. 411-429.

Bagnasco, A. and Le Galès, P. (2000): European Societies and Collective Actors? In Bagnasco, A. and Le Galès, P. (eds.) (2000): Cities in Contemporary Europe, 1 - 32. Cambridge University Press, London.

Barnes, Trevor, J. (2003): The 90s Show: Culture Leaves the Farm and Hits the Streets. Urban Geography Volume 24, Number 6, pp. 479-492.

Bell, D. (1973): The Coming of Post-industrial Society: A Venture in Social Forecasting. New York Basic Books, London.

Bianchini, F. and Parkinson, M. (1993): Cultural policy and Urban Regeneration: The West European experience. Manchester University Press, Manchester.

Castells, M. (2000): The Rise of the Network Society. The Information Age: Economy, Society and Culture, Volume 1. Second Edition. Blackwell Publishers, Oxford.

Coaffee, J. and Healey, P. (2003): 'My Voice: My Place': Tracking Transformations in Urban Governance. Urban Studies, Vol. 40, No. 10, 1979-1999.

Evans, G. (2003): Hard-Branding the Cultural City – From Prado to Prada. International Journal of Urban and Regional Research, Vol. 27, No. 2, p. 417-440.

Fainstein, Susan S., Hoffman, Lily M., and Judd, D. R. (2004): Cities and Visitors. Regulating People, Markets, and City Space. Blackwell, New York.

Florida, R. (2002): The Rise of the Creative Class: And How It's Transforming Work, Leisure, Community and Everyday Life. Basic Books, New York.

Goldsmith, M. (1995): Local Government in Europe. In Judge, J., Stoker, G, and Wolman, H. (eds.) (1995): Theories of Urban Politics. Sage, London.

Haila, A. and Häussermann, H. (2003): The European City: A Description Or New Paradigm? The End of the European City: New Urban Europe Between West and East. Eurex-article, Eurex (currently unpublished draft).

Hannigan, J. (2003): Symposium on Branding, the Entertaiment Economy and Urban Place Building: Introduction. International Journal of Urban and Regional Research, Vol. 27, No. 2, p. 352-360.

Harding, A. (1997): Urban Regimes in a Europe of the Cities. European Urban and Regional Studies, Vol. 4, No. 4., 291-314.

Harvey, D. (1989): From Managerialism to Entrepreneurialism: The Transformation in Urban Governance in Late Capitalism. Geografiska annaler, 71 B, No 1. p. 3-17.

Jessop, B. (1994): The transition to post-Fordism and the Schumperterian workfare state. In Burrows, R. and Loader, B. (eds)(1994): Towards a Post-Fordist Welfare State? Routledge, London.

John, P. (2001): Local Governance in Western Europe. Sage, London.

Kearns, G. and Philo, C. (eds.) (1993): Selling Places. The City as Cultural Capital, Past and Present. Pergamon Press, Oxford.

Kooiman, J. (ed.) (1993): Modern Governance. Sage, London.

Kooiman, J. (2003): Governing as Governance. Sage, London.

Le Galès, P. (1998): Regulations and Governance in European Cities.

International Journal of Urban and Regional Research, Vol. 22, No. 4, 482-506. Blackwell Publishers.

Le Galès, P. (2002): European Cities: Social Conflicts and Governance. European Societes. Oxford University Press, Cornwall.

Lefèvre, C. (1998):'Metropolitan Government and Governance in Western Countries: A Critical Review. International Journal of Urban and Regional Research, Vol. 22, No. 1, 9-25.

MacCannell, D. (1999): The Tourist: A New Theory Of The Leisure Class. University of California Press, Berkeley.

Markusen, A. and King, D. (2003): The Artistic Dividend: The Art's Hidden Contributions to Regional Development. Project on Regional and Industrial Economics, Humphrey Institute of Public Affairs, University of Minnesota.

Martinotti, G. (1999): A City for Whom? Transients and Public Life in the Second-Generation Metropolis. In Body-Gendrot, Sophie and Beauregard, Robert A (1999): The Urban Moment. Sage Publication, Springfield.

Mollenkopf, J. and Castells, M. (Eds.) (1992): Dual City: Restructuring New York. Russel Sage, New York.

Piore, M., J. and Sabel C., F. (1984): The Second Indusrial Divide: Possibilities Od Prosperity. Basic Books, New York.

Kearns, G. and Philo, C. (1993): Culture, History, Capital: A Critical Introduction To The Selling Of Places. In Kearns, G. and Philo, C. (Eds.)(1993): Selling places. The City As Cultural Capital, Past And Present. Pergamon Press, Oxford.

Sassen, S. (1994): Cities In The World Economy. Pine Forge Press, Thousand Oaks, California.

Sassen, S. (2001): The Global City: New York, London, Tokyo. Princeton University Press, Princeton, New Jersey.

Schwab, B. (2002): Metropolitan Governance And Cultural Policy. Democratic Legitimacy In Regional Systems To Finance Urban High Culture: The Tension Between Politics And Artistic Feedom.Conference Paper for the 30th ECPR Joint Session of Workshops, workshop 12: The Politics of Metropolitan Governance 22-27 March, 2002, Turin, Italy.

Scott, A., J. (1997):The Cultural Economy of the Cities. International Journal of Urban and Regional Research, Vol. 22, No. 2, 323-39. SAGE Publications, London.

Thrift N. J. (2000): Performing Cultures in the New Economy. Annals of the Association of American Geography, Vol. 91, pp. 674-701.

Vivion, A. and Le Galès, P. (1998): Politique culturelle et gouvernance urbaine: l'exemple de Rennes. Revue Politiques Et Management Public, Vol. 16, No. 1., Institut de Management Public, Paris.

Ward, S. V. (1998): Selling Places. The Marketing and Promotion of Towns and Cities 1850-2000. E and FN Spon - Routledge, London.

Weber, M. (1958): The City. Heinemann, London.

Whitt, J.A. (1987): Mozart in the Metropolis: The Arts Coalition and the Urban Growth Machine. Urban Affairs Quarterly, Vol. 23, No.1, 15-36.

Zukin, S. (1995): Culture of the Cities. Blackwell Publishers, Oxford.

The European City in Transition

Edited by Dieter Hassenpflug und Frank Eckardt

www.peterlang.de

Reimund Seidelmann / Ernst Giese (eds.)

Cooperation and Conflict Management in Central Asia

Frankfurt am Main, Berlin, Bern, Bruxelles, New York, Oxford, Wien, 2004.
XVIII, 272 pp., num. fig. and tab.
Schriften zur Internationalen Entwicklungs- und Umweltforschung.
Edited by the Zentrum für internationale Entwicklungs- und Umweltforschung
der Justus-Liebig-Universität Gießen. Vol. 10
ISBN 3-631-52446-3 / US-ISBN 0-8204-6590-9 · pb. € 51.50*

The newly independent states in Central Asia face development, transformation
and regionalization challenges. These include the definition of their domestic
and foreign national politics, the build-up of peaceful regional cooperation and
the management of the islamic fundamentalism, sustainable socio-economic
development and the rehabilitation of the environment – in particular water
resources. Apart from country studies the volume presents results from two
collaborative research projects on Central Asia regarding water resources and
political developments. It combines views from politicians and scientists both
from Central Asia and Germany towards these matters and gives an overview
about the most pressing problems as well as ideas for their solution in the Central
Asian region.

Contents: Current problems and conflicts within the Central Asian region ·
Overview about countries of the region and their recent developments ·
Transformation and nationbuilding, economic development, regional security
and cooperation · Water resources. Islamic fundamentalism and energy

Frankfurt am Main · Berlin · Bern · Bruxelles · New York · Oxford · Wien
Distribution: Verlag Peter Lang AG
Moosstr. 1, CH-2542 Pieterlen
Telefax 00 41 (0) 32 / 376 17 27

*The €-price includes German tax rate
Prices are subject to change without notice
Homepage http://www.peterlang.de

Peter Lang · Europäischer Verlag der Wissenschaften